AF608245

CULTURES OF THE FRAGMENT

Uses of the Iberian Manuscript, 1100–1600

HEATHER BAMFORD

Cultures of the Fragment

Uses of the Iberian Manuscript, 1100–1600

UNIVERSITY OF TORONTO PRESS
Toronto Buffalo London

Toronto Buffalo London
utorontopress.com

ISBN 978-1-4875-0240-9

Toronto Iberic

Library and Archives Canada Cataloguing in Publication

Bamford, Heather, 1978–, author
Cultures of the fragment : uses of the Iberian manuscript, 1100–1600 /
Heather Bamford.

(Toronto Iberic ; 37)
Includes bibliographical references and index.
ISBN 978-1-4875-0240-9 (cloth)

1. Manuscripts, Medieval – Spain. 2. Manuscripts, Medieval – Portugal.
3. Manuscript fragments. I. Title. II. Series: Toronto Iberic ; 37

Z106.5.S7B36 2018 091.094609'02 C2018-901050-9

University of Toronto Press acknowledges the financial assistance to its publishing program of the Canada Council for the Arts and the Ontario Arts Council, an agency of the Government of Ontario.

Canada Council for the Arts Conseil des Arts du Canada

Funded by the Government of Canada | Financé par le gouvernement du Canada | Canada

Contents

Figures

Acknowledgments

I first came to study medieval and early modern manuscripts at the University of California, Berkeley's Bancroft library, and my work there and elsewhere on the campus was the seed for this book. I am indebted to many people based or once based in the Bay Area. I wrote the first piece of this project in one of Jesús Rodríguez Velasco's seminars, and it was there and in coversations since that I learned to put some of the book's most central ideas into writing. Hans Ulrich Gumbrecht encouraged me to write about fragments, to consider both the philological and theoretical questions they posed, and helped me to finish an unorthodox dissertation. I am grateful to Vincent Barletta for his guidance and invaluable insights on the book's scope and organization over a period of several years. Lively conversations with José Rabasa and Tara Daly on different books in Continental philosophy informed my thinking for several of the chapters.

Working on BETA, PhiloBiblon, I learned a great deal about medieval manuscripts and am grateful to Charles Faulhaber and Óscar Perea-Rodríguez for the opportunity. I am indebted to Ignacio Navarette for his input on the book's corpus and for his support in many other professional endeavours. It was in Berkeley where I first met Alberto Montaner, a person whose erudition I can only hope to have rubbed off on parts of this book. Israel Sanz Sánchez's friendship and insights were key supports in writing this book. Many friends and colleagues living near and far helped with evidence and specific examples or with the book's theoretical arguments, including Yasmine Beale-Rivaya, Jerry Craddock, Sam England, David Hult, Cathy Jaffe, Eileen Joy, Seth Kimmel, Kat Lecky, Albert Lloret, Nicola Masciandero, Sol Miguel-Prendes, Simone Pinet, Dan Remein, Isidro Rivera, Emilie Bergmann, Laurie

Finke, Ryan Giles, George Greenia, Jorge Terukina, David Wacks, and members of the MLA Committee on Scholarly Editions, including Paul Armstrong, Susan Brown, and Kevin Brownlee.

I am very fortunate to have a group of supportive colleagues and friends in Washington, DC. I am indebted to Christopher Britt for the sacrifices of time and possibly sanity that he has made to help me in this and many other endeavours. Masha Belenky and Sergio Waisman have provided feedback on drafts of various pieces of this book. In engaging conversations over lunch and coffee, Lynn Westwater, Leah Chang, and Holly Dugan helped move this project forward. Kathryn Kleppinger has read drafts of several parts of the book and, with Manuel Cuellar, has been an excellent companion in weathering different parts of our profession. Jeffrey Cohen, Jonathan Hsy, and Alexa Huang have imparted much appreciated wisdom at different moments. Emily Francomano's reading of the manuscript greatly improved this book, and her steadfast support and friendship many things more.

Thank you to *La corónica*, the *Journal of Medieval Iberian Studies* (Routledge, Taylor & Francis), and *Postmedieval* (Palgrave) for allowing me to include revised fragments of previously published material from the following articles: "Fragment as Phenomenon and Philological Subject: Two Cases of Chivalric Binding Fragments," *La corónica* 39, no. 2 (2011): 29–60; "A Romance *Kharja* in Context," *Journal of Medieval Iberian Studies* 5, no. 2 (2013): 169–83; and "Ruins in Motion," *Postmedieval: A Journal of Medieval Cultural Studies* 4, no. 2 (2013): 192–204. I extend my sincere appreciation to the two anonymous readers for their wealth of helpful suggestions, all of which had a profound impact on the book. I thank Suzanne Rancourt for her support of this project with all its eccentricities and am humbled by Carla DeSantis's wonderful copyediting. I am grateful to Arístides Fernando Gil Fatás for his assistance with the translations. I express my appreciation to the librarians and staff at the libraries that conserve some of the manuscripts examined here, most especially the University of California's Bancroft Library, where I spent hours as a graduate student, even and perhaps especially so when I had nothing in particular to study. Thank you to those running the relevant reading rooms at the Biblioteca del Monasterio de El Escorial, the Biblioteca Nacional de España, the Bibliothéque nationale de France, the Cambridge University Library, the Bodleian Library, and the Real Academia de la Historia.

I have relied on encouragement of a long-standing group of friends originally based in Washington State, now dispersed. Rebecca

Kirkpatrick, my friend of some thirty-five years, and Chelsie Antilla and Jochelle Pereña were some of my first interlocutors. They are still with me as I write, as is our literature teacher Susan Bauska of The Annie Wright School, who was the first to teach us to read and write critically.

Finally, I am grateful to my parents who early on provided me with the encouragement and opportunities that make the publication of a book more possible. I thank my grandparents, who took good care of me as an undergrad in Philadelphia, and my grandmother Mimi, who knew so well the importance of intuition and of courage born of magic. This project had a motley trajectory: it cross-crossed the United States, languished in difficult transitions, and was met with the fantastic noise of young children. It would have never been possible without my husband Sam. I dedicate this book to him and to our sons.

Note on transliteration and translations: with the exception of quoted material, including published editions of primary sources, Arabic and Hebrew words are transliterated without diacritics, as many of the words used here are widely used either in English or in the study of the literature and culture of medieval and early modern Spain. All translations are mine unless otherwise noted.

CULTURES OF THE FRAGMENT

Uses of the Iberian Manuscript, 1100–1600

Introduction

In the late 1990s, workers restoring the Aljafería, an eleventh-century Islamic palace in Saragossa, Spain, made a puzzling discovery. They found folios of two different fourteenth-century Qur'ans in one of the ceiling coffers. A series of inscriptions written in Arabic on the rafters was also found, visible only from the ceiling itself. Although they did not form a complete prayer, it is clear that the inscriptions were inspired by Qur'anic text and contained some of the ninety-nine Beautiful Names of God (the Adored, the Sustainer, the Greatest, the Benevolent) and phrases from suras (chapters of the Qur'an) on the greatness and oneness of God (20/6–8, 57/3, and 59/22–4). The Aljafería Palace had been built as the residence of the Banu Hud, an Arab dynasty that ruled the Islamic principality of Saragossa from 1039 to 1110. Surprisingly, the Qur'an folios and inscriptions were not found in a room used during Muslim control of the palace, which lasted until 1118, but in a room built by Muslim workers constructing a room for Pedro IV, who ruled from 1336 to 1387.

Some two centuries after the Qur'ans found in the rafters were copied, an experienced and learned Morisco scribe compiled and copied forty-five texts or selections of text for either an imam or *alfaquí* (expert in Islamic law) who administered the zakat (obligatory alms); they included pieces of the Qur'an, hadith and religious texts, *wasiyya* (advice), and texts on divinatory practices and traditional beliefs.[1] The codex, T19 conserved in the Real Academia de la Historia, appears to have had a similar function to many, if not most, Morisco manuscripts – the preservation of Islam – and also resembles other Morisco manuscripts in that it contains many different works. Today, some of these texts, including those that were partial to begin with, are missing and others are fragmentary, either acephalous, lacking internal folios, or incomplete at the end.

This book is about the uses of manuscript text that produced fragments in medieval and sixteenth-century Spain. It examines the importance of fragments to the production and circulation of manuscripts in these periods and also studies how the fragment impacts the way in which these periods have been studied in the modern age. By fragments, I refer to pieces of material text separated from their whole texts as a result of an intentional act; the term is used in this book for not only isolated bits of manuscript material with a damaged appearance, such as binding fragments, but also any piece of a larger text that was intended to be a fragment or that was necessarily a fragment for lack of a better model. The definition thus includes two seemingly opposite phenomena. While in the case of the former the text has ceased to have any intellectual value, in the latter the reason for the creation of the fragment is often the very text it contains. We might conceive of these phenomena as constituting two different types of fragments, one primarily destructive and the other at least partly constructive, but they actually point to two central characteristics of fragments as a class: in addition to lack, even the most ragged, partial fragment can convey a sort of completeness.

Most Iberian manuscripts, including those of some of the best-known works of Spanish literature, can be described as fragments, containing fragments, or fragmentary. Among Castilian works with epic content, for instance, the *Cantar de Mio Cid* (*The Song of My Cid*) is most likely incomplete at the beginning and lacks two internal folios, the *Mocedades de Rodrigo* (*The Youthful Deeds of Rodrigo*) and the *Poema de Fernán González* (*The Poem of Fernán González*) have lacunae that hinder reading, and the *Roncesvalles,* though some think it relatively whole, has been reduced to a hundred verses as a result of having been used as a carrying device.[2] Latin epics, liturgical documents, chivalric romances, and other diverse texts were destroyed for use in binding notarial, legal, musical, literary, and other texts, or as a result of intentional censorship. Community leaders, bibliographers, secretaries, families, and other users collected worthwhile or simply available selections of text to form codices that today are labelled "miscellanies" or "anthologies," according to the designator's perception of the intentions of the compilers and other users of such collections. For example, a significant part of what is known as Aljamiado literature, the literature of the Iberian Mudejar and Morisco communities, exists in miscellaneous codices containing selections of diverse works or occasionally works united by a theme.

Fragments are provocative for what they lack, offering far more questions than answers with respect to their earliest context, content, and use. While a fragment by common definition is incomplete, or what Jean-Luc Nancy and François Lacoue-Labarthe describe as an endless deferral of anything resembling a resolution of elements or events, Friedrich Schlegel, in the context of intentionally created Romantic fragments, affirmed the fragment's ontological concreteness and even wholeness. Authors such as Coleridge, Byron, Shelley, and Keats published unfinished texts that were met with praise by readers who considered them agreeable and fashionable. In *Athenaeum* fragment 206, Schlegel compares the fragment to a "small work of art" that is isolated from the world around it but complete in itself, like a "hedgehog."[3] It is a wholeness consisting of a "chaotic universality" produced by illimitable opposing forces (Schlegel), or in the words of Anne Janowitz: "... the beginning of something that remains unaccomplished."[4] Lacoue-Labarthe and Nancy insist that the completeness conveyed by a fragment does not entail perfection, homogeneity, or stasis, but what they call "individuation" and involvement in a process of becoming.[5] Maurice Blanchot, in contrasting Romantic views of fragments with postmodern ones, similarly writes of the limitations of conceptualizing fragments as restricted islands from which one moves forward or backwards only with great difficulty: "In truth, and particularly in the case of Friedrich Schlegel, the fragment often seems a means for complacently abandoning onself to the self, rather than an attempt to elaborate a more rigorous mode of writing. Then to write fragmentarily is simply to welcome one's own disorder, to close up upon one's own self in a contented isolation, and thus to refuse the opening that the fragmentary exigency represents: an exigency that does not exclude totality, but goes beyond it."[6] The fragment functions both as a remainder of the individuality of the formerly complete manuscript or version of the whole text and as individuality, a characteristic that has led to a dearth of definitions of the fragment in the context of manuscripts, or rather has given rise to a series of contradictory, primarily theoretical definitions.[7] A fragment has a dialectical relationship with its once whole. In order for a fragment to be a fragment, it must be identifiable as having come from something greater. A fragment conveys lack in its appearance or in its content but also conveys self-sufficiency, sometimes precisely because of all that it lacks, in that the user is unable to imagine its missing content convincingly.

These two sides of the fragment, those of deficiency and independence, are both represented among manuscript fragments. One side insists that a fragment has lost something in comparison to a totality, while the other suggests that the fragment has the capability of standing alone and referring to its totality, thereby constituting a fragment that conveys something more than only lack. Whereas physically destroyed fragments like the *Roncesvalles* fit easily into the first category, and texts intentionally selected for anthologies, such as the fragments that a Morisco called Mohanmad de Vera chose to comprise a carefully constructed Islamic treatise, map seamlessly onto the second, there are plenty of fragments between the two extremities and others that could fit into either category. For instance, while many codices that contain myriad texts may seem unmanageable, it is possible in other cases to conceive of the multiple texts in a codex as so many chapters of a "new," unified text, as Nuria Martínez de Castilla Muñoz has proposed of the Aljamiado manuscript T19 in her *Una biblioteca morisca entre dos tapas* (A Morisco library between two covers) and mentioned above.[8] In other cases, while a text might appear fragmentary today, it may have been perceived as relatively complete in its period of circulation, as is true of the Latin panegyric *Prefatio de Almeria*, known in Spanish as *El Poema de Almería* (The poem of Almería), which strove to sing of the 1147 siege of Almería but ended without doing so. While some of the extant manuscripts of the poem note the premature ending, and in one case propose that it was cut short by an act of censorship, the poem was considered sufficiently cohesive and complete enough to be copied at least nine or ten times in the sixteenth, seventeenth, and eighteenth centuries.

The ability of a fragment to convey both lack and self-sufficiency is latent in Hans Ulrich Gumbrecht's definition of the term. Perhaps unintentionally, his characterization allows for the fragment to exceed its status as fragment by coming to substitute for its whole: the term fragment "applies to any object that we identify as part of a larger whole without implying, however, that this part of a larger whole was meant to be a metonymy, representing the whole."[9] A fragment may not have ever been intended to represent its whole or more drastically substitute for its whole, but this certainly can and does occur in working with fragments. Even the now highly fragmentary chivalric romances that became fodder for early modern bindings, particularly those representing the only extant handwritten copy of a given romance, can be used to divine characteristics of their once-whole manuscripts and to substitute more generally for a now largely missing manuscript tradition, if only for lack of any other viable solution.

More than simply theorizing a dual metonymic and anti-metonymic character of the fragment, however, this book aims to account for why the large majority of Iberian fragments came into existence. Specifically, I challenge the commonplace notion that fragments came about accidentally. The majority of manuscript fragments were created on purpose, as a result of the use of manuscript material for a wide variety of practical, intellectual, and spiritual purposes – from binding material to excerpting for an anthology, to talismans. These fragments are thus created rather than born.[10] Both the activities that created fragments and the fragments themselves are part of a phenomenon we can call "manuscript culture."

A simple, literal definition of manuscript culture is one in which the written word is committed to a surface by hand or, as Dagenais describes it in underscoring its importance to understanding ethical reading in the Middle Ages, "a culture of the handwritten word."[11] While "by hand" and "handwritten" may seem straightforward enough, defining the reach of "culture" is more complex, a subject more frequently associated with historical anthropologists and ethnographers than philologists.[12] At the start of his *Order of Books,* Roger Chartier nevertheless proposes two meanings of culture that consider work in the history of the book and reading, and that anticipate future work, even if he frames these definitions as meanings that we spontaneously ascribe to the word culture: "The first [meaning] designates the works and the acts that lend themselves to aesthetic or intellectual appreciation in any given society; the second aims at ordinary, banal practices that express the way in which a community – on any scale – experiences and conceives of its relationship with the world, with others and with itself."[13] Aesthetic and intellectual responses to texts are not necessarily independent of one another, but in the realm of manuscript studies, the intellectual tends to subsume the aesthetic, and also the spiritual and apotropaic.

Scholarship on manuscripts and early printed books in the last several decades has sought to examine medieval and early modern intellectual responses to texts composed and circulated in these periods, with a focus on reading and writing activities. This research has involved an examination of the processes of manuscript production and circulation and the details that often lie hidden behind the scholarly print edition – which are perhaps best captured or rather recreated in a digital edition – including oral performance, visual culture, and annotations, or what Stephen Nichols calls the material specificity of a given medieval text or "manuscript matrix."[14] Similarly, there is growing recognition that the scholarly edition, notably the digital scholarly edition, is what the Modern Language Association of America's Committee on Scholarly Editions has recently called an "analytic surrogate for the textual landscapes that it describes" rather than a closed, permanent entity.[15]

This awareness for the openness of a digital edition goes hand in hand with prior work on the networks in which books are involved and the ways in which the meanings attributed to their forms and contents depend on the habitus of the multiple publics that use them.[16] Work that situates medieval and early modern reading, note taking, information management, and compilation practices in a sociological framework, which D.F. McKenzie calls the "sociology of texts," evinces the malleability of the book and its human actors, and the connections between the manuscript book and social phenomena and institutions such as literacy, censorship, libraries, and monasteries.[17] The study of manuscripts in their sociocultural context and the materialist study of individual manuscript texts in their distinct "textual situations," as Andrew Taylor describes them, has helped to replace conceptions of the book as a pre-interpreted object, or as what Jerome McGann calls "a book already read," with conceptions of it as more of a process, a living organism, and the "locus of past human experiences" operating in a culture with multiple possibilities for authorship.[18]

Scholars in Renaissance reading and marginalia, including Anthony Grafton and Lisa Jardine, Bradin Cormack and Carla Mazzio, and William Sherman have developed the notion of "use" to refer both to strategic gathering and collecting practices of readers and to notes that bear little connection to the text near which they were found.[19] Medieval and early modern readers have come out of the shadows to some degree, although more often than not remain anonymous, with an awareness that readers determined texts by copying those parts of a text that they or someone else found useful or interesting.[20] Harold Love's coining of the term "scribal publication" represented significant progress towards understanding the uses of the manuscript book in the age of print, a subject since studied extensively in the context of sixteenth- and seventeenth-century Spain by Fernando Bouza.[21]

The centrality of the fragment to the diverse intentional reading and writing activities that comprise manuscript culture is clear, but the many manifestations of fragments and fragmentation have yet to be studied collectively and in sufficient depth. The fragment is clearly an important part of medieval florilegia and Renaissance memory and commonplace books. As scholars in English studies have shown, commonplace books were veritable libraries of extracts containing passages culled primarily from printed books that could serve as seeds for thought and writing.[22] Works like the mid-twelfth-century *Florilegium Gallicum* (Gallic florilegium) contained several hundred mostly short and sententious extracts of classical authors, serving as an important teaching tool and source of classical texts for medieval readers and circulating in both complete and partial forms. As Bouza has shown in reading a treatise on the Hieronymite monk Miguel de Salinas's *Rethórica en lengua castellana* (Rhetoric in the Castilian language; 1541) entitled "De la forma en que se deue tener en leer los autores" (On the way in which authors should be read) as well as the notes (*notata*) of several Spanish humanists, early modern Iberians had some of the same reading and compilation preferences as humanists in the rest of Europe.[23] As Dagenais has examined in studying the fragmentary manifestations of the *Libro de buen amor* (*Book of Good Love*), many of these practices were explicitly fragment driven. These practices include harvesting quotations and extracts from different books to compile lists of commonplaces for use as needed, in addition to other techniques like the composition of brief summaries of books of interest and the writing of glosses in the margins of manuscripts or printed books, which sometimes served as the foundation for new texts.[24] In the context of fifteenth-century Iberian writing culture and social networks, Ana Gómez Bravo has indicated that Iberian textuality was flexible due to the plastic nature of the support.[25] This flexibility led to a culture of mobile paper and parchment in the form of the circulation of single leaves or quires that could be written on, folded, or added to existing *cuadernos* (quires, notebooks) and registers. Leaves or quires could be gathered in one of several common modes of paper compilation, such as booklets, rolls, and *envoltorios* (folders, wrappers, bundles).[26] Some compilers and copiers of fragments, including Moriscos like the one who compiled the codex discussed above (T19), produced manuscripts in workshops that held writing and binding materials, as well as codices from which to cull useful or textual fragments, with some codices containing a single work and others multiple works in Arabic, Aljamiado, or both.[27] Here I call this collection and copying of fragments and in some cases their careful arrangement "intellectual fragmentation," a fragmentation that results from a cognitive engagement with manuscript text through thinking, interpretation, learning, or remembering.

Views on whether intellectual fragments are carefully arranged or appear haphazard depend on our perceptions of the intentions of their users. Fragments actively raise many questions regarding intention, not only of the authors of the texts within them but also of their users – most critically the user or users that created them – with one of the key defining characteristics of this use being whether the creator valued the text. While intention is particularly central to this book's main thesis that the large majority of Iberian fragments are intentional fragments, it has long been a central though largely unrecognized issue in manuscript and printed-book studies.[28] When McKenzie refashioned textual and historical bibliography as a sociology of texts, he effectively expanded the evidential possibilities for bibliography.[29] In many circles, bibliography became manuscript studies and brought with it a consideration of the nontextual evidence of manuscripts as both material and symbolic, as well as a consideration of text of little hermeneutic value that may have previously escaped study. Manuscript studies also led to an inquiry into the many bodies and minds that had touched the book, from authors to scribes, readers, and owners – a recognition that the book was truly a "product of human agency."[30] Ferreting out these actors would take not just substantial research but also inevitably at least some speculation as to the motives of different users who impacted the life of the book. In this way, there is a multiplicity of intentions reflected in a single copy, and each copy is a conglomeration of the decisions of many people.

While authors and their intentions are of very clear interest for Lachmmanian-style scholarly editing, the intentions of other actors may be just as critical for other sorts of work with manuscripts, notably for the codicological work of identification and description that precedes scholarly editing. The use of terms like "miscellany," "anthology," and "compilation" often depend on the success by which we can convince ourselves that we have identified the intentions of the scribes, compilers, and owners of a given manuscript, most particularly with regard to their management or apparent lack of management of fragments, with the use of "miscellaneous" often meaning how few details or even general ideas about previous contexts of the manuscript we can actually understand. On the other hand, compilation, if we follow a medieval thinker like Isidore of Seville (Isidoro de Sevilla, d. 636), refers to a new work generated through the selecting, excerpting, and arranging of texts already valued in the cultural tradition. Drawing on Macrobius, who likened the compiler to a plunderer of the entire library of accumulated texts (*compilator bibliothecae*), Isidore writes that the compiler is "qui aliena dicta suis praemiscet, sicut solent pigmentarii in pila diversa mixta contundere" (one who mixes things said by others with his own words, as paint dealers are accustomed to pound together various mixes in a mortar).[31] A compilation in this sense encompasses not only the intentions and desires of a prospective owner and of the compiler, whose intentions might be assumed to be more specific than the producer of an anthology or miscellany, but also indirectly the intentions of the authors of the works from which the excerpts were taken.[32] Similarly, in the case of an anthology, which can be distinguished from a compilation in that it is a collection of fragments of separate texts related in theme, one can entertain not only the intentions of the authors of the selected texts but also the intended theme of the anthology. Commonplace books can reflect a wide variety of purposes and include a wide variety of material, the selection of which Julia Boffey and John Thompson suggest can be influenced by local, practical, domestic, and even political considerations. Perhaps even the creators of these books could not trace completely their own logic employed in selecting certain passages.[33]

Other users apart from compilers, including readers and owners, have their own intentions, some of which are even more difficult to surmise. A central problem in manuscript studies is anonymity and the obvious yet often unstated fact that our understanding of the bibliographic past is conditioned by decisions made by earlier readers and older antiquarians.[34] In writing of early medieval English compilation, Seth Lerer remarks that those who assembled compilations are largely unknown or at best usually fall into one of several categories.[35] At the same time, it is in some senses the ultimate goal of the scholar to identify or at least offer a plausible description of these compilers in addition to the texts and poems they compiled. Writing of the large assemblies of Middle English poetry, Lerer observes that this places the manuscripts and their texts in a liminal world between the concrete and the conjectured, suggesting that despite New Critical attention in the early twentieth century, the poems remained, in the words of Raymond Oliver, "'poems without names,' documents not so much of authorial prowess or of cultural context as of autonomous aesthetic value."[36] In the case of composite codices filled with a variety of fragments and full texts, we are at times uncertain of the identities of the authors or even of the texts themselves. While scholars are more likely to overinterpret the organization of a given codex than to attribute the current arrangement to less intentional acts or to chance, much of what ended up in miscellaneous manuscripts depended on what was available to be copied.[37] We are also nearly always unsure of the user or users who participated in the fragmentation of the texts included, whether intentionally or otherwise, assuming that we are even reasonably confident that the fragmentation was the product of human rather than natural or animal intervention. Even when the general circumstances of a given testimony's fragmentation are fairly transparent, many questions often remain. These questions render the pieces at times not only "poems without names" but also fragments without contexts, including textual contexts, contexts of use, and most importantly contexts of creation.

Anonymity can be even more pronounced in the aspects of manuscript culture in which reading and writing activities are secondary to another activity or to several activities. This is often the case for fragments that were produced or used for spiritual purposes, such as protecting people and spaces, or in accordance with religious practices, like the Jewish mezuzah or even, if passively, a genizah (literally, to hide, to put away) like the Cairo Genizah (hereafter, Genizah), a repository that held illegible, obsolete, or fragmentary Hebrew books and documents of religious and sometimes nonreligious content that could be further fragmented upon deposit. These fragments force either a broadening of the definition of reading or a placing of reading outside of the most central use of fragments entirely. While in the case of the mezuzah the text was clearly important but not read every time it was touched, the text of the Genizah fragments was officially disused but nevertheless "in a literal sense, indispensable."[38] The power of fragments created for spiritual purposes relied more on principles of contact and more generally on a strong belief in a fragment's ability to function magically rather than serving as a locus of interpretation. Jews, Christians, and Muslims all made talismanic use of the mezuzah and more generally of pieces of text, including verses of the Qur'an, the Bible, and brief prayers. As Ana Labarta has shown by drawing on data from the Valencian Inquisition between 1566 and 1609, many of those it tried for witchcraft, including for the use of amulets and talismans, were Christians: of the sixty-four people tried for that offence, there were forty-six Christians and eighteen Moriscos.[39] The talismanic power of text was intimately linked to the body. A variety of fragmentary and, in some cases, complete Christian prayers were put to talismanic use, such as a prayer that León III had sent to Charlemagne that circulated in early modern manuscript copies ("Oración de los dichos e ordenaças de la santa madre Yglesia").

Their power depended on carrying or wearing the prayer on one's person.[40] The well-known final scene in Diego de San Pedro's *Cárcel de amor* (*The Prison of Love*), in which Leriano tears two letters of his beloved Laureola and drinks them in a cup of water, has received much critical attention. Some critics, emphasizing the nonhermeneutic function of the letters, have read Leriano's consumption of the letters as an act that mimics communion, sortilege, or cannibalism.[41] More extreme yet is the case of Francisco de Mora, an architect who worked for Philip III (1598–1621). In his *Dicho para el proceso remisorial de la canonización de santa Teresa* (Declaration for the remissorial process of the canonization of Saint Teresa; 1610), after relating how one of Teresa's autographs cured his servant's toothache, he tells of his discovery of a blank folio in the saint's copy of her *Vida* (Life), in which she had written that this page is blank, continuing, "Esta hoja quedó en blanco, pase adelante" (This page is blank, continue on).[42] He steals the folio so as to possess any piece at all of Saint Teresa's handwriting but also goes on to steal some of the flesh from her writing arm, which he later ingests in a cup of water.

Though at first there might seem to be little connection between spiritual and practical uses of manuscript material, both can entail destruction of text and little to no actual reading. In the case of the fragmentation of manuscripts for practical purposes, this destruction is all too apparent. As Delphine Demelas has recently pointed out, however, early modern restoration efforts did exist, such as those in which monks and other copyists amended a particular fragmentary medieval text with other copies of the text.[43] These efforts, though admittedly much less researched and understood than destructive efforts, were eclipsed by practical uses of manuscript material. Starting in the late Middle Ages and extending into the Industrial Revolution and beyond, leaves cut out of biblical, liturgical, legal, musical, and literary manuscripts were used as pastedowns, reinforcing strips, pasteboard pads, flyleaves, and as the wrappers of bookbindings, largely due to the rise in book production that followed the invention of the printing press.[44] In monastic binderies, old or poor copies of manuscripts lying about were employed to stiffen the bindings of newly copied or printed folios at the end of the fifteenth century.[45] Among extant Iberian literary manuscripts, the use of medieval manuscripts for practical purposes is particularly pronounced among chivalric manuscripts, as nearly all of the extant chivalric manuscript material is fragmentary as a result of having been used in what José Manuel Lucía Megías has called an "instrumental" fashion. The great majority of these fragments, after having served as binding reinforcement, covers for early modern ledgers and other books, and folders for legal proceedings, have not been extensively studied or studied beyond transcription and edition.[46]

The story of binding fragments is by no means new to medievalists and early modernists, but the full potential of these fragments as study subjects, combined with a serious analysis of the reasons for their existence and an acknowledgment of these reasons as an important part of manuscript culture, has yet to be fully realized. There has nevertheless been progress of late; a field is clearly emerging, as evinced by projects like the Books within Books (BwB) network, with partners in a dozen countries working to catalogue extant Hebrew binding fragments with comprehensive descriptions and to evaluate their conservation needs.[47] The University of Texas at Austin Harry Ransom Center's *Cultural Compass* blog describes a successful crowd-sourcing project to identify binding fragments or "manuscript waste," which used informal pictures posted to Flickr and drew on the expertise and hypotheses of both established scholars and independent researchers.[48] To coincide with the Medieval Academy of America 2010 Annual Meeting, Yale University's Law School Library held an exhibit entitled "Reused, Rebound, Recovered: Medieval Manuscript Fragments in Law Book Bindings," featuring a selection of fragments culled from their 150 printed books containing manuscript waste. Apart from manuscript waste, however, another practical use, fragmentation by palimpsest, has attracted scholarly attention and technology enthusiasts – though not especially from scholars working with Iberian manuscripts, with the exception of Ángel Escobar's important efforts.[49] It is generally agreed that the large majority of palimpsests, including Iberian ones, appear to have been created for want of material or lack of space. A minority, however, such as the Latin epic the *Carmen Campidoctoris* (*The Song of the Campeador*), appear to have arisen as a result of censorship, the most extreme intellectual motivation for creating fragments. One of the few publications that treat aspects of Iberian fragments is a guide on recovering fragments of manuscripts, printed books, and other documents prepared by Taurino Burón Castro for the Biblioteca Nacional de España in 2002.[50]

While often raising more questions than answers, the intentional creation of fragments evinces the diversity of intentional activities and practices that comprise manuscript culture, and accounts for a good part of the material and textual state of Iberian manuscripts. To describe these activities and practices, I build on the notion of book "use" discussed above, but unlike the scholars working in the history of Renaissance reading and note-taking practices,[51] I employ "use" to refer not only to reading and writing activities explicitly involved in the production, circulation, and consumption of manuscript texts, but also to practical and spiritual uses of the actual manuscript material, the primary goal of which is not the communication of information or engaging the user in a hermeneutic experience. *Cultures of the Fragment* thus studies fragments and the conditions of their creation in order to disrupt the causality between a manuscript text's legibility and usability, between its usability and meaning, and between usability and productive engagement. The book contests, even in the realm of technical manuals, Cormack and Mazzio's statement that "for a book to be usable, it must of course be legible."[52] Investigating fragments and the sometimes unorthodox parts of manuscript culture that led to their creation unsettles the connection between the use of manuscript material and the creation of meaning, at least of the hermeneutic sort. The practical and spiritual uses outlined above attest to the medieval and early modern presence of other engagements with manuscript material, sometimes at odds with and sometimes in conjunction with reading.

Just as manuscript use and manuscript culture more broadly extend beyond reading activities, manuscript culture is not uniquely a medieval and early modern phenomenon and should be considered in a trans-historical framework. To expand on a remark that Chartier made in 1994, "works are produced within a specific order that has its own rules, conventions, and hierarchies, but they escape all these and take on a certain density in their peregrinations – which can be in a very long time span – about the social world."[53] This timespan extends to our own era and includes present-day engagement with manuscript material. Fragments serve both as practical examples and as a critical framework to examine the ways in which academics, cultural officials, and the public at large fill in the gaps of time, space, and epistemology that stand between the present and the medieval and early modern periods. Modern philologists, collectors, and officials of cultural institutions have found their own uses for medieval and early modern manuscripts and fragments. Philologists have reconstituted and thoroughly studied certain fragments and manuscripts containing fragments, while other fragments have received scant attention and been left unidentified among the myriad texts of a composite codex. Some fragments have been carefully transcribed and subjected to initial philological study, but then critically set aside for decades at a time or indefinitely, as in the case of the binding fragments of the *Amadís de Gaula* (*Amadis of Gaul*). Today, whole and partial manuscripts are auctioned at major houses like Christie's and Sotheby's, and sold to private collectors or public institutions.[54] One can buy single waste fragments or numerous waste fragments pulled from nineteenth-century bindings, sometimes mounted in albums and sold for several thousand dollars or more. Single leaves or groups of leaves are sold individually or as sets, a practice whose prevalence can be easily gauged by searching for "medieval manuscript leaf" or "illuminated leaf" in online auction catalogues. In fact, the practice is so common that it was the subject of a 2014 *New Yorker* article entitled "Scattered Leaves," which told the story of Elaine Treharne's experience with a 1460s Christian devotional whose leaves had been stripped for individual sale not a century or more ago but, to her surprise, in the fairly recent past.[55]

Manuscripts are also displayed in museum exhibits on Morisco manuscripts, Andalusian material culture, chivalry, or another theme, as either the focus or one element of an exhibit.[56] It is in the confines of the glass case that manuscripts and other objects often become catalysts for discussions on the meaning and ownership of cultural heritage, the representation and celebration of certain aspects of the past, and proof of the utility of medieval and early modern manuscripts for audiences larger than the academy. The difficulty of displaying manuscripts, in the sense that they cannot be open to more than two folio sides (one verso, one recto) at a time, underscores that manuscripts are more than reading material. In exhibits, even if a manuscript contains a complete text, the text effectively becomes a fragment due to the limitations of displaying physical books. Furthermore, due to the reading difficulties that manuscripts present to all but experts and dedicated amateur enthusiasts, exhibited manuscripts draw our attention to the many intangible aspects of what UNESCO (United Nations Educational, Scientific, and Cultural Organization) calls "tangible heritage," along with all of the ambitious political, cultural, and sentimental work these objects are often expected to perform.[57] The intangibility and illegibility of glass-encased manuscripts aptly conveys the inaccessibility of the manuscripts as texts to the general public and the separation between physical manuscripts – displayed not to be read but as art or cultural heritage – and the philological work often contained in the exhibit catalogue.

Cultures of the Fragment writes these modern-day uses of manuscript material, some of which tend more towards the spiritual than the purely intellectual, into manuscript culture, thus examining the diverse practical, intellectual, and spiritual uses inherent in manuscript culture from the medieval period through to the present. Each chapter aims to identify the defining characteristics of fragments, with particular attention to physical appearance, intention, metonymy, and audience. Each chapter analyses aspects of practical, intellectual, and spiritual fragmentation in a key Iberian literary tradition, including Hispano-Arabic and Hispano-Hebrew poetry, *mester de clerecía* (craft of the clergy) works, Latin and Castilian epics, chivalric romances, and the literature of the Moriscos. All of the chapters also briefly examine present-day uses of medieval and early modern manuscripts related to the fragments treated in this volume. These uses range from the creation of scholarly editions and other philological activities, including scholarly practices with augmenting or fragmenting effects, to the use of medieval and early modern manuscripts and fragments in museum exhibits and issues of curatorship and rights to ownership. The first three chapters focus principally on scholarly procedures in working with fragments created through practical, spiritual, and, to a lesser extent, intellectual uses. The last two chapters treat spiritual and intellectual use in detail, considering the complex and sometimes high-stakes intentions surrounding the creation of fragments.

Chapter 1 begins the book's inquiry into the ways in which medieval and modern users have approached fragments by exploring the meaning of fragment in the realm of the epic. While the majority of Iberian epics are not actual fragments, they are all fragmentary in some way, even if only minimally so. Each evinces a different reason for fragmentation, including practical use, such as the employment of manuscript material as a personal item, extreme intellectual use including censorship, and unknown causes. The chapter addresses the importance of metonymy and intention in working with fragments, arguing that there are certain physical features, contextual factors, and perceptions of medieval and early modern users' intentions that convey fragmentariness today: physical appearance, perception of whether the work was intentionally or accidentally rendered incomplete, and the success by which a testimony serves as a metonym of its whole, both in its time of circulation and today. The chapter works with both canonical Castilian epics (*Cantar de Mio Cid*, *Roncesvalles*, and *Mocedades de Rodrigo*) and two less studied twelfth-century Latin epics (the *Carmen Campidoctoris* and the *Chronica Adefonsi Imperatoris* [*Chronicle of Alfonso the Emperor*], a prose chronicle about the reign of Alfonso VII of León, emperor of Spain from 1126 to 1157). The chapter also examines how different reasons for fragmentation affect editorial intentions and the way in which editors have approached missing epic text.

The second chapter centres on a well-known practical use, treats it in a practical manner, and continues to examine the role of metonymy, this time in the context of chivalric binding fragments. The growth of the printing press in the sixteenth century led to the fragmentation of a wide range of literary, liturgical, legal, and other types of texts for use in the binding of other manuscript and printed books. I examine two sets of fragments found in the twentieth century in early modern bindings – fragments of the sole extant manuscript of the *Amadís de Gaula* and text and image fragments from *Tristán de Leonís* (Tristan of Leonis) – to argue that the manuscripts became disused as texts in the early modern period primarily for practical reasons and perhaps due to the success of their printed editions. These same fragments nevertheless remain largely ignored as texts, a result of the paucity of the fragments' text, the philological challenges they pose, and, as in the early modern period, the availability of similar text in printed editions. The chapter reverses this disuse and applies a hermeneutic approach, analysing a selection of the *Tristán* miniatures and portions of the text of the *Amadís* fragments. My analysis allows these pieces to overcome their status as fragments and effectively become metonyms of their once-whole manuscripts.

The third chapter continues to examine scholarly intentions and practices by considering multiple sorts of fragmentation, this time in the context of the medieval Iberian Andalusian poems discarded in the Genizah of a Cairo synagogue, with additional consideration of spiritual use. The poems, known as *muwashshaha*s and primarily written in Arabic or Hebrew, have been of particular interest to Iberianists due to the presence of Spanish (more properly Andalusí Romance) in the final verses (*kharja*) of a small number of muwashshahas. Interest in the kharjas in Romance, known as the "Romance kharjas," has led some critics to study them independently of their muwashshahas, in effect as critically generated fragments, with text predominately in Spanish. The chapter analyses physical muwashshaha fragments from the Cairo Genizah to argue that, rather than having suffered a single, twentieth-century intellectual or "critical" fragmentation, the Romance kharjas have undergone many practical, intellectual, and spiritual fragmentations over time. Some of these fragmentations have been accidental due to textual misunderstandings; some were motivated by literary or artistic choices (disuses, rewritings, and erasures of parts of text), and others by practical or spiritual needs (the fragmentation of muwashshaha manuscripts and their consignment to the Genizah). The chapter focuses on the muwashshahas of two well-known poets writing in Hebrew in the Iberian Peninsula during the Middle Ages – Yehuda Halevi (1075–1141) and Moshe Ibn Ezra (1055–after 1135) – as well as a related muwashshaha by Ibn Baqi (d. 1145 or 1150), a poet writing in Arabic.

The fourth chapter focuses on a less examined purpose, spiritual use, and the challenges it poses to study, through two discoveries of fragmentary texts. The first text consists of two parts, fourteenth-century Qur'an folios and inscriptions of the names of God left in the rafters of the Aljafería Palace in Saragossa during the reign of Pedro IV of Aragón, while the second is a fourteenth-century roof shingle containing part of a Christian prayer popular in a medieval epic, the *Ordo commendationis animae* (Order of the commendation of the soul), possibly taken from the *Poema de Fernán González*. I examine medieval and early modern Islamic, Jewish, and Christian practices, including the use of Qur'anic verses for talismanic purposes, the mezuzah, and Christian inscriptions and birthing amulets, to argue that the power of these spiritual fragments does not derive from reading the text they contained or from the text's accuracy but from knowledge of the text's physical presence in the area in which it was intended to have an effect. Drawing on theories of presence, where "presence" refers to the effects of present people or things on bodies and consciousness, or to a persistence or survival of the past, I propose that the physical presence of the fragment (rather than reading) is similarly important in some uses of medieval and early modern manuscripts today, most notably in museum exhibits.[58]

The final chapter turns directly to the Moriscos, focusing on intellectual fragmentation in their clandestine manuscript culture. The chapter argues that an intellectual fragment always both refers to and undermines its source text or referent. This undermining can take various forms, including extreme compilation, excessive editing at the level of the sentence, and lengthy but incomplete citations of the work that convincingly stand for their referent. The chapter examines the Morisco Mohanmad de Vera's creation of fragments in his florilegium, comprising three works of significant diffusion among the Moriscos: Iça de Gebir's *Breviario Sunni* (Sunni breviary), a translation of the Sunna for Castilian Muslims; the advice or *wasiyya* of Muhammad to his cousin and son-in-law, Ali Ibn Abi Talib; and a Morisco version of the tenth-century jurist and ascetic (d. 983) Abu al-Layth al-Samarqandi's *Tanbih al Ghafilin* (Warning to the neglectful), a work of ethics, hadith, and moral tales known among the Moriscos as the *Libro de Samarqandi* (Book of Samarqandi). I study De Vera's neatly ordered compilation in conjunction with more loosely compiled and typical Morisco codices that also contain fragments of his source texts. The last part of the chapter briefly considers Morisco manuscripts as a personalized book culture through comparison with manuscripts containing magic texts.

The afterword, "Material and Digital Tangibility," examines the way in which the fragment and the UNESCO categories of tangible and intangible heritage elucidate the intangible character of physical manuscripts. While in a practical sense these categories function quite well, when analysed critically and in the context of a specific form of heritage, they can be used to interrogate uncritical uses of the term materiality and to explore the meaning and limitations of something that could be called digital tangibility. In most contexts of use, tangible fragments and even complete manuscripts require intervention and even production prior to productive use, whether in the form of physical conservation, transcription, interpretation, or the creation of paratexts that create an understanding of the main texts. Intangibility and tangibility thus exist on a continuum and are also a process, as is manuscript culture itself.

While showing the fragment to be a key but scarcely studied part of manuscript culture, *Cultures of the Fragment* seeks to answer not only fundamental questions surrounding the fragment, including all of the sometimes contradictory phenomena to which the very term "fragment" refers, but also what fragments born of different uses – practical, spiritual, intellectual – have in common. The various uses studied here not only account for the creation of many Iberian fragments but also elucidate uses of manuscript material that have thus far been poorly understood or insufficiently studied, most particularly the employment of books for spiritual and practical purposes. The book works to engage its corpus of fragments and fragmentary texts with four key phenomena impacting manuscript use, both past and present: physical appearance, intention, metonymy, and audience. In studying spiritual and practical fragments and those fragments created as a result of intellectual intention, *Cultures of the Fragment* aims to move beyond the binaries that so often structure discussions of manuscripts within medieval and early modern studies, including fragmentary and whole, religious and magical, and popular and erudite.

Chapter One

Fragment and Fragmentary in the Iberian Epic

The preservation of so few Iberian epics in Spanish has led to a lengthy and often highly creative search to discover more. This search has consisted of a careful mining of ballads (*romances*) and prose chronicles for content and specific words, most famously by Menéndez Pidal, and a celebration of all extant pieces and a reconstruction of others, such as the *Siete Infantes de Lara* (The seven princes of Lara). The fragment and the scholarly processes of reconstitution and substitution that accompany it are central to the epic in both theoretical and practical terms. In Menéndez Pidal's *Reliquias de la poesía épica española* (Relics of Spanish epic poetry), the fragment not only describes the state of some of the texts that are actually extant but also serves as the central piece of his methodology and what Catherine Brown has called his "synecdochic reasoning" with regards to the epic. A fragment of text is not simply a fragment, and the romances are as convincing as material epic scraps:

> La crítica no positiva afirma, como cosa necesaria, que existieron en España otros poemas sobre Carlomagno, y para asegurar que existió uno sobre *Sansueña* y la reina Sevilla, los romances nos dan absoluta certeza, igual que si tuviéramos delante de los ojos alguna mísera hoja de tal cantar convertida en bolsa, vocadero, pantalla o tapa de encuadernación. (Menéndez Pidal, *Reliquias*, xviii)

> (Nonpositivist criticism necessarily affirms that other poems on Charlemagne existed in Spain, and in order to be certain that one existed on *Sansueña* and Seville, the romances give us absolute certainty, as if we had before us a miserable page of that poem that had been converted into a bag, hat, shade, or book cover.)[1]

All of the epics we possess are fragmentary, whether lacking a few or hundreds of stanzas. Among works of epic content in Spanish, the *Cantar de Mio Cid* lacks two internal folios and is generally thought to be acephalous. *Mocedades de Rodrigo* is incomplete at the end and may contain lacunae, and the *Poema de Fernán González* contains lacunae that hinder reading. Even if *Roncesvalles* is relatively complete, as some scholars have argued, its two folios likely survived because they were put to practical use as a bag or folder.[2] Iberian Latin epics have also come down to us in fragmentary form. For instance, two twelfth-century panegyrics, the *Poema de Almería* and the *Carmen Campidoctoris*, are both incomplete at the end.[3] The mid-twelfth-century *Poema de Almería* ends without describing the conquest of Almería and is extant only in early modern and eighteenth-century manuscripts. The *Carmen Campidoctoris* (hereafter *Carmen*), on the other hand, is a palimpsest, with its last twelve or thirteen stanzas scraped and overwritten with a letter composed upon the death of Holy Roman Emperor Federico Barbarroja I, known for his political, military, and organizational savvy. He died in 1190, the upper limit of the date range that Ángel Escobar and Alberto Montaner have proposed for the composition of the *Carmen*.[4]

This list of epics does not include those partially reconstructed from chronicle prose, *romances*, or other epics that are lost but for which there are varying degrees of evidence of prior existence, such as statements in one or more chronicles. In writing about the many incomplete, highly fragmentary, and lost works of medieval Spanish literature, the late Alan Deyermond observed that it is difficult to know at what point a work preserved solely in fragmentary form is better classified as lost rather than extant.[5] A work is clearly lost if all that is left is but a few words (or none at all), and clearly extant if all the text is conserved save a few verses. What, though, does one do with a work that has lost a fifth, a fourth, a third, or even more of its content? Deyermond used what he acknowledged was an arbitrary criterion to determine whether or not a work was lost: if less than half of what was thought to be a work's content was extant, as with the *Roncesvalles*, or if only a fragment were extant, then the work was lost.[6] Deyermond also included lost versions of extant works if they were thought to have been significantly different from what has survived, though the degree of difference between the lost and extant versions remains unclear. The lost works themselves, with "lost" conceived pessimistically as works with less than half of their content extant, were hardly useless, however. For instance, Menéndez Pidal considered "relics" not only those epics for which there was a material testimony but also those for which he had simply evidence of a tradition. Deyermond observed with some disgust that hypotheses about authorship, date of composition, and other contextual details are often advanced with more confidence when no work exists to contradict the theories of the scholar or scholars.[7] As a result, the study of lost epic, in contrast with the many entombed binding fragments, for instance, has at times gone beyond what the evidence supports, giving rise to a situation in which the "hypothetical is the real" and yielding detailed accounts of poems or traditions that may not have even existed.[8]

While all the Iberian epics are at least minimally fragmentary, the majority are not actual fragments. The diversity among these fragmentary epics is ample. Though its original length is a matter of debate, *Roncesvalles*, for instance, is for many both fragmentary and a fragment. Few people, however, would label the *Mocedades de Rodrigo* a fragment, even if its hypothesized lacunae, interpolations, and what some have argued is a piecemeal composition lead them to describe it as fragmentary. The same could be said of the *Poema de Fernán González*, whose problematic lacunae render it fragmentary, but not a fragment. The *Cantar de Mio Cid* (hereafter *Cantar*) likewise could be called fragmentary, but its missing internal folios (47–8 and 69–70) and hypothesized acephalousness would make it a problematic fragment for most scholars, particularly since it is universally regarded as the most complete epic in Spanish, or as Roger Wright puts it, the only real epic that Hispanists possess.[9] Further, the emotive power and careful composition of the first extant scene in the *Cantar* have inspired some scholars to posit that there is no missing first folio at all. According to this point of view, the first extant episode was actually intended to come first, rather than a fifty-odd-verse scene relating the arrival of the royal decree of exile and possibly an allusion as to the cause of the exile, all typically filled in with text from the prosified version of the *Crónica de Castilla* (*The Chronicle of Castile*).[10]

Though most Iberian epics are are not actual fragments, the fragment is a useful means for examining the ways in which Hispanists have perceived, approached, and actually edited Castilian and Latin fragmentary epics whose damage resulted from a variety of uses. This chapter studies how lack and completeness are conceptualized in studies and other uses of the epic. I consider the time and nature of the fragmentation of the epics and the way in which that lack is perceived today. The chapter argues that there are certain physical features, contextual factors, and perceptions of past users' intentions that convey fragmentariness, whether simply in the sense of the adjective "fragmentary," which can exclude the designation of fragment, or in the sense of actually labelling something a fragment. These physical features, contextual factors, and perceptions include physical appearance, the perception of whether the text intentionally or accidentally became incomplete, and the success by which a fragmentary testimony serves as a metonymy of its whole, both in its time of circulation and today.

Physical Appearance and Intention

What makes a fragment? The most basic criterion for a fragment is that it must be apparent, though not necessarily explicit from its physical appearance, that it is a piece of a whole that is not present. Apart from this basic relationship of separation of piece from whole, a rough, poor, or mostly destroyed appearance is often associated with fragments, as is the urge to speculate about the form and content of the once whole, in the event that it actually existed. This fundamental requirement of the ability to discern that a text is part of some totality does not necessarily mean that we can definitively confirm the existence of a whole or even imagine this whole very well at all. Instead, there is something about the appearance of the material or the quality of the text that appears at odds with what we assume to be the intention of the author and at times the intention of the creator of the copy. Another intention still is that of the person or persons responsible for the fragmentation, provided that the reason for fragmentation is not known or is suspected to have been an accident. Speculation and imagination about intentions – all quite unscientific-sounding practices – along with what Gumbrecht has called "conjuring" the absent text and material, inspired by the material presence of the actual fragment, are important parts of attempting to identify that something is in fact a fragment.[11]

Intention is also an issue for more complete manuscripts and other areas of interest in manuscript studies, though apart from the intentions of authors, it remains largely unrecognized.[12] With McGann's insistence on the social as opposed to personal and psychological character of literary work, McKenzie's sociological and archaeological approach, and New Philology's material hermeneutics, the text has become an affected, living entity.[13] This entity stood in contrast to other approaches for which the production of meaning depended on the "automatic and impersonal operation of a system of signs," whether that system was one in control of the text's language or one in charge of the organization of the form of the book.[14] As Chartier has noted, this change was thus a revision of bibliographic and New Critical approaches that ignored the presence of authors, scribes, and owners in the history of manuscripts and printed books. While recovering the author was an important correction, it was not without its complications, for along with the author came scribes, owners, and printing houses and their workers, all of whom had their own intentions and actions, which in nearly all cases cannot be discerned with any certainty. In the foreword to *Bibliography and the Sociology of Texts*, McKenzie observes the conjectural quality of new bibliography:

> Paradoxically, this extension of knowledge about the context of book production, while it induced a skepticism about the kinds of truth some forms of analytical bibliography might yield, also opened up the discipline in at least three ways. First, because the conditions of production were so much more complex than had hitherto been thought, it released the subject from the straitjacket of induction, giving it a new imaginative life in the speculative range it now demanded. Second, and ineluctably, in seeking to recover the complex conditions by which texts and their multiple meanings can be made, it drove inquiry into ever widening circles of historical context. ... Third, it directed critical attention to other forms of visual evidence in the books themselves as determinants of meaning.[15]

As McKenzie illustrates, this approach, while showing the complexity of conditions of production and more importantly the scope of "context" for a book, allows the material form of the book to impact the creation of meaning. Sometimes this meaning initially appears absent or wholly unattainable but later emerges after spending more time with the book, such as in attempts to find order in a messy composite codex. The same can be true for composite codices containing fragments and, perhaps to a lesser extent, for fragments with a destroyed appearance. In other cases, however, we can divine few to no intentions at all, so the meaning sought never quite arrives. In manuscript studies, the difficulties of determining the nature and scope of the intentions for a given piece of material text is directly reflected in the challenge of defining the meaning and content of historical context and in knowing how to interpret and use the visual evidence that McKenzie mentions.

Speculating as to how a fragment came to become a fragment and the reasons for its physical appearance is thus no small task. An added difficulty is that physical appearance is not always an accurate indicator of completeness. Many would say that this is not the case for *Roncesvalles*, however, perhaps the only Castilian epic that is definitively a fragment. Even if one argues that *Roncesvalles* is a discrete or mostly discrete entity, it is clear that at least some of the text was intentionally made fragmentary after its text had ceased to have any literary or other intellectual value for at least one user. We know that since being copied in the 1300s, part of *Roncesvalles* has been used for at least two purposes other than reading, both uses after or perhaps immediately after the manuscript had been reduced to just two folios. In addition to the use of the folios as a folder that was sewn on three sides, they appear to have served as a bookmark. The folios were found loose in Navarre in a collection of codes entitled *Libro de Fueros de todo el Reyno. Año de 1366* (Book of charters of the entire kingdom. The year of 1366), appearing after folio 172.[16] Immediately before the location where the *Roncesvalles* folios were found, there is an unfoliated quire whose sheets are narrower than those used in the rest of the manuscript, suggesting that the epic folios served as a type of signal or divider in the manuscript.[17]

With so many unknowns, including the widespread issue of anonymity with regard to the many users in the life of a manuscript, we use what we have, often quite creatively, either by choosing to recognize the pieces we do possess as wholes or by trying to fill in the pieces. In the face of the fragmentariness of *Roncesvalles* and the *Carmen*, Jules Horrent urged caution against using the pieces that survive, whether relatively plentiful or comparatively scanty, as a means to speculate about once-whole manuscripts.[18] In his work on *Roncesvalles*, Horrent offers some reconstruction of scenes but stops short of Menéndez Pidal's detailed imagination of the Battle of Roncesvalles and what precedes it. Horrent writes that despite Menéndez Pidal's profound erudition and enumerable insights, he might have gone too far with his theories on the *Roncesvalles*:

> Au terme de notre effort, que distinguons-nous? Beaucoup d'ombres, quelques lueurs. C'est peu; mais oserait-on aller plus loin sans témérite? Avec les moyens dont nous disposons, la prudence la plus extrême est requise. Il ne faut travailler à une tentative de reconstruction qu'avec le maximum de certitudes. Le moindre doute contraint à s'abstenir. Qu'est-ce, en effet, que mener une telle recherche? C'est à l'aide de textes détournés

> de leur destination propre, imaginer l'existence de telles feuilles de parchemin rapportant tel récit particulier.[19]
>
> (At the end of our effort, what can we determine? Many shadows, some light. This is but scant, but dare we go further without being reckless? With the resources we have, the most extreme caution is required. We must work on a tentative reconstruction only with maximum certainty. What, in fact, does it mean to do such research? It is using texts diverted from their proper destination to imagine the existence of those sheets of parchment relating that particular story.)

Menéndez Pidal dedicated a significant portion of his study to the poem's extant content and what may have been its now lost content; he is known for his estimation of the original poem as up to five thousand verses long, a Spanish *Chanson de Roland* (*The Song of Roland*) and longer than the *Cantar*.[20] Menéndez Pidal does admit that conjecturing about the lost content is difficult, noting that it would actually be easier if the one hundred extant verses were divided between two different scenes, allowing one to plot the events between them with greater certainty and to establish a network, lessening the island effect of the extant text, which in this case does not make for easy reconstruction:

> Pocos elementos tenemos para conjeturar lo que sería la totalidad del poema a que nuestros cien versos pertenecen. Sólo poseemos de él una corta línea del interior de su argumento, y será muy aventurada la prolongación de esa línea que en ambas direcciones intentemos. Si al menos los cien versos perteneciesen a dos escenas apartadas entre sí, podríamos con más acierto trazar la línea del argumento que las unía.[21]
>
> (We have few elements to conjecture as to what the whole of the poem to which our one hundred verses belong would be. We have only a brief line of the interior arument, and it would be very risky to extend this line in both directions as we may be tempted. If at least the one hundred verses belonged to two separate scenes, we could trace with greater certainty the plot line that united them.)

Even in cases where we have more text but not necessarily more certainty as to specific events of what is missing or its style, character construction, and the like – and even when our speculation is less wild than imagining absent parchment folios into pseudoexistence – Horrent and later Montaner and Escobar wisely urge caution. Regarding the *Carmen*, Montaner and Escobar warn against employing a metonymic philology:

> La opinión más razonable es, a nuestro entender, la de Horrent ... quien ha señalado la ineficacia de operar por analogía de la parte conservada sobre la perdida, como han hecho Curtius (1939) para suponer un poema de mayor extensión total y Menéndez Pidal (1938) para deducir que el poema se acababa con la batalla de Almenar o, a lo sumo, la de Tévar, puesto que nada exige ni un desarrollo del tercer combate en proporción a su parte preparatoria ... ni que otros sucesos de mayor importancia histórica recibiesen un tratamiento correspondiente a la misma.[22]
>
> (In our view, the most reasonable opinion is Horrent's ... who has pointed out the ineffectiveness of operating by analogy of the conserved part on the lost one, as Curtius (1939) has done, to propose a longer total poem, and Menéndez Pidal (1938), to deduce that the poem ended with the battle of Almenar, or at the most, with the battle of Tévar, since nothing requires that the development of the third combat be of the same proportion as that which came before ... nor that other events of greater historical importance would receive an analogous treatment.)

However, avoiding the use of the extant text to hypothesize, whether internally or in print, about what is missing is easier said than done. The sole manuscript of the *Carmen Campidoctoris* ends abruptly, obviously so. The *Carmen* was originally copied as if it were prose on folios 79v–80bis r, but now ends in medias res on folio 80v with the beginning of the first verse of a new stanza: "tunc deprecatur" (Then he prays; figure 1). The text was scraped and overwritten in the thirteenth century by a monk at the Ripoll monastery with a text originally composed in the late twelfth century; the overwriting may have occurred after some time had passed since the scraping.[23] The scraping affects the last nine and one-half lines of folio 80v and the first nine on folio 80bis, and it has been calculated that the scraping is responsible for the loss of a dozen stanzas, according to the verse/stanza ratio of the extant text. The scraping itself is very thorough, even meticulous, making it difficult or impossible to see the text beneath, though this is not unique to the text of the *Carmen*. As Escobar notes, the number of partial and complete Greek and Latin palimpsests in Spanish libraries is modest, but of those surveyed and catalogued by Escobar, similar scraping is present

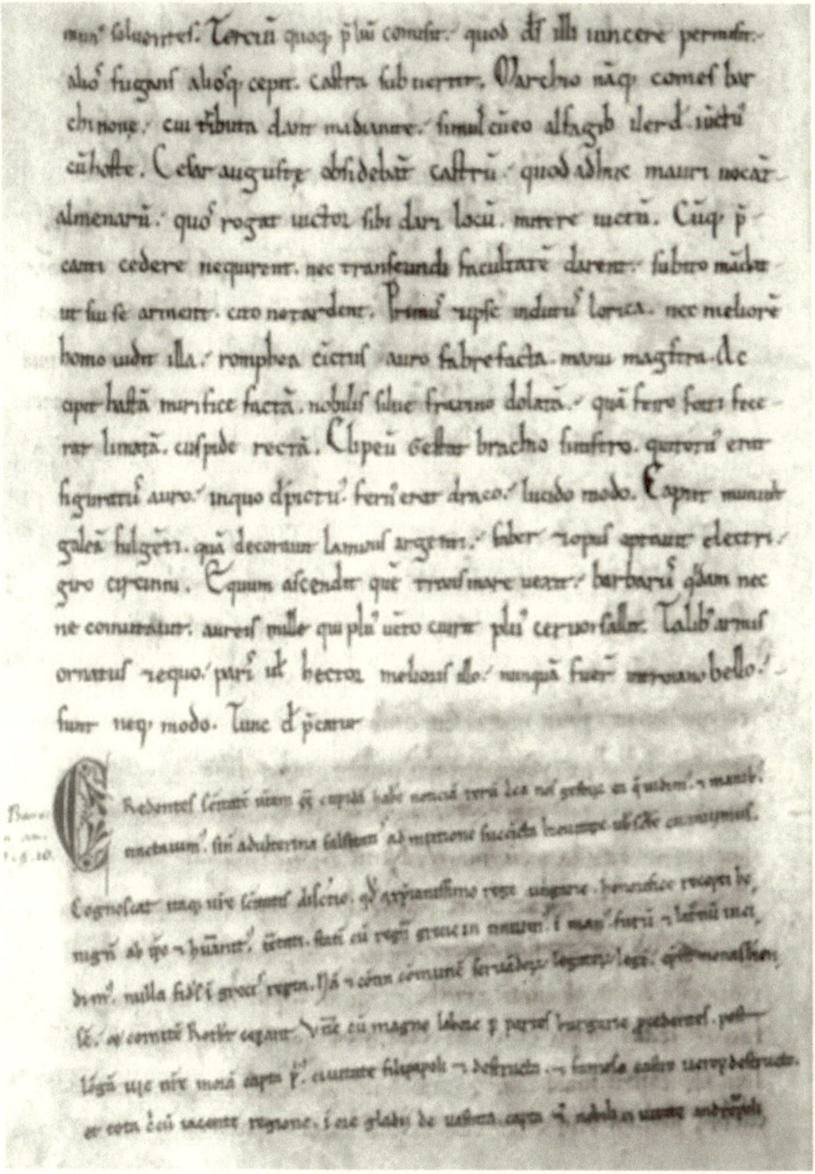

Figure 1 Abrupt end of the *Carmen Campidoctoris*, BnF, fonds latin 5132, 80v

on some folios in one codex of the Biblioteca Nacional de España (BNM) on Escobar's list, MS 6367, which transmits Burchard of Worm's (950/65–1025) *Decretum* (*Decree*) written over a Visigothic prayer book dated to 1105. With regard to Ripoll, there is at least one other Latin manuscript in which text from what appears to be the eleventh century was overwritten in the twelfth or thirteenth centuries; while the reuse of parchment via palimpsests was not necessarily a widespread practice in Ripoll, this similar case suggests that this second manuscript was likely not scraped for reasons of censorship (Archivo de la Corona de Aragón, Barcelona, Rivip. 1031).[24]

In terms of the content lost, we could hypothesize without much conjecture the completion of the conquest of Almenar (1082) and the battle between the Cid, guiding the troops of the king of the *taifa* (independent Muslim-ruled principality) of Saragossa, Yusuf Ibn Ahmad al-Mu'taman Ibn Hud, and al-Mundir al-Hayib 'Imad ad Dawla, king of the *taifa* of Lérida, who had the aid of not only the king of Aragón but also the Count of Barcelona (Berenguer Ramón II) and the Count of Cerdaña and Berga (Guillermo Ramón I). The remainder of the poem, though, cannot be so easily reconstructed or its folios imagined, despite Montaner and Escobar's convincing theories for the balance of the poem: that it continues to centre on the Cid's prowess in *lides campales* (pitched battles), probably two more of them, rather than on his aptitude for defeating Muslims.[25] It is noteworthy that until the interruption of the *Carmen*, the Cid engages in battle only with Christian opponents.

While imperfect, this reconstructive work with the *Carmen* would still be better than what we could do with *Roncesvalles*. The extant text essentially relates scenes of mourning, telling of Charlemagne's search for Roland's body and his discovery of the bodies of Bishop Turpin and Oliver before finding his nephew's corpse in the battlefield of Roncesvalles. What follows is a long lament by Charlemagne, his fainting, and the Duke Aymón of Dordone's search for and discovery of the body of his own son, Reinaldos de Montalbán. What text has survived has been thoroughly studied by both Menéndez Pidal and Horrent, along with other scholars, such as Francis Carmody, Angelo Monteverdi, and Martín de Riquer.[26] These studies remain crucial for the examination of the *Roncesvalles*, particularly so as relatively few new efforts have been published in the last twenty years.[27] Enzo Franchini's state-of-the-question piece published in *La corónica* in 1995 reaffirms critical interest in the less literary aspects of the work, including the dating of the poem and copy, formal aspects like metrics, language, and geographic origin, and the poet's sources. He concludes that *Roncesvalles* was composed in the thirteenth century, at the latest between 1325 and 1350, and that the language of the original was Spanish related to the Burgos region near the Rioja. He further argues that the poem's author drew in part on a source from a region above the Pyrenees, undoubtedly French but not Provençal, and that both linguistic and historical-literary arguments suggest a Burgos origin.[28] These important points have dominated scholarship along with what Elena Rossi-Ross calls logical and conceptual aspects of the poem, which include some speculation regarding its storyline or about lost content.[29]

In terms of *Roncesvalles*'s lost content, while it is easy to detect the presence of a Francophile spirit and a lack of a Hispano-nationalist attitude about the Battle of Roncesvalles, it is difficult to provide more than a rough outline of the plot, as Menéndez Pidal proposed in his foundational study: Charlemagne, accompanied by Roland, conquers Hispania with the exception of Saragossa before returning to France, putting Roland in charge of the rearguard. Roland is then surprised by the Moors, and the Battle of Roncesvalles ensues, costing the king of Saragossa, Marsín, his right hand. The Moors reorganize and successfully attack the French, until Roland sounds his horn to ask for Charlemagne's help. What follows is the death of Roland's compatriots Oliveros and Reinaldos, then of the hero himself, and Charlemagne's discovery of Roland's corpse among the battle's casualties.[30]

This piecing together of facts and conjecture of lost plot points, while interesting and successful in drawing some attention to the work, does not restore it to something that better resembles a whole. Important to note as well is evidence that by as early as 1236, the date of composition for Lucas de Túy's *Chronicon mundi* (Chronicle of the world), the perspective towards the battle had changed from a focus on the Franks who died in the Battle of Roncesvalles to the warriors responsible for the slaughter of the Franks.[31] This detail calls for pause before concluding that Spanish poets once entertained Spanish audiences with the exploits of Charlemagne's invasion of Spain and the massacre of the Spanish by the Franks.

It is notable, though not at all illogical, that even with highly fragmentary texts scholars aim first to resolve very particular questions, especially those of date and origin. Rossi has tried to defragment the *Roncesvalles* in another way, however, making the poem into a whole unit able to be appreciated aesthetically, primarily as a result of its ability to create affect and evoke pathos through a series of *planctus* (laments;

Charlemagne for Roland, Charlemagne for himself, and Aymón for his son Reinaldos). There are thus two main approaches to addressing fragments; each is a version of filling the void, and each often carries with it what David Greetham has called an attitude of dismay towards the gaps that fragments present to us.[32] The first is to speculate about lost content and other contextual unknowns, such as authorship, dating, and length. The second is to allow the existing piece or pieces to become a whole, either by convincing oneself that the fragment was originally intended to be a fragment or by overcoming, at least for the moment of study, the pieces' fragmentary status and allowing for an appreciation of at least some of the aesthetic aspects of the text we conserve.

Another way of attempting to reconstitute a fragment is through comparison with a complete or more complete work, such as the *Chanson de Roland* or the *Siete Infantes* in the case of *Roncesvalles*. The *Siete Infantes* offers insight into the ways in which *Roncesvalles* reworks parts of the *Chanson de Roland*, as Riquer proposed in 1959 and to which Jane Whetnall returned in the 1990s.[33] Yet another approach is to reimagine the genre of the extant piece or pieces as something more manageable and shorter, so that less appears to be lacking. Whetnall, for instance, draws on Menéndez Pidal's observation that our knowledge of *Roncesvalles* would be much greater if we possessed parts of two different episodes with a linking narrative to argue that it is more of a ballad than an epic; this theory has relatively recent supporters, including Wright, but has also been dismissed by Carmody and Horrent.[34] If considered a ballad rather than an epic, *Roncesvalles* would lack just a modest introduction, the finding of Turpin, and perhaps a more satisfying ending to be a "discrete, self-contained *cantar*."[35]

While Whetnall's (following Riquer) theory is not altogether convincing, it is provocative, particularly in what it tells us about the perception of fragments. For Whetnall, it is difficult to believe that we would happen to preserve two consecutive folios, out of so many others, that contain such a cohesive episode. But is it really so unlikely? The use of manuscript material in a definitively practical manner, even a very small selection of manuscript material, does not preclude its prior or even concurrent use in a way that values its text intellectually. The extraction and intellectual use of the *Roncesvalles* folios, or perhaps, more likely, those extant and a few more, would mean that they were previously grouped together, perhaps with others, so that even when they were employed for a means that did not value their text, it may have preserved some cohesiveness. On the other hand, in destroying a manuscript for use of its physical material, using consecutive folios that are similar in size would be logical. It is also not obvious that the extant *Roncesvalles* episode is actually that cohesive. Even in providing counterarguments to the ballad theory, Whetnall maintains that *Roncesvalles* is cohesive but explains its brevity and its selection as the product of a user's selection of the best part of an incomplete exemplar. She argues that it was intended to be the only episode copied in the manuscript, an intentional intellectual fragment that simply became even more fragmentary:

> It could be that the scribe who copied it down around 1300 was simply reproducing the most coherent remnant of an incomplete exemplar. If so, we are bound to wonder why it was deemed worthy of a fair copy. However, if the exemplar itself contained only the episode we have, adherents of the fragmentation theory would have to concede either that the process of epic disintegration was well under way by the thirteenth century, or that whoever authorized the original transmission was anticipating a process that had yet to occur in the oral transmission of the poem.[36]

The manuscript evidence to support the theory that the *Roncesvalles* was an epic is no better than the evidence to support that it was a ballad, a fact that underscores that the material object can actually prompt more questions than provide answers. The eagerness to find and identify texts as epics is responsible for a series of lengthening or shortening of actual texts or texts that have been mined and reconstructed from chronicles, with some of these epics more convincing than others. At the same time, however, we cannot allow the number of folios that remain to determine our estimation of a once-whole poem. In the present case, with an actual manuscript contemporary with the *Cantar* and with both manuscripts antedating not by decades but by centuries their ballads, the epic theory is simply more plausible, and *Roncesvalles* more likely a fragment than simply fragmentary.

Metonymy/Whole

Whetnall's ballad theory is just one of several ways of imagining fragmentary epics into wholeness and one of many means by which they might serve as metonymies of their wholes. Fragments require a recognition that they are both partial and capable of communicating something in their own right, which often involves treating them as though they lacked less than they actually do. It is clear that responses to *Roncesvalles* vary widely, from a consideration of the folios as lost to a perception of them as nearly complete, with the former view being more common. The extant *Roncesvalles* thus ranges from more commonly being considered a far-fetched metonymy of its lost epic whole to a quite convincing one. Another issue yet is whether more complete works can necessarily come to substitute for their wholes more effectively without recourse to highly compensatory theories.

In this vein, there are Iberian epics that appear relatively complete, but that may or actually do contain significant lacunae and have at times been studied in compensatory frameworks. The unique manuscript of the *Mocedades de Rodrigo* is one such case. The *Mocedades* is extant in a single manuscript from the Bibliothèque nationale de France, Espagnol 12, copied between folios 188ra–201vb at the end of the fourteenth or beginning of the fifteenth century. The manuscript is aesthetically pleasing, with fairly regular use of *calderones* (pilcrow signs), some decorated initials, and a neat two-column format.[37] Immediately prior to the *Mocedades de Rodrigo* is the *Crónica de Castilla* (hereafter *Chronicle*), a post-Alfonsine chronicle adapted from the fourth part of the *Estoria de España* (The history of Spain) in the fourteenth century and told from the perspective of the nobility. The *Chronicle* has a clear interest in the Cid, narrating the Cid's exile, his demands in the Toledan court, and the moment in which ambassadors from Navarre and Aragon come to ask for his daughters' hand in marriage. Considering the paucity of Iberian epics, the *Chronicle* and the *Mocedades* have logically been studied as two separate works, rather than the *Mocedades* as a lengthy poetic epilogue or extension of the *Chronicle*. As Jesús Rodríguez-Velasco has noted, they are nevertheless aesthetically linked in the manuscript, as they are copied in the same hand, on the same quire set, and with the same *ordinatio* (physical arrangement of texts) and style of rubrication.[38]

The failure of a consistent physical appearance to entail cohesiveness is reflected in the copy. As summarized in the introduction to Leonardo Funes and Felipe Tenenbaum's 2004 edition of the *Mocedades*, critics since Eugenio de Ochoa (1844) have noted its oddities.[39] Marcelino Menéndez Pelayo explicitly mentions that the *Mocedades* is fragmentary, even a heterogeneous and poorly strung together collection of fragments or the notes of a degenerate jongleur copied by an incompetent scribe.[40] In addition to reading in places as if it were the product of a piecemeal and perhaps sloppy composition, it is generally said that the *Mocedades* has several lacunae, or at least a few incomplete sections, and that it is definitively incomplete at the end. Several of the *Mocedades*'s proposed lacunae are present in the most careless section of the copy, folios 196 and 197 that relate the defence of Castile from the treacherous counts and the battle with five allied Moorish kings. While this section has a fairly large percentage of crossed-out and overwritten words and some changes in the width of the columns, there are no breaks in the text or other indicators that something is missing (figure 2). Probable gaps similarly occur elsewhere without notice. The last lines of the manuscript, while not providing an actual end to the text, at least appear to supply a fairly complete end to the manuscript itself, and the manuscript notably ends with the treaty of peace with France, which is the same ending found in the prose narrative in the *Crónica de Castilla*. The much less aesthetically appealing, fifteenth-century copy of the *Poema de Fernán González*, conserved in the library at El Escorial, is also incomplete at the end and evinces the changes and deletions that can occur in a copy in which multiple scribes and readers intervene. These changes include modernizing the poem's thirteenth-century language, committing errors of transcription, and changing lines and reducing the number of syllables. Lacunae in the *Fernán González* manuscript occurring towards the beginning, middle, or end, whether as a result of problems of transcription or even perhaps oral to written transmission, appear without explicit notice.[41] The *cuaderna vía* (literally, fourfold way) verse form of the *mester de clerecía* epic in most cases, however, fairly clearly reveals the absence of lines.[42]

In other cases, however, a text's abrupt conclusion is clear in the manuscript itself, even if not explicitly indicated and even if the manuscript does not have a particularly fragmentary appearance. This is the case with the Cidian Latin epic the *Poema de Almería*, the poetic epilogue of the *Chronica Adefonsi Imperatoris*, a chronicle dedicated to Alfonso VII of León and Castile's (1105–57) internal political affairs and to the external battles he fought with the Muslims. All eight extant manuscripts of the *Chronica Adefonsi Imperatoris*, with the oldest dating from the sixteenth century and the most recent from the eighteenth, contain lacunae at the beginning of the text and end without treating the conquest of Almería.[43] In all but two cases, the copies conclude without noting the abrupt end of the poem. BNM 1505, a sixteenth- or seventeenth-century manuscript in which Juan de Mendoza wrote notes and translated the work anew into Spanish, interprets the interruption of the *Poema de Almería* as a deliberate act of destruction by an ill-intentioned man: "Aquí faltan las ocho oxas desta historia, cuya falta vi con gran dolor y

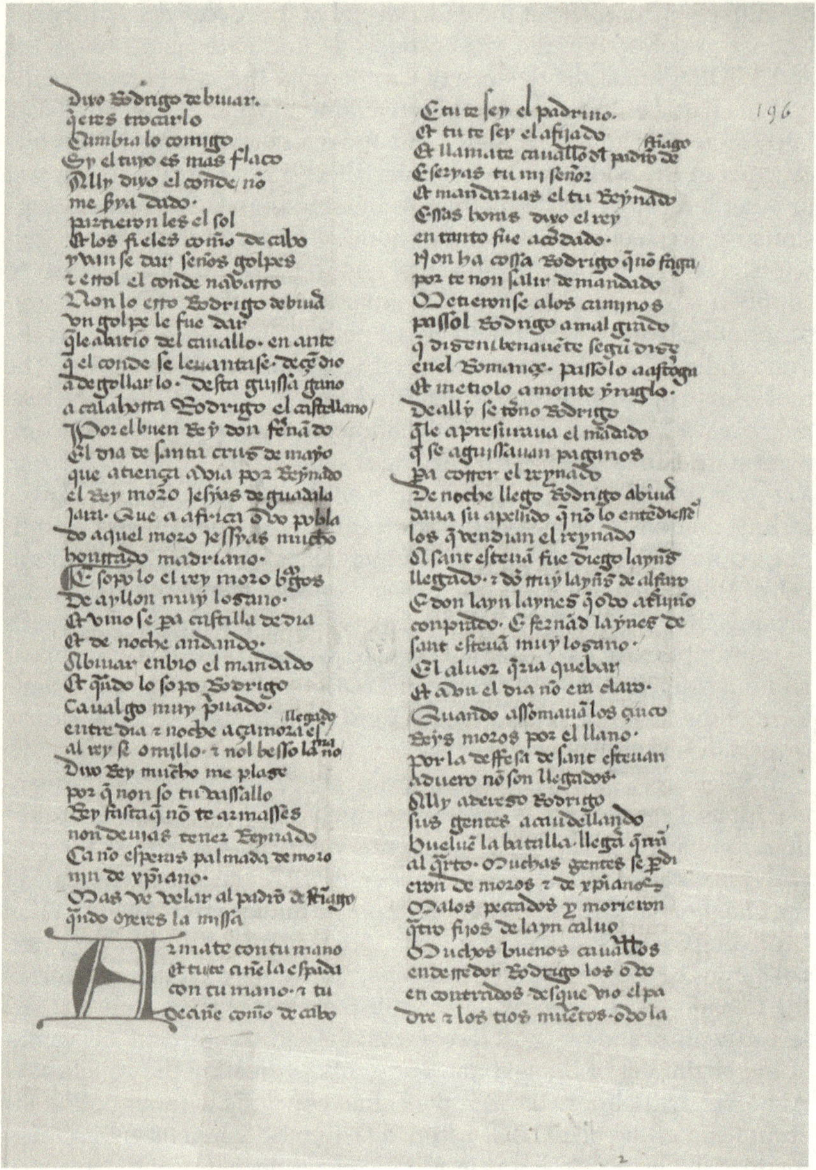

Figure 2 *Mocedades de Rodrigo*, BnF, fonds espagnol 12, 196r, complete folio (*above*) and detail of column A (*on facing page*) with obvious corrections but no lacunae noted

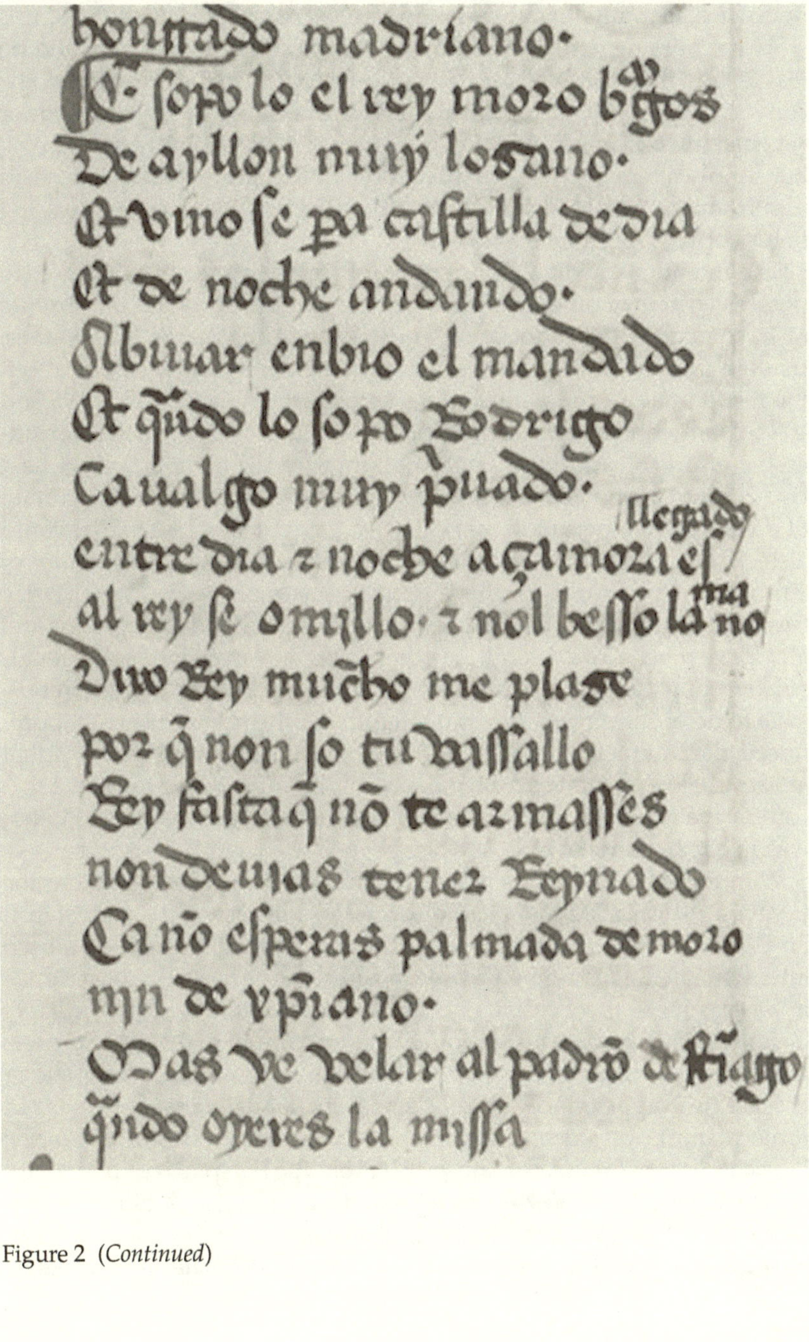

honrrado madriano.
E sopo lo el rey moro de bayos
De aylon muy losano.
Et vino se pa castilla de dia
Et de noche andando.
Albuar enbio el mandado
Et quando lo sopo Rodrigo
Caualgo muy priuado.
entre dia e noche a çamora es llegado
al rey se omillo e nol beso la mano
Dixo Rey mucho me plaze
por que non so tu vassallo
Rey fasta que non te armasses
non deuias tener Reynado
Ca non esperas palmada de moro
nin de xpiano.
Mas ve velar al padron de Santiago
quando oyeres la missa

Figure 2 (*Continued*)

no menos sentimiento del malvado que las cortó" (Eight pages of this story are missing here, whose absence I noticed with great pain and no less feeling than the evildoer that cut them out). On the other hand, the copyist of MS 1279, also from the BNM and dated to the sixteenth or seventeenth century, does not explicitly raise the possibility of foul play but simply offers instead an explanation for the abrupt end that excuses him from any culpability, indicating that there was something missing in his copy: "Deerat in exemplari."

The intentions behind the creation of fragments, even when we do possess written or other indications in the manuscript, are often obscure or have gone without notice or study. We might assume, for instance, that the lacunae of the *Mocedades* manuscript were not purposeful but the result of an incomplete model, particularly between folios 196 and 197 – if only because the scribe appears to have exerted such a considerable effort to produce a page that appeared complete, with a neat two-column format, the regular use of a *calderón* to mark the beginning of a verse, and a period to mark its end.[44] An incomplete model could also explain part, but likely not all – due to the very visible presence of editorial intervention – of the fragmentariness of the *Poema de Fernán González* manuscript, whose incomplete and modified appearance and text leave much to be desired. In other cases, however, while the details surrounding the fragmentation of the pieces are sketchy, it is often possible to determine a very general intention of the user or users that produced the fragment. With some fragmentary texts, such as those that are acephalous or that end abruptly, it might appear easy to posit a reason for the fragmentation, even if it is only to determine that its cause was likely an accident or otherwise beyond the control of its users.

With regard to the *Poema de Almería* that finishes, if incompletely, the *Chronica Adefonsi Imperatoris*, Heraclio Salvador Martínez and Maurilio Pérez González have proposed that the poem could not have been intentionally made fragmentary or incomplete precisely because it ends in medias res, a theory that assumes that censorship is either unlikely in general or that any censor would be more careful in the act of censorship by avoiding a midline stop.[45] The desire to maintain a complete or at least neat appearance, despite actual incompleteness, is present in some manuscripts such as the *Mocedades* and to a lesser extent in the *Poema de Fernán González* manuscript. From the perspectives of themes, explaining the *Poema de Almería*'s premature ending and failure to sing of the fall of the Muslim stronghold of Almería in 1147 as the result of some irremediable circumstance, like an incomplete model, seems particularly plausible since the *Poema* ends with a definitively Christian message from the bishop of Astorga. This ending is perfectly consistent with the anti-Muslim sentiments expressed throughout the poem, as in "Extitit et testis Maurorum pessima pestis" (Testament of this was the perverse plague of the Moors) and other verses:

Inter pontifices presentes Astoricensis
Hoc cernens presul, cuius micat inclytus ensis
Plus quam consortes, confortans uoce cohortes,
Alloquitur gentem iam prorsus deficientem.
Vocibus et dextra sunt magna silentia facta,
"Psallat in excelsis celorum gloria" dixit.
"Pax sit et in terris genti Domino famulanti.
Nunc opus ut quisque bene confiteatur et eque,
Et dulces portas paradisi noscat apertas.
Credite, queso, Deo, Deus est profecto deorum
Necnon cunctorum Dominus manet hic dominorum,
Qui fecit lectus nobis miracula solus.
Constant et celi ..."[46]

(Among the present bishops, seeing this, the bishop of Astorga, whose illustrious sword shines, comforting in words more the troops than his equals, rallies the troops, since they were at the point of collapse. With shouts and his right hand he achieved a silence, saying, "The glory of the heavens sing to the Lord in the highest. And peace be to the people who serve the Lord. Now it is necessary that each one confess well and completely, and know that he has the sweet doors of paradise open. Have faith, I ask, in God; he is without a doubt the God of Gods and also the Lord of all Lords, the only one that has performed miracles of reading for us. And the heavens show ...")

The *Poema de Almería*, likely written not long after the actual fall of Almería in 1147, ends in a way that is thematically consistent with the rest of the work, making the poem a fairly unlikely candidate for censorship. There is nevertheless evidence that at least two early modern scholars considered the poem a victim of intentional destruction. The Spanish bibliographer Nicolás Antonio and the historian, philologist, and poet José Pellicer de Ossau Salas y Tovar (1602–76) observed that the seventeenth-century copy of the *Chronica Adefonsi Imperatoris* and the *Poema de Almería* that the infamous pseudohistorian Román de la

Higuera possessed (BNM, MS 590) was mutilated.[47] Together with other chronicles, both the *Poema de Almería* and its chronicle were at one time attributed to Julián Pérez, a historian whom Higuera invented. After noting the mutilated state of Higuera's copy, Pellicer attributed its fragmentariness to foul play, suggesting that Higuera himself excised many pages, which Pellicer thought would have contained the name of the author, so as to attribute the work to Higuera's invented historian, Julián Pérez:

> En este codice se halla letra de la mano, que se dize haver supuesto el Cronicon de Iuliano; y que para que no se pudiesse comprobar la suposicion de poner esta cronica del emperador don Alonso I el prefacio de Almería, en Nombre de Iulian Perez, como dize parece, que se cortaron las hojas ultimas, que contenian el fin de prefacio de Almeria, que acaba su ultima coluna, en esta clausula: *Constant et celi,* hasta la qual imprimiò Sandoval. Las hojas que faltan segun el vacio que se ve en el codice, no son pocas. Y en ellas estava sin duda *el nombre del auctor* ...[48]
>
> (In this codex, there is handwriting in the hand that is said to have composed the *Cronicon of Juliano*; and so that this supposition of putting this chronicle of the emperor Alfonso I, the preface of Almería in the name of Julian Pérez could not be verified, the last pages that contained the end of the preface of Almería were cut, which ends its last column with this clause: *Constant et celi*; Sandoval even printed it this way. The leaves that are missing according to the hole that can be seen in the codex are not few. And in these, without a doubt, was *the name of the author*.)

Even apart from Antonio and Pellicer's accusations, we know that the sixteenth- or seventeenth-century copy in which Juan de Mendoza wrote notes and from which he translated the work anew into Spanish (BNM, MS 1505) attributes the incompleteness to foul play, specifically an ill-intentioned man (*malvado*) who had cut the leaves, whereas another manuscript simply notes the abrupt ending in Latin (*Deerat in exemplari* [It was missing in the copy]).

Returning to Higuera's copy, it is very possible, based on evidence like the extant but incomplete sixteenth-century manuscript, that Higuera's incomplete copy was simply the norm in the seventeenth century. In contrast to what may have been the case with the *Mocedades* and *Poema de Fernán González*, Higuera's foul play reminds us definitively that a manuscript may not have ended midverse for a reason beyond the control of the scribe. In the other Latin panegyric mentioned above, the *Carmen Campidoctoris*, the text was deliberately made fragmentary or incomplete. With the *Carmen*, what is up for debate is whether the destruction was the result of explicit censorship to eliminate something offensive, the result of a more neutral version of censorship in which the content was judged simply less important than the work copied over it, or for a practical reason that required little consideration of the work's content or that arose after the text ceased to have any intellectual value.

The creation of palimpsests for reasons of censorship, whether consisting of a few folios of a manuscript or an entire manuscript, is generally regarded as rare in most contexts. As Elias Lowe has noted and Escobar has echoed, the principal cause of palimpsest is a lack of material on which to write, a purely economic and supply issue present in the medieval period and before.[49] In this vein, the notion that medieval Christians created palimpsests to censure profane antique texts has now been largely replaced by the idea that the erased texts were nearly always outdated, including pre-Vulgate versions of the Bible, liturgy no longer used, texts in difficult hands and styles such as *scriptura continua* (writing without spaces or punctuation), rarely used languages, or redundant works like extra copies of the Vulgate.[50] While the creation of a palimpsest typically does not result from explicit censorship, it does always involve the privileging and prioritization of a second text over one previously written. In the case of the *Carmen*, the careful rasping of its last dozen or so stanzas have combined with other factors to lead Giulio Bertoni, Wright, Alejandro Higashi, Escobar, and others to propose that the poem's text was not scraped for practical reasons, such as a lack of space, but for reasons of censorship.[51] The *Carmen* ends with the words *tunc deprecatur* (Then he prays), the first verse of a stanza, now lost, that would have introduced the Cid's battle with the Count of Barcelona, Berenguer Ramón II, known as "el Fratricida," as he was rumoured to have planned the murder of his twin brother Ramón Berenguer II during a hunt. The stanza that precedes *tunc deprecatur* comments on the grandeur of the Cid's armour and his horse, noting that he has no rivals, either historical nor contemporary (see figure 1):

XXXII Talibus armis ornatus et equo
– Paris uel Hector meliores illo
nunquam fuerunt in Troiano bello,
sunt neque modo –
XXXIII tunc deprecatur ...[52]

(Never was there anyone better furnished with arms and horse than he, neither Paris nor Hector in the Trojan war, nor anyone today. Then he prays ...)

As Escobar and Montaner have noted, description of arms is typical in the *Carmen*, making the content of the last full stanza nothing out of the ordinary.[53] *Tunc deprecatur* or "the Cid prays," as Colin Smith translates, is similarly nothing unusual, with resonances in the *Historia Roderici* (The history of Rodrigo), including the epistolary exchange between the Cid and Berenguer.[54] At the same time, however, this praying is often a request for aid and success in battle; in this case, it would be aid and success for the Cid over Berenguer, which may have seemed offensive in Catalonia at that point in the thirteenth century. However, if the rasping were motivated by the fury of an offended monk at the Santa Maria de Ripoll monastery where the *Carmen* manuscript was found, why would he simply scrape a portion of the poem rather than the entire text? On the other hand, why even begin the section in which the rasping occurs, if it were the offending part? Was a partial salvage due to the long tradition in Ripoll of the composition of Latin poetry, from the ninth to the thirteenth century? Or, rather, was it the fame of and respect for the Cid that led to the preservation of part of the *Carmen*, or is this last hypothesis, as Wright has argued, likely coloured by our modern appreciation of later texts on the Cid?[55] In offering arguments for a later date of the *Carmen*, Michael Harney has proposed that the poem appears to be strongly driven by a desire to explain who the Cid is and to justify the glorification of his feats.[56] Despite the Cid's undoubted importance but perhaps lesser fame than we might initially assume, by the thirteenth century, when the stanzas of the *Carmen* were likely overwritten, had it become increasingly offensive to invoke the defeat of Berenguer Ramón II, since at that time Barcelona was more powerful and had finally united with Aragon?

Yet another possibility is that the monk who scraped the *Carmen* paid little attention to its content beyond determining that the poetic content was less valuable than the letter. This possibility is also problematic, however; if the monk read not for content but for a stylistic or rhythmic reason, such as pauses, why did he not stop at the end of the stanza with "sunt neque modo"? The scribe that penned the letter written after the death of Federico I Barbarroja in the space of the scraped stanzas of the *Carmen* did take care with respect to the format of the manuscript page: it appears that he tried to maintain the same interlineal space as the scribe who had copied the *Carmen*, but then changed to a smaller interlineal space on folio 80bis, and an even smaller one on folio 80bis v (see figure 1 above). This apparent interest in maintaining the interlinear space of the *Carmen* followed by a progressive decrease in this space could indicate that the scribe incorrectly assessed that he would not have enough room. In this way, despite our present-day knowledge that it was unnecessary to scrape some twelve stanzas of the *Carmen* for reasons of space, that fact may have been unknown to the copyist.

Though our knowledge of users' intentions is often limited, reading portions of the conserved text can prove useful. The present analysis of the *Carmen* and the *Poema de Almería* involves reading part of each poem as a means of shedding light on the user responsible for its incompleteness, whether by rasping or, in the latter case, by possibly removing or failing to copy the last part of the poem. However, in some cases of what at least on some level is intentional fragmentation, as with *Roncesvalles*, any use of the extant text as a means to explain the reason for the creation of the fragment has no real value. With the hundred-odd verse text of *Roncesvalles*, it is not clear why anyone would make a folder or bag from an epic poem or use it as a divider. Was it that the codex containing the poem was irrevocably damaged and that practical use was deemed the most appropriate salvage effort? Was the user truly in dire need of a folder or divider? This question elicits a simple answer, as with the use of manuscripts for book covers, endpapers, spine linings, and pasteboard layers beginning in the fifteenth century: quite possibly, the poem was not regarded as a poem at all but simply as physical material ready to hand. A partially analogous case in which both text and its material form ceased to have intellectual value is fragment 19 of the *Tristán de Leonís* fragments, held at the BNM, which Adolfo Bonilla y San Martín has said served as a folder for a few quires belonging to the nineteenth-century Spanish scholar Agustín Durán, containing his notes on Vélez de Guervara's *El diablo cojuelo* (*The Limping Devil*).[57] While this use of folios as a folder may seem regrettable, it may be only for this use or, even more likely, the use of folios as signals or dividers that any part of *Roncesvalles* was saved at all. An even more important but equally unanswerable question as to the reason for this practical use is whether the user who fashioned the folder or bag also had the rest of the *Roncesvalles* manuscript in his possession.

Apart from literally being much more complete than *Roncesvalles*, some Iberian epics acquire increased completeness from their manuscript contexts or through creative interpretations. The *Mocedades*, for instance, has long been considered a problematic epic, compared unfavourably at various points since the nineteenth century with the seriousness and verisimilitude of the *Cantar*. The *Mocedades* nevertheless gradually gained credibility, thanks to the efforts of critics such as Deyermond and Samuel Armistead. Deyermond and Armistead respectively laid the groundwork for the possibility of a learned, pro-Palencian author and of the *Mocedades*'s accounts of episodes that appear in chronicles, including the one that precedes it in the BnF manuscript, the *Crónica de Castilla*, as well as the *Mocedades*'s relation with the *romancero* (ballad) genre that followed.[58] Matthew Bailey found a positive benefit in the *Mocedades's* rough composition, suggesting that its crudeness "privileges us with insights into the aesthetics and mechanics of medieval epic composition in a way that the Mio Cid, for all its fine expression, could never do."[59] In this vein, we can consider that the *Mocedades* was composed in a culture that still used oral transmission and in which manuscript text served as much as a memory aid as an archive.

For some, however, the *Mocedades* still demanded various sorts of restitution, even from critics who appeared to appreciate it to the degree it did survive. Armistead's 1955 dissertation began an inquiry into the *Gesta de las mocedades de Rodrigo* (Original song of the youthful deeds of Rodrigo), posited as a lost epic poem that served as the basis of the *Mocedades* we have today. Funes and Tenenbaum took this query several steps further, describing the layered, heterogeneous, and composite character of the *Mocedades* as fragmentary and attempting to solve it – then partially undoing their solution – by tracing and reproducing what they call the "proceso compositivo" (process of composition) of the work.[60] This process includes what the editors consider a traditional epic poem that is now lost, the *Gesta*, and what they call the *Refundición* (The rewritten poem), an epic poem entirely in verse and essentially identical in content to what remains in the manuscript that reworked and added to the *Gesta*. This interesting, though not unproblematic, approach is both deconstructive and constructive. On the one hand, the marking of what they interpret as different moments in the life of the *Mocedades* by three different texts, which are also three versions of the same text, allows Funes and Tenenbaum to create a plausible hypothesis of the history of the *Mocedades*. In the context of this hypothesis, the editors consider the *Gesta* as the lost epic, fashioned by removing four clearly delineated fragments consisting of some 123 verses relating to Palencia, which were likely added in the fourteenth century by a learned poet with an interest in underscoring and adding to the prestige of the diocese of Palencia.[61] In this way, restoring an epic can entail a reduction or even fragmentation of an extant text and the production of what is essentially a new text that in epic terms is more complete, even though it is shorter than what actually exists. Those who posit a primitive epic text thus have to treat sections that do survive as fragmenting interpolations, even though the *Mocedades* might have been a perfectly viable and even aesthetically pleasing text at the time of its creation.

Less can thus be more in the realm of reconstituting epics, while a reconstitution of the extant text can involve a reduction in its number of words. Even when there is no text to subtract but rather quite a bit of text to add, an epic can be recognized as complete or at least slightly less mysterious in other ways, including its manuscript context. With regard to being considered complete, the scraping of the last stanzas of the *Carmen Campidoctoris*, for instance, can appear slightly more comprehensible when viewed in light of the documents that surround it in its composite codex. The codex contains some twenty-one different works, many of which were composed between 1090 and 1190, with the notable exception of the text related to the Council of Nicea that precedes the *Carmen*. The codex begins with a chronicle of the First Crusade (1096–9), Fulcher de Chartres's *Historia Hierosolymitana* (The history of Jerusalem), an anonymous sermon to honour the Virgin Mary, and, of particular interest, a fragment of the *Gesta Barcinonensium comitum* (Deeds of the counts of Barcelona), probably of the first composition (1162 and 1184). A thirteenth-century monk might have perceived a contradiction between the first composition of the *Gesta Barcinonensium comitum*, a work that ends with the reign of Ramón Berenguer IV de Barcelona (1131–62), and a panegyric that sings of the defeat of Berenguer Ramón II, thus resulting in the scraping of the stanzas that relate to the earlier Berenguer's defeat. Further, while the erasure constitutes a disconcerting lacuna for modern-day scholars, it can also be seen as providing coherence to the codex as a whole in the thirteenth century. The date of Barbarroja's death falls within the date ranges proposed for the *Carmen*. If the latest date for the *Carmen* is accepted, it could be claimed that the substitution of the defeat of the Conde de Barcelona and other events for a text about the death of Barbarroja is a displacement of part of one text from 1190 for another dated from that same year, the *Epistola de Barbarroja* (Epistle of Barbarossa), even if that displacement was purely accidental.

This substitution argument, which is its own sort of synecdochic reasoning, nevertheless does little to remedy the text that the poem lacks, even if it provides some information regarding the logic of the compilation of the *Carmen*'s manuscript context and its possible process of fragmentation. It is clear that incompleteness at the end yields a wide variety of effects. A lengthy, nearly or relatively complete work like the *Mocedades* is an unquestionably good candidate to serve as an effective metonymy of its whole, but the whole to which one aspires depends upon one's goals: a whole version of what was once in the BnF manuscript; or a version entirely in verse of what is in the manuscript (the *Refundición* of Funes and Tenenbaum); or the now lost *Gesta* that Funes and Tenenbaum recreate in their edition. While things are bleaker in terms of text loss in the *Carmen*, it is clear to which whole we should aspire. We can remember here Deyermond's statement about how some critics more confidently advance hypotheses about lost rather than extant work. In cases of fragmentation and attempts at restoration, there is necessarily a detection of loss, but there is also sometimes a dissatisfaction with the extant text that can vary in intensity depending on the perceived value of the work that survives. With the *Mocedades* as presented in Funes and Tenenbaum's edition, the critical work looks beyond an extant text that appears complete in search of a more epic epic, one entirely in verse and without any seemingly extraneous passages that detract from its primary plot.

The *Mocedades* is, however, a strong metonymy of its whole today if the whole is the complete *Refundición* and a fairly good touchstone of the *Gesta*, though in the latter case a reconstruction of the *Gesta* displaces the actual epic that we conserve. The reconstruction of the *Gesta*, which really is a different text rather than a purer version of the extant *Mocedades*, entails that the *Refundición* is a derivative work compiled and copied by a scribe directed either by his own intentions and motivations or by those of his masters. From this point of view, the proposed missing bits of the extant *Mocedades*, while important, are somewhat offset by what is perceived as the added Palencian material that must be removed to produce the *Gesta* and the very fact that it is considered necessary to produce a *Gesta* at all.

For its part, *Roncesvalles* initially appears to be at the other end of the spectrum, in the sense that the task of the philologist or literary critic is not simply to remove sections that are insufficiently epic – or, as in the case of the *Poema de Almería*, to imagine the missing final episode whose content is known with a fairly high degree of certainty – but to imagine nearly the entirety of an epic, in the event the critic believes it to have been one. The *Carmen* occupies something of a middle ground; even though it has fairly significant content gaps, it is material at the end; even in cases in which we cannot pinpoint the content directly, the commonness of incompleteness at the end among medieval and early modern manuscript texts normalizes the loss to a degree.

Of the epic or epic-content texts examined or mentioned here, all end in medias res except the acephalous *Cantar* and the highly fragmentary *Roncesvalles*. The status of fragmentary as opposed to fragment is thus more commonly associated with works that are relatively complete elsewhere or that have lacunae that can be remedied, at least in terms of identifying the general context of the lost verses. Further, fragmentariness, particularly incompleteness at the end, is more commonly associated with accident rather than an intentional act, sometimes for reasons of having very little manuscript evidence to suggest otherwise. However, the *Carmen* was deliberately rendered fragmentary and the *Poema de Almería* may have been, at least according to one early modern intellectual and one other manuscript witness. Knowledge that a work was made fragmentary on purpose plays some role in its status as fragment rather than simply fragmentary, whether the text was rendered a fragment by using a very physical mechanism but for intellectual reasons, like the *Carmen*, or for practical reasons, as with at least part of the *Roncesvalles*. In the context of these Iberian Castilian and Latin epics, if intentionality is associated not only with fragmentation but also with the designation of fragment, are any of the other epics that are incomplete at the end truly fragments?

The *Cantar* is not a fragment and likely not even fragmentary, as its missing content enjoys a substantial degree of consensus; in the case of the first fifty verses, it can be supplied from a specific chronicle. We might say the same of the *Mocedades de Rodrigo*, as the content of the ending of the poem can be extrapolated to some degree from other sources, namely that Rodrigo would return home triumphant, ready to marry Jimena, and become the most famous warrior in Spain's history.[62] Apart from its length, though, the clearest reason why the *Mocedades* is not a fragment is that its problem is most commonly seen as one of excess rather than lack, albeit an excess intended by the copyist or reviser of the extant text. Even when its oddities are tolerated and left to rest in their place in the Paris manuscript, as in the case of Bailey's 2007 edition and translation, the Palencian material and other text (including what may have been glosses) are still regarded, probably rightly, as interpolations.[63] The challenge for some in working on the *Mocedades* is thus not so much a reconstruction of the extant text, as is more true of the less careful *Poema de Fernán González* manuscript, but a removal or reordering of the extant text and a reconstruction to some degree of a hypothetical original text.

The opposite is true with *Roncesvalles,* for which, as with the *Carmen Campidoctoris,* one of the most frustrating questions is determining the nature of the missing content. Due to the intentional nature of their fragmentation and the relative vagueness in speculating about their lost content, each is both fragmentary and a fragment. Even in the event that we regard the *Roncesvalles* as a relatively complete episode, it is still somewhat fragmentary. We can, however, concurrently consider it an outright fragment, but a fragment that has coherence in itself. The *Poema de Almería,* on the other hand, is likely more accurately fragmentary, as there is evidence of circulation of the epic in a fragmentary condition in the early modern period and uncertainty as to the intention behind the fragmentation, despite Pellicer's hypothesis regarding Higuera's bad intentions.

While the adjectives "fragmentary" and "incomplete" can be considered interchangeable, it is very clear that the term "incomplete" indicates a loss significantly less grave than what the noun "fragment" conveys. There are nevertheless several points of contact between characteristics of fragments and works that are fragmentary. In the Iberian epics studied or cited here, an epic fragment is a product of an intentional act, as opposed to an accident or unknown cause, as is more frequently the case with fragmentary works. However, epic fragments and fragmentary epics are both associated with foundational nineteenth- and twentieth-century reconstructions of an epic's traditional trajectory, along with its lost content and sometimes the verses that may have comprised the lost epic whole; the best-known case of an epic that does not exist materially is Menéndez Pidal's reconstruction of *Siete Infantes* verses from two different chronicles, the *Crónica general de 1344* (General chronicle of 1344) and the *Interpolación de la tercera crónica general* (Interpolation of the third general chronicle). Further, both epic fragments and fragmentary epics are associated with careful transcriptions and editions, such as Menéndez Pidal's lengthy and still relevant study of the *Roncesvalles.* A difference, however, is that epic fragments are fairly infrequently the object of literary study or studies explicitly attuned to their aesthetic aspects, unlike the *Cantar,* and even the *Poema de Fernán González* and the *Mocedades* to some extent: with these last two, however, the subject of study focuses more on edition, assonance, verse length, the poems' evolution, and language. It is worth noting that epic fragments that may not function well as literary works today may well have been quite operable when performed orally in fragmentary form in the Middle Ages.

The difficulty of studying fragments today has lent itself to traditionalist approaches, especially reconstruction efforts, as opposed to approaches with roots in Joseph Bédier's "individualist" or neoindividualist thought (such as Deyermond's) with a focus on the extant text.[64] Further complicating codicological and editorial work, oftentimes a fragmentary work has defects other than missing text, such as interpolations, lacunae, and other inconsistencies that indicate a poor-quality copy. Even in a relatively complete text, these are characteristics that lend themselves to approaches similar to those applied to brevity.

The fragmentariness and scarcity of Iberian epics have thus given rise to a wide range of approaches, including many that are, logically, highly compensatory. Some epic fragments were more readily plucked from chronicles than others, and what remained of other texts, like the sole episode of *Roncesvalles*, did not lend itself as easily to the creation of a narrative or "encasement in text," as, say, the *Siete Infantes de Lara*.[65] The *Carmen*, on the other hand, is problematic in that many denouements could have concluded the epic. *Roncesvalles* and the *Carmen*, the only Iberian epic fragments, are counterpoints to the *Siete Infantes* in that they show that physical testimonies are not a panacea. The story of fragmentariness goes beyond the texts themselves and the material that conserves them. It includes the way in which the texts became fragmentary, the perceptions of early modern users, and our modern-day perceptions, desires, and overall valuation of the texts. The question of whether each of our extant epics serves as a successful metonymy of its whole is far more complicated than it might first appear. The whole to which one aspires, whether we appear to know quite a bit about it (as in the case of some interpretations of the *Mocedades*) or not much at all (*Roncesvalles*) is clearly the creation, even if a well-founded one, of the critic.

Chapter Two

From Bound to Metonym: Early Modern and Modern Disuse of Chivalric Fragments[1]

With the expansion of the printing press in the sixteenth century, copies of nearly every type of medieval and early modern text in Europe, from the texts of Aristotle to the *Summa theologiae*, the Bible, and myriad literary and legal texts, were subject to a practice that likely dates to the first codices ever produced: the fragmentation of manuscript leaves and their use for practical, nonhermeneutic and nonaesthetic purposes, or what Anthony Wood has called "servile uses."[2] Leaves and partial leaves were recycled and employed as pastedowns, reinforcing strips, pasteboard pads, flyleaves, and as wrappers for other books. Single folios or sections of folios gave stiffness or lining to items of apparel, including hats and shoes. As we saw in chapter 1, manuscript fragments like *Roncesvalles* served as material for personal accessories like bags and folders. Leaves composed lampshades, gun wadding, seal bags, and rags for cleaning dirty shoes and candlesticks.

Damage to manuscripts also resulted from early modern and modern users who loved books to death and could not resist pulling them apart for various personal interests. Some particularly beloved or attractive leaves were separated for safe keeping or sale. Manuscript miniatures were removed for use as wall decorations or to adorn travelling cases. In both the early modern and modern periods, initials were removed for both commercial and transitory personal uses. By the seventeenth century, there is evidence of interest in generating fragments for the purpose of creating examples of ancient handwriting.[3] The modern age has made its own mark on medieval manuscripts, with marginal material eliminated in the rebinding of books and with the practice, which reached its height in the nineteenth century, of cleaning the margins of annotations so that manuscript pages would be more appealing to wealthy collectors.[4] In the nineteenth century, museums, which used fragments for teaching purposes in the name of art and design education, fuelled dismemberment and a fragment market. Scholarly ambition itself has led to the marring of certain leaves, primarily through the use of chemical reagents, to decipher text. Some partially complete Bibles, psalters, and Qur'ans sold at leading auction houses like Christie's and Sotheby's were subsequently separated and sold as individual leaves.[5] Pairs of leaves and nonconsecutive lots of leaves from religious manuscripts have turned relatively high profits on the auction block. Christopher de Hamel began his 1995 Sol. M. Malkin Lecture in Bibliography at the University of Virginia with an anecdote about a late colleague who cut disks of vellum from a fifteenth-century choir book to repair a blown gasket in his car.[6]

This chapter studies a particular practical use in detail in a practical manner by examining the use of manuscript text as binding material and proposes a possible approach to these fragments. One subset of Iberian manuscripts that is particularly well represented among manuscripts used as binding material is chivalric romances. Manuscript copies of the *Amadís de Gaula*, the *Tristán de Leonís*, the *Lancelot*-Vulgate, the Portuguese *Liuro de Josep Abaramatia*, and others were torn to pieces, more valued for their material than their texts, which had become available in print form. The chapter analyses the disuse of two chivalric manuscripts as text and/or images in the early modern period and their employment as binding material. Drawing on two sets of fragments found in early modern bindings in the twentieth century, fragments of the sole extant manuscript of the *Amadís de Gaula*, and text and image fragments of the *Tristán de Leonís*, I argue that, while in the early modern period the manuscripts were disused as reading or viewing material primarily for practical reasons and due to the success of their printed editions, today the fragments remain largely ignored as texts and images. This modern disuse results from the scarcity of the fragments' text or images, as well as from scholarly approaches that focus primarily on description and transcription, and inadvertently explain the fragments away, leading to a return to the printed editions. Here I continue to reflect on the role of the critic; I examine the ways in which we might use these and other fragments philologically, aiming to reverse their disuse and to return the fragments to hermeneutic use through an analysis of a selection of the *Tristán* miniatures and portions of the text of the *Amadís* fragments. The analysis allows the pieces to overcome their status as fragments and to become metonyms of their once-whole manuscripts, a practice explored in a theoretical manner in the first chapter. This chapter engages the fragments in a metonymic philology that identifies and studies extant continuities rather than searching for missing symbolic codes; this metonymic philology can function on material that was originally intended to be read and engaged hermeneutically and on images that primarily served as a guide to the plot.

The chapter first examines a group of fifty-nine pieces of text and images from a fifteenth-century manuscript of the *Tristán de Leonís* (hereafter *Tristán*), one of two extant medieval Castilian versions of the *Tristan en prose*. The testimonies of the *Tristán* in prose reflect two lines of transmission. The first consists of two fourteenth-century folios in Galician Portuguese, while the second includes the following: an incomplete manuscript of 131 folios held at the Vatican Library, whose text is known as the *Cuento de Tristán de Leonís* (Story of Tristan of Leonis); two different fourteenth-century fragmentary testimonies in Catalan, which combined are eight folios; the fifty-nine fragments of interest to this chapter, BNM, MSS 20262/19 (one folio) and 22644/1–51, the first found in 1902, the others in 1998; and the sixteenth-century print editions. A manuscript similar to the one of which the BNM fragments once formed part was likely the source for the printed editions, including: Valladolid (1501), printed by Juan de Burgos; Seville (1511), Jacobo Cromberger; Seville (1520), Juan Varela de Salamanca; Seville (1525), Juan Varela de Salamanca; and Seville (1528), Juan Cromberger.[7] The *Carta de Iseo y respuesta de Tristán* (BNM, MS 22021; Isolde's letter and Tristan's response), discovered in 1976 in a private collection, is an independent text inspired by the *Tristán* story. This *Carta* derived from the printed editions as well, as did the only preserved continuation of the *Tristán*, the *Tristán de Leonís el Joven* (Tristan of Leonis the Young), printed in Seville in 1534. Of the fifty-nine BNM fragments, this chapter focuses primarily on a selection of the twenty-seven extant image fragments, particularly the contiguous ones.

The second group of fragments in this chapter comprises the four pieces of the sole extant manuscript testimony of the *Amadís de Gaula* (ca. 1420). The fragments are held at the Bancroft Library in Berkeley, California (UCB) and were first published by Antonio Rodríguez Moñino in 1957. Rodríguez Moñino has identified the pieces as corresponding roughly to book 3 of Garci Rodríguez de Montalvo's *Amadís de Gaula* (1508), but the text of the fragments has important differences. In contrast to the printed editions, the manuscript lacks the fourth book that Montalvo identifies as one of his contributions to the *Amadís* and also has different chapter divisions. Further, it is clear that the manuscript possesses its own style and a unique way of communicating events to readers. In the 1960s, Antonio Rodríguez Moñino requested that the *Amadís* fragments be bound in leather by Emili Brugalla, one of the Iberian Peninsula's best-known twentieth-century binders. The fragments form their own small book, perhaps an attempt, in addition to improving usability and for conservation, to recover a past wholeness.[8]

As destructive as the disuse of the *Amadís* and *Tristán* manuscripts as text or images might appear, it is indicative of a tradition: the reuse of manuscript leaves in the binding of other manuscripts and for other practical purposes. As in the case of many fragments found in the past two centuries, particularly those discovered in the process of repairing or replacing bindings, little is known about the codices from which the *Amadís* fragments were extracted. In Rodríguez Moñino's initial study of the fragments, he simply states that Antonio Moreno Martín (d. 1990), a well-known bibliographer from Almería, discovered them upon changing the bindings on some old volumes and that they were found in two separate discoveries, the second undertaken at the request of Rodríguez Moñino himself.[9] The contents and the age of the tomes from which they came are unknown, and the wide parameters of Moreno's library, spanning the thirteenth through the twentieth centuries and totalling some one hundred thousand volumes, make it foolish to hazard a guess. In the case of the *Tristán* fragments, however, more is known. Fifty-nine fragments (BNM, MS 22644/1–51) were extracted from the nineteenth-century binding of BNM, MS 12915, a late fifteenth-century codex containing works of canon law that formed part of the library of "San Francisco de Segovia," as noted in its first paper folio.[10] The first parchment folio of MS 12915 contains residue from a fragment, number 25. Another fragment from the same *Tristán* manuscript, found separately by Adolfo Bonilla y San Martín in 1902, served as a folder for the nineteenth-century scholar Agustín Durán's notes on Vélez de Guevara's novel *Diablo cojuelo* (1641).

The *Tristán* and *Amadís* fragments are by no means the only Iberian chivalric fragments found in bindings. As Lucía Megías has observed, though the Matter of Britain was highly successful in the Middle Ages, as indicated by allusions in literary works and its presence in daily life in the form of the names of people and animals, there are only some ten extant Arthurian manuscripts in Iberian languages, many of which he calls "instrumental" fragments used as binding material.[11] Apart from the two sets of fragments that concern us here, among the extant fragmentary chivalric testimonies employed in the binding of other books are two fourteenth-century parchment folios in Catalan of the *Lancelot*-Vulgate, which served as a cover for a sixteenth-century account book, and another parchment folio that served as either cover or wrap; two fifteenth-century parchment folios of the Portuguese *Liuro de Josep Abaramatia* (Book of Joseph of Arimathea); three fourteenth-century parchment folios of the *Suite de Merlin* (Merlin continuation) in Galician Portuguese used to reinforce the binding of the first and second parts of the third edition of Pierzossi's *Chronicon* (Bâle: Nicolas Kesler, 10 February 1491); two now lost fourteenth-century parchment folios in Galician Portuguese of the *Livro de Tristán* (Book of Tristan) that comprised part of the binding of a 1501 copy of the testament of the Marqués de Santillana made in Guadalajara; and four fifteenth-century paper folios of the *Tristán*. Apart from these binding fragments, the sole extant folio of a manuscript *Tirant lo Blanc* (*Tirant the White*) was used for another practical purpose: as a folder to contain documents related to a court case involving one Johan de Loriz and Pero Maça de Liçana, dated 11 October 1454.

The fragments above evince general trends in practical use in the late-medieval and early modern periods, and even in the nineteenth century, but cannot explain exactly why our fragments were seen as more useful for their material than for their texts. Of the chivalric manuscripts just cited, several were disused as texts and employed in early modern bindings or put to another practical use in the early modern period, particularly as folders, as with Catalan folios of the *Lancelot*-Vulgate that served to cover the sixteenth-century account book mentioned above and the sole extant folio of a *Tristán* manuscript. Both sets of the *Tristán* fragments that concern us here were disused as text in these same ways in the nineteenth century.

Nicolas Pickwoad and others have logically attributed the frequent fragmentation of manuscripts in the early modern period to the advent of printing and the subsequent availability of large numbers of medieval manuscripts as ready material, including illuminated manuscripts, grammars, those with musical notation, and chivalric romances.[12] The increased output of printed books and changes in trends in liturgical practice, education, and literature were accompanied by a purging of manuscripts from libraries, whether for replacement by printed versions of the same texts or by new texts altogether.[13] This purging was especially pronounced in monastic and conventual libraries in northern European countries with the establishment of Protestantism, but it is clear that Catholic Europe also made frequent use of medieval manuscripts as binding material and saw to the removal of books of entertainment, like chivalric romances, from their collections.[14] Sixteenth-century Spanish historians including Ambrosio de Morales (1513–91) and Jerónimo de Zurita (1512–80) lament the loss of medieval manuscripts from monastic libraries. As Lucía Megías and others have noted, Zurita shares his concern for the destruction of intellectually worthy and expensive manuscripts with Antonio Agustín Albanell, the humanist historian, jurist, and archbishop of Tarragona, in a letter that dates from 1579 or 1580. Speaking of books that he had donated to the Saragossan Aula Dei monastery, Zurita asks the archbishop for assurance that the manuscripts will evade both printers and bookmakers, and find a safe haven in the monastery. He also hopes, however, that the manuscripts will be of some intellectual value:

> En cuarenta años que han pasado que los voy recogiendo y escapando del poder de impresores y libreros, que andan comprando pergamino para despedazallo; y aun estos días han venido a mis manos algunos de poder de libreros, que los habían ya condenado por esto, que son de estimación, y acuden a mí por lo que más vale que lo que a ellos cuesta, tomándolos a peso del pergamino o papel; porque todavía es mejor que allí se conservan en buena guarda, pues pueden ser de algún provecho algún dia, que estar al mismo peligro de perderse.[15]
>
> (In the past forty years I have collected and saved books from printers and booksellers that buy parchment in order to tear it to pieces; and even recently I have come upon some books in the hands of a bookseller that had been condemned to this, which are of value, and that come to me for more than what those that pay for them according to the weight of parchment or paper; because it is still better that they be conserved carefully, such that they can be of some use some day, rather than be at risk for loss.)

Zurita's contemporary Ambrosio de Morales similarly notes the loss of good reading material for the sake of its support in several Leonese monasteries. Preceding a list of the books that remained in the San Bernardo de Carracedo monastery, Morales writes that while many of the library's volumes have been lost for a lack of appreciation of their content, some remain: "Libros han tenido muchos, y hanlos dado para pergamino viejo: todavía quedan estos" (They had many books and have given them away for their old parchment: these still remain).[16] Similarly, of the Santa María de Sandoval and San Benito de Sahagún monasteries, he writes respectively: "No hay duda sino que huvieron Buenos Libros antiguos mas todo está ya perdido" (Without a doubt there were old Good Books, but now all is lost) and "De la Libreria se han perdido muchos Libros, que alli huvo, muy antiguos" (Many books have been lost from the Library that were there, very old ones).[17] Morales writes at length of his experience in the San Pedro de Montes monastery, suggesting that the books there should be treated as relics, recalling Menéndez Pidal's classification of lost and found epic parts as relics. In reality, Morales held that the books should be valued even more highly than the saint's other personal effects, since he had put them to intellectual use:

> Ethimologias de S. Isidoro, sin principio, ni fin, maltratado. Vitae Patrum, deshojado: tienen las vidas de S. Paulino, Santo Augustin, S. Geronimo, y pocas mas: fue gran volumen. Un pedazo de los Morales de S. Gregorio. Beati Basilij, institutio Monachorum, pequeño. Como es gran lastima ver estos Libros tan despedazados, asi pone devocion tomarlos en las manos, pues son como Reliquias, en consideracion que el Santo los trató mucho, y estudió en ellos, y asi tienen una mayor estima que una cinta, ò un pedazo de su ropa, si pudiera haber.[18]

> (The *Etymologies* of Isidore of Seville, without beginning or end, treated badly. The *Vitae Patrum* [Lives of the Fathers], stripped of its leaves: they have the lives of Saint Paulinus of Nola, Saint Augustine, Saint Jerome, and little more: it was a large volume. A piece of the *Morals* of Saint Gregory. The *Order of Monks* of Saint Basil, but little. As it is a great shame to see these books so torn to pieces, it inspires devotion to take them in our hands, because they are like relics, considering that the saint used them a lot, and used them for study, and thus they have greater value than a ribbon, or a piece of clothing could have.)

The fact that the *Tristán* and *Amadís* fragments were "despedazados" reveals that their text was of lesser value than their material, even if that text was not considered offensive or a factor of any kind in the decision to tear them up. At first glance, one of the most surprising aspects of the *Tristán* fragments is the fact that they include images, leading one to wonder why, if they were not appreciated for their text, they were not saved for their decorative value, even if the images were considered relatively unsophisticated and not particularly attractive. Apart from religious texts including *Beatos* (*Beatus* manuscripts) and Bibles, we conserve very few Iberian illuminated manuscripts, with the most famous being the manuscripts of the *Cantigas* (*Songs of Holy Mary*), *Calila e Dimna* (*Calila and Dimna*), and of course the *Zifar* (*Book of the Knight Zifar*). We know, however, that popularity and even holiness certainly did not stop the disuse of text as reading material, and it appears that this also applied to at least some images. Meradith McMunn's study on the fragments of the *Roman de la Rose* (*Romance of the Rose*) nevertheless shows that illuminated *Rose* manuscripts – whose images do consistently exceed in quality those of the early modern *Tristán* manuscript – were less likely to be fragmented than plain ones, as there are proportionally fewer illustrated fragments than complete manuscripts.[19] Illustrated *Rose* manuscripts did prove to have staying power, in that they continued to be produced in the sixteenth century after the appearance of printed editions, some of which were also illustrated.[20] In other cases, however, it is clear that the content and appearance of the available manuscripts was not a major factor as to whether they were disused for intellectual and aesthetic purposes or used instead to replace excised material. McMunn cites a fourteenth-century manuscript currently in the collection of manuscript dealer Heribert Tenschert in which three miniatures were cut and replaced with other miniatures that have very little to do with the content of their nearby text.[21] Pickwoad argues that even when a leaf appears to have been used for decorative purposes for a new book, there is little evidence that subject matter or content inspired the use of the decorated leaf:

> When manuscript waste was used it was generally plain text leaves that were used, though occasionally binders do seem to have succumbed to a decorative impulse when confronted by a large initial on a manuscript leaf, especially where it was to be used on a small book, though there is no evidence to suggest that they were in any way influenced by the subject matter of the book. Such covers can be found just as easily on a volume of secular songs as on a work of serious theology, and there are many surviving examples where it is clear that decorated initials did not influence the way parchment was used. Some binders were seemingly oblivious to the decorated initials which they folded in around edges of a cover or through which they laced sewing support slips and fore-edge ties.[22]

The online galleries from the Yale Law Library's 2010 exhibit *Reused, Rebound, Recovered: Medieval Manuscript Fragments in Law Book Bindings* evince Pickwoad's claims, in that many of the exhibit's book covers and pastedowns made from leaves with musical notation and leaves containing illuminated initials have no connection to the main content of the codices.[23] Alternatively, we can cite the modern case of the piecemeal sale of leaves of books of hours at rare-book stores and at auction, a practice in which there is clear interest in the individual images or, rather, in as many images as the buyer can afford, but no significant interest in conserving the manuscript intact as a means of studying the miniatures as a group.

The taking apart of a series of miniatures, whether to repurpose the material for love or disregard of the images, extends into the present. In this vein, the *Tristán* image and text fragments could be considered doubly lamentable from a modern perspective. Their presence does, however, support the notion that fragmentation for reasons of censorship in the early modern period was fairly rare, a notion directly in line with Lowe's 1964 seminal study, which proposed the conditions and criteria that led to the creation of early medieval palimpsests, namely that they came about due to a shortage of material or an inability to afford what was available.[24] Georges Declercq has recently reiterated the reasons why palimpsests were created, each of which may have impacted the decision to reuse the *Tristán* in a practical manner: the quality of the support, the physical state of the book containing the pages to be reused, and the presence of a second copy of the text to be overwritten, or in our case of paper manuscripts, reused in another way.[25]

Tristán Fragments

While there are diverse reasons why the *Tristán* manuscript was put to practical use, the fragments themselves evince the variety of effects that can result from this sort of employment. Like the other twenty-some *Tristán* fragments pulled from the nineteenth-century binding, the images evince various types of dilapidation and fragmentation. A third of the miniatures have transfer from textual fragments stuck to their surfaces. Some of the textual fragments, meanwhile, contain blue and red ink transfer from miniatures. On three miniatures, the ink is so badly corroded that their images are scarcely detectable at all. Miniatures 20a, b, and cv arrived in three separate strips that have subsequently been put back together.[26] Miniature 25r was attached to and subsequently removed from a guard folio of the manuscript from which the fragments were pulled (BNM, MS 12915).

Despite their appearance, there is nevertheless some semblance of coherence in the miniatures. It is evident that they were once large in scale and not particularly detailed. Many of the scenes, people, animals, and structures they portrayed more clearly in the past can still be identified, including characters of the story, such as Palomades, Tristán, Galeote, Iseo, Brangel, King Arturo, Lanzarote, King Marco, and Saigremor, some of them identified with a label in the miniature. Some miniatures are consecutive (6ar and 6br; 9ar and 9br) or in close proximity (35ar, 35br), providing an opportunity to deduce, as Lucía Megías has noted, the frequency of miniatures in the codex and the relationship between them, including examining them as a series.[27] Some miniatures preserve text that describes the miniature's content or the names of the characters featured (1r, 6br, 9abr, 14r, 18v, 20abcv, 25r, 30r, 33r; and MS 20262/19), while others depict particularly large figures or highlight specific characters, acting in part as portraits (Iseo, 4v; Brangel, 5r; Tristán and Galeote, 2r). Some fragments have miniatures on both faces.

The frequency of the miniatures in the once-whole manuscript was high, with sometimes two illuminations for a single chapter of the sixteenth-century printed book. Such is the case in the scene depicting the defeat of Palomades's brother, both of whom were foes to Tristán, and the subsequent liberation of the temporarily captive Arturo, king of Britain (figure 3). Approximately half of the images include titles in red. Instead of portraying a single, concrete, preterit event, the titles often evoke processes, encouraging the observer to witness the gradual realization of an action in the past, including Palomades (in love with Queen Iseo and thus an enemy of Tristán) searching for some squires and finding Brangel (Queen Iseo's damsel) in the forest after Queen Iseo had ordered her death out of jealousy of the maid's relationship with the king (6br) and Tristán rescuing King Arturo in the Gasta Floresta after the king had been captured and threatened by the Doncella del Arte (Artful damsel) with death if he would not marry her (9br).[28] As Lucía Megías has indicated, the miniatures highlight specific exploits, particularly those of Tristán.[29] The titles of the miniatures are interpretive, in that they describe the content that was selected for depiction among all the events of a given chapter. They are also interpretive in the sense that the artist's portrayal is a reading of the people and objects mentioned in the story. The titles nevertheless fall short of inserting the images into the ideological framework that Lucía Megías has proposed.

While the images themselves do contain symbolic coding, the images' titles, scale, and lack of intricate detail, as well as their frequency – which

Figure 3 The defeat of Palomades's brother and the liberation of King Arturo, *Tristán de Leonís*, BNM, MS 22644, 9abr

Lucía Megías has noted can be inferred from other consecutive series of preserved folios – suggest that their primary function was to make the characters more present and familiar to readers, rather than to offer a sophisticated ideological commentary on the narrative.[30] In this section, I argue that attempting to decode the miniatures' individual parts may in some cases not be the most productive way to put them back to use. In visual richness, the *Tristán* miniatures stand in contrast to the majority of the 240 elaborate, high-quality medieval images of the *Libro del caballero Cifar* (*Book of the Knight Zifar*) manuscript, for instance.[31] In the *Cifar*, it appears that those responsible for determining the content of the miniatures had read the text fairly carefully. In some cases they went beyond the content of the chapter titles, sometimes, as Christopher Donahue has observed of the interpolated *Flores de filosofía* (Flowers of philosophy) section and other scenes of instruction, for lack of content in the text that lends itself to representation or to avoid representing the same content multiple times.[32] The chapter titles and miniatures of the *Tristán*, on the other hand, are tightly correlated, save one case that I analyse here.[33]

François Garnier's criteria for studying medieval iconography offer one logical approach to the *Tristán* miniatures, a method of analysis that could be used to support claims as to the miniatures' ideological function. Garnier's method posits that the medieval image explains people, places, and things using a codified symbolic grammar, rather than simply picturing them.[34] The size and location of the figures within the miniature, along with the figures' positions, gestures, expressions, and attitudes are all symbolic and indicate the characters' intentions, rather than simply depicting the characters described in the text. While excellent in many cases for complete pictures and perhaps for some fragmentary ones, this symbolic representational method needs supplementation for fragmentary and even whole images whose relationship to the text is unclear. It is also important to distinguish between the use of a symbolic grammar in the image to represent attitudes described *within* the text and an image's advancement of an ideological reading *of* the text. Further, as Donahue has observed in relation to the *Cifar* miniatures, there is a difference between a team of artists' use of a set of conventions for hierarchic positioning, gestures, interior and exterior backgrounds, architecture, representations of warfare, animals and the possibility that these conventions constitute an ideological reading of the text or an image ideology. Instead, these features may tell us more about an illumination team's ability to follow a common set of instructions so that they could finish a project – an enormous one at that – in a timely manner.[35] Moreover, the possibility that the images reflect attitudes and beliefs of the artists' own times is a good one, and thus any ideology conveyed by the images is in part a function of a world fairly far removed from that of the chivalric text. This is not to say that the miniatures depict the artists' reality, but that their reality – or what Michael Camille calls a reality that the artists hoped to shape – combines with that of the text. As I explain below, this reality may be even more likely to have influenced the production of the images than any reading of the text.[36]

One series of images that illustrates these last points depicts part of the *Tristán* story in which King Mares of Cornwall and Tristán are at odds over Iseo, King Mares's wife. This section includes a scene in which King Mares goes to Arturo's court to seek vengeance on Tristán for the shame Tristán's affair with Iseo has brought upon him, as well as a scene of feigned reconciliation between Mares and Tristán. The first image shows King Arturo and Lanzarote speaking with Brangel outside of her tent right before Tristán and Iseo emerge from it (figure 4). The second miniature, essentially a stain and barely identifiable apart from the arms and legs of a standing knight, might depict Tristán or possibly Tristán and Lanzarote, since the corresponding chapter relates that Tristán and Lanzarote have just recognized each other after having unknowingly fought in a tournament (figure 5). The next fragment, number 18, presents text on its recto that is contiguous with the text on folios 17 and 19, but also presents an image on the verso showing Mares, Iseo, Tristán, and Arturo on horseback in a scene not described in the folios' text, a scene which could only have occurred after Arturo arranges Mares and Tristán's reconciliation (figure 6). Although Mares is mentioned at the end of the chapter that ends on folio 18r, he is not at all the focus of the chapter, as the last sentence indicates: "E dexemos lo agora estar E [torne]mos al rrey mar[es] de cornualla" (And we leave him be for now and turn to King Mares of Cornwall).

The feigned reconciliation that takes place in the following chapter includes several iconic scenes of the Tristan tradition that would make appealing subjects for a miniature, such as the series of tricks employed to reduce Mares's suspicion of Tristán and Iseo, including the famous placement of the sword between the sleeping lovers to illustrate the couple's supposed fidelity or, as in the 1501 edition, a scene showing Arturo's negotiation of the truce. Miniature 20, extant in three strips, nevertheless depicts Mares going to Arturo's court with twenty knights to seek vengeance on Tristán (figure 7). Miniature 18 (figure 6), representing the feigned reconciliation, would thus logically come after the one shown on folio 20, save perhaps the fact that the miniature shows Arturo, Tristán, Mares, and Iseo making a collective journey to Camelot that does not appear in any of the surrounding chapters. One journey to Camelot that would be a logical possibility for miniature 18 is Tristán and Lanzarotes's entry into Camelot after having been invited by Arturo and *before* Mares's arrival.

Figure 4 Brangel speaking with King Arturo and Lanzarote from the door of her tent, BNM, MS 22644, 14r

Figure 5 The figure of a knight, possibly Tristán, BNM, MS 22644, 17v

Figure 6 Tristán and Lanzarote's entry into Camelot (?), BNM, MS 22644, 18v

Figure 7 Mares going to Arturo's court with twenty knights to seek vengeance on Tristán, BNM, MS 22644, 20abcv

The title of miniature 18v, the seemingly misplaced – in terms of its image, not the text on its recto – miniature, identifies the characters depicted and indicates that Arturo, Mares, Tristán, and Iseo go to Camelot where the temporary reconciliation eventually takes place. This journey to Camelot occurs before Tristán is forced to return with Mares to Cornwall to provide the people with a reason for his association with Iseo. Attempts to decode the individual elements of the miniature do not answer why it actually appears in this location. Lucía Megías has suggested that this image constitutes a symbol of the disingenuous truce to come between Mares and Tristán.[37] This is, in many respects, a convincing interpretation, as Lucía Megías's analysis of the coding of the miniature indicates: Tristán as protagonist and Iseo's true love in the most central and thus important part of the miniature; only Tristán and Iseo's horses are visible, indicating their connection; and the unequal heights of King Mares and Iseo in the background, with Iseo positioned such that her back is to her husband to indicate dishonesty.[38]

Upon considering the other miniatures among the fragments, however, Lucía Megías's argument leaves several questions unanswered. There is no indication that such a symbolic premonitory gesture symbolizing the reconciliation of Tristán and Mares would occur in the manuscript. In every other case of the extant miniatures, the images simply depict material included in their preceding chapters, recalling that the chapter that precedes miniature 18 treats the combat between Lanzarote and Tristán and the journey of Tristán, Lanzarote, Arturo, Iseo, and Brangel to Camelot. The two miniatures that follow similarly represent chapter content, communicating two different processes: Mares's arrival at King Arturo's court with twenty knights to seek vengeance on Tristán, and Arturo's travel to the monastery where Lanzarote and Tristán were resting after having fought in a series of challenges with the fairy Morgana.

In the two other extant series of miniatures, there is similarly nothing to suggest symbolic meaning in the pictures, apart from the network of gestures and use of space in medieval iconography studied by Garnier, which again could in part be conventions of the miniaturists. The series consisting of miniatures 6av, 6bv, and 8v focuses on a single character's involvement (Palomades) in a sequence of episodes that begin with Iseo's ordering her damsel Brangel's death after having perceived an excessive familiarity between her husband and her lady. The extant miniature prior to 6a depicts Brangel crying, tied to a fruit tree and awaiting death, but soon to be pardoned or in the process of asking for pardon of the squires (not extant) whom Iseo orders to kill her. Miniature 6a (figure 8), which corresponds to the same printed chapter to which the image depicting Brangel corresponds, shows Palomades conducting the maid to the convent. Miniature 6b (figure 9), as the miniature title suggests, depicts Palomades's search for the squires who had left Brangel in the forest after deciding not to kill her. The following miniature, 8v (figure 10), again depicts Palomades with his hand at his sword, in conversation and demanding Iseo of Mares.

The series comprised of miniatures 6ar, 6br, and 8v is thus consistent to a fault, in that it perpetuates the focus on Palomades when it might have been much more provocative – and appropriate, considering the main events of the text – to represent something else in miniature 6br. The text prior to 6bv includes such important events as the queen's lament for not having seen Brangel for some time (despite having ordered her death) and her order for Brangel to be delivered to her, dead or alive. The images, when viewed consecutively as they appeared in the once-whole manuscript, depict a Palomades in motion, which in this case takes the form of his moving gradually to the outer edge of the manuscript page, as though having started by finding Brangel in the forest and working onward, in this case to the right, until he arrives in Camelot and takes Iseo. A similar appearance of motion and montage is found in the second extant group of contiguous miniatures: 9ar, 9br, and 11v. This series also centres on the exploits of one character: Tristán's successive defeat of Palomades's brother, his saving King Arturo from death, and his riding away with the recently saved king. As in the series that begins with 6a, the last two images of this second series (9av and 9bv; figure 3) can be viewed simultaneously.

The placement of miniature 18v (figure 6), which appears in the section of the romance that treats the feud, desired vengeance, and feigned reconciliation surrounding Iseo, was probably a mistake. Specifically, it is likely that the person responsible for placing the miniature at this juncture noticed that the conclusion of the chapter (on 18v) conveys that Tristán, Iseo, and Brangel go to Camelot at Arturo's invitation. The miniaturist or person who planned the miniatures thus read the word "Camelot" and the idea of journey, and anticipating both the resolution that came afterwards and Tristán's subsequent forced journey to Cornwall, depicted this journey by mistake.

Figure 8 Palomades escorting Brangel to a monastery for women, BNM, MS 22644, 6ar

Figure 9 Palomades seeking the squires who left Brangel in the forest, BNM, MS 22644, 6br

Figure 10 Palomades demanding that Mares surrender Iseo, BNM, MS 22644, 8v

Amadís Fragments

A mistake is hardly the most satisfying explanation for miniature 18, but it is more plausible than a purposeful act of destruction or a symbolic gesture. In any of these cases, it is difficult to determine the miniature's present hermeneutic possibilities or what they were intended to be at the time of its creation. Even when material can be fairly easily deciphered, transcribed, and described, its hermeneutic potential can be ambiguous. This can also occur when the majority of the fragment text correlates very closely with the extant editions, as with the *Tristán* text fragments. It is less of an issue when one considers the text on the fragments that does not appear in the editions at all or, rather, the text in the editions that does not appear in the fragments. Regarding the *Tristán* text fragments, in nearly all cases the fragments' text closely aligns with Juan de Burgos's 1501 edition, although there are some nine episodes in which there are fairly significant additions or suppressions.[39] Without generalizing too much about a diverse group of episodes, a few observations can be made. Fragment 10 contains a significant passage absent from the 1501 edition that provides insight into how Arturo is trapped and enchanted by the Doncella del Arte, who uses a ring, and the reason why he kills her. In the episode on the fragment, Arturo is truly the protagonist, rather than Tristán, and the reader is taken through the stages as prisoner, escapee, and destroyer of the Dueña del Lago (Lady of the Lake), with emphasis on the process rather than simply on the destruction of the Doncella and her castle with everyone in it, as is the case in the edition: "El rey tomó un espada de los que eran muertos e cortóle la cabeça, e los diablos la llevaron delante todos. Luego se encendió el Castillo e quemóse él e las gentes que eran en él." (Burgos, *El libro*, 45.104; The king took a sword from one of the dead and cut off her head, and the devils carried it before everyone. Then the castle was burned and all the people in it.) Another example is the correspondence between the fragment text that relates the death of Iseo and Tristán and that of the editions. Though there is text missing in the fragments, it is evident that along with other events surrounding the death of Tristán and Iseo, such as the war against Mares and punishment of Aldaret, Iseo's lament for Tristán is clearly more lengthy in Cromberger's edition, in which it is peppered with rhetorical questions for herself and readers, while she confesses and laments her wrongs and wonders about her possible future: "¿Mas qué digo agora?, que mis pecados han permetido este mal que me está agora presente, que Dios se venga de los injustos como yo?" (82.177; But what do I say now? That my sins have brought this wrong upon me that is now present with me, that God take vengeance on the unjust like me?).

These observations are modest, yet when studied in conjunction with other divergences, they have yielded several convincing theories to explain the origins of the adaptations and to describe the adaptations themselves, including theories of plagiarism and the influence of sentimental romance.[40] In the case of the *Amadís* fragments, so few in number and without any images that present opportunities for other types of engagement besides reading, study of the fragments is anxiety provoking. Since these fragments are both brief and not contiguous, they make it difficult to generalize about the once-whole manuscript and its relationship with the printed editions, as with the divergent parts of the *Tristán* fragments. Further, while the *Tristán* images might have wider interest among philologists, librarians, and other curators as the only extant Iberian chivalric image fragments, many of which Megías has shown can be at least partially decoded using Garnier's criteria, the physical appearance of the *Amadís* fragments is consistent with other chivalric binding fragments: plain, two-column text with red chapter headings preceded by a *calderón*.

Fragments can thus fall into disuse for several reasons, including if their text is too similar to extant printed editions, if they are noncontiguous pieces of what was once a manuscript of many folios, or, as with the *Tristán* miniatures, by failing to consider and actually accept the modest results of less meaning-oriented approaches. In the case of the *Amadís*, however, imagining a whole manuscript or even the text that would complete the missing lines in the fragments seems an entirely more risky venture. Nearly all of the very few studies on the fragments conclude that the pieces cannot tell us much of anything. Perhaps due in part to their California location, we count just one article dedicated to the fragments in over nearly fifty years.[41]

What, then, is actually known about the *Amadís* fragments, and what can they tell us? The fragments correspond roughly to four noncontiguous chapters of book 3 of Garci Rodríguez de Motalvo's version of the *Amadís*: chapters 65, 68, 70, and 72. They are bound in a book in a different order from the one in which they were discovered and in a chronology that diverges from Montalvo's version, with Montalvo's chapters 65 and 68 reversed. As Rodríguez Moñino observed in his initial study, in addition to providing concrete evidence of a manuscript tradition of the *Amadís*, they reveal that Montalvo was indeed not the creator of Esplandián, Amadís's son, or of the epithet "Caballero de la Verde Espada" (Knight of the Green Sword), one of Amadís's identities. It is for these last two pieces of information that one of the smallest of the four fragments, the one containing the name Esplandián, has been considered the most valuable of all.[42]

While it might be most desirable for the purposes of this study to read the *Amadís* fragments in their own right and without recourse to Montalvo's edition, this proves extremely difficult. The manuscript text is very brief and a minute portion of what it once was. The four individual manuscripts nevertheless can not only tell us something about Montalvo's edition, or the once-whole manuscript, but also together comprise a highly imperfect collective from which to advance hypotheses. A comparison of 2r, for instance, with the corresponding passage in Montalvo's chapter 65 reveals several small but fairly significant differences between the manuscript and print versions. In 2r, Amadís, his brother-in-law Don Bruneo de Bonamar, and squire Gandalín arrive at an island and encounter a confusing scene. The fragment is the second largest of the four, containing some one hundred words, with twenty-nine partial lines of text in one column and twenty-nine complete lines in the other. Many details of the arrival are missing, all of which are clearly articulated in chapter 65 of Montalvo's edition:

> Don Bruneo dixo:
>
> – ¿Vedes, señor, qué hermosa tierra?
> – Tal me paresce – dixo Amadís.
> – Pues paremos aquí, señor, dixo don Bruneo – unos dos días, y podrá ser que en ella fallemos algunas estrañas aventuras.
> – Aquí se haga – dixo Amadís.
>
> Entonces mandaron al patrón que acostasse la galea a la tierra, que querían salir a ver aquella ínsola, que muy hermosa les parescía, y también para si algunas aventuras hallassen.
>
> – Dios vos guarde della – dixo el maestro de la nao.
> – ¿Por qué? – dixo Amadís.
> – Por vos guardar de la muerte – dixo él – , o de muy cruel prisión; que sabed que ésta es la Ínsola Triste, donde es señor aquel muy bravo gigante Madarque, más cruel y esquivo que en el mundo ay. Y dígovos que passa de quinze años que no entró en ella cavallero, ni dueña, ni donzella, que no fuessen muertos o presos. (3.45.974)[43]

(Don Bruneo said:

– Do you see sir? What a fair land!
– So it seems to me, said Amadís.
– Then let us stop here, sir, said Don Bruneo, – some two days, and it may be that on it we find some rare adventures.
– So let it be done, said Amadís.

Then they gave orders to the captain to bring the ship inshore, for they wanted to disembark to see that island, which seemed very beautiful to them, and also in order to find some new adventures.

– God protect you from it, said the master of the ship.
– Why? said Amadís.
– To guard you from death, said he, – or from very cruel imprisonment, for know you that this is the Sad Island, where that very fierce giant Madarque is lord, more cruel and harsh than any other that there is in the world. And I tell you that in fifteen years, no knight or matron or maiden ever disembarked on it who was not killed or imprisoned.)[44]

Folio 2r of the fragments conveys a story similar to the Montalvo passage quoted above, describing Amadís and his companions' arrival at the island and a perception of the battle on shore. We know from Montalvo's chapter 65 that the island is the "Ínsola Triste" (Sad Island) and that the group arrives there en route to Gaul. In the fragment, the mention of the positioning of the ship and of shields, in addition to Amadís, Don Marinero, or Amadís's groups' pronouncement of "¡Dios confunda!" all appear in column A:

[...] quanto el mandasse pus[...]	[...] el [...]
[...] fecho sin mas tardar	[...] o [...]
[...] Dios si non quereis que todos	do [...]
[...][ci]ertos τ el lo dizia tan	sali [...]
[...]mente que ellos pensauan qu'el	aquella [...]
[...][mu]y cerca de lo fazer sy	τ asi
[...][fizi]esen su mandado τ de	que [...]
[...] el tienpo τ tomaron el remo [τ]	τ catas [...]
[...[[lleva]ron la naue contra la ynso[la]	cauall[ero] [...]
[...]por unas alturas [...]	su en [...]
[...]n ya quanto por la tierra	ras que [...]
[...] las aguas que descen[den]	tas as[...]
[...] montaña τ quando fueron	pelig[...]

[...] dixo don mariñero ved
[...]so en aquella ribera entre
[...] resplandecen escudos
[...] no[n] los vio τ di[xo]
[...][Di]os confunda
[...] τ ante los
[...] omes τ
[...] se bollir
[...] dezir nin
[...] ad que viera
[...] [o]tros que pa
[...] vanan τ me
[...] parescia

mas [...]
es que un [...]
vieron [...]
en su[...]
pera τ [...]
escude[ros] [...]
gero [...]
ros [...]
mejor [...]
en si lo [...]
falles [...]

(UCB, MS 115, 2r)[45]

In the manuscript, it is not certain whether the shipmaster ("el maestro de la nao") in Montalvo's edition, possibly "don marinero" (Mr sailor) in the fragment, is in fact the one who informs Amadís and his men about the cruelties of Madarque and the mortal dangers of the island. It appears strange, nevertheless, that, if the manuscript's Don Marinero plays the same warning role as the shipmaster in Montalvo's version, any of the men would be so disconcerted as to shout "¡Dios confunda!" (God confound) upon seeing a battle on the shore, particularly after a remark about having seen shining shields. Despite what could be a contradiction to the character as Montalvo presents him, it seems unlikely that any of the direct discourse or possible direct discourse in the fragment ("ved ... so en aquella ribera entre ... resplandecen escudos ... Dios confunda" ["look … upon that shore among … shields shine … I'll be damned]) would be Don Marinero's addressing the group of men. "Don Marinero," for its lack of article, is most probably a vocative. Further, if Don Marinero were in fact the subject of the "dixo" (he said) in line 14, it would be necessary to supply the verbs *ver* and *decir* in the line that precedes "¡Dios confunda!" with another singular subject, either one of Amadís's companions or perhaps the protagonist himself.

The ambiguity in fragment 2r with regard to exactly who orders the ship's approach to the island and who actually directs attention towards the shields combines with the questions of to what and to whom "su mandado" (his/their order or messenger) refers to suggest the fortuitous nature of the arrival at the island. This chance arrival stands in contrast to the situation in Montalvo's edition, in which the men collectively decide to approach the island: Bruneo provides the initial idea, the shipmaster the motivation with his story, and Amadís the final agreement. In the fragments, however, it seems more likely that Don Marinero is not nearly as informed as Montalvo's shipmaster, and that if any context for the island is in fact given, he is not the one who provides it. It is possible, then, that the arrival at the island and the encounter with Madarque, Galaor, and King Cildadán occur without prior knowledge of the island's ominous reputation. In the fragments, there is thus possibly no expectation of combat and little or no suspense about what could occur once they land. In this vein, whether it is the squire Bruneo or Amadís who notes the presence of shields in the manuscript, the shields, as Montaner has pointed out, do not appear to have an emblematic or heraldic function, serving, rather, primarily to signal the presence of a combat without raising suspicion and suspense about which knights the combatants might be.[46]

If the chain of communication for deciding to approach the island is not altogether clear in the manuscript, it is certain that the manuscript presents specific divergences from Montalvo's edition with regard to the particulars of Amadís's entry into combat with the giant. In noting the proper nouns in the fragment and in reading the corresponding chapter of Montalvo's edition (3.65), it is evident that folio 2v relates the scene in which Amadís and his men come upon King Cildadán of Ireland, Amadís's brother Galaor, and his dwarf vassal Ardián, whom they must rescue from the giant Madarque. There is no extant mention of the giant in the fragment, only what is likely a reference to Amadís's assault on Cildadán and Galaor. As Montaner notes in his study, one apparent difference between the text of the fragment and Montalvo's edition is that it is Amadís who decides to rescue Cildadán, Galaor, and Ardián, having himself recognized and identified both Ardián and Galaor by their appearance or their manner of fighting (figure 11) in UCB, MS 115, folio 2v:

[...] mas	
[...] su	[...]los lo mejor que podian y Ama[dis] [...]
[...] mas	venir de contra alla dan[do] [...]
[...] tan rre	a Ordian el su enano τ v[io?] [...]
[...]an roto	en varones como [...]
[...] andauan	res caualleros del mundo a[...]
[...][A]madis	nosció luego τ bien cuyda[ba] [...]
[...]ntado	don Galaor era el un[o] [...]
[...]nque	dos que querian matar τ to[mo] [...]

[...]rir o ma	armas muy toste e di[xo] a don [Bru-]
[...]a los ca	neo que tomase las s[us?] [...]
[...]se pue	[cu]idaba que era don Galaor... [mon-]
[...]la ynso[la]	taña τ quando Amadis [...]
[...]si tan	do conosçiolo Ordian que [...]
[...]o el quiere	sobreseñales que'el trai[a] [...]
[...]a alla tan	de yr contra el dando m[uchas] [...]
[...]de los	vozes ay señor A[madis][...]
[...]os suyos	sea Dios que vos tr[...]
[...] τ ama	buen señor [...]
[...] que ma	don Galaor [...]
[...] toviese	Cildadan [...]
[...] un po	Dios los [...]
[...]des boces	de amos que [...]
[...] sueño	τ entonces m[...]
[...]dustra	to mas pu[...]
[...] omes	τ Amadis [...]
[...] matar	de consu[...]

In contrast to Montalvo's edition, after recognizing Ordián (Montalvo's Ardián), Amadís continues as the subject of the first part of the fragment and is likely the subject of "v[io]" (right column, line 4) and "[co]nosció" (right column, line 7; recognized): "E A[madís vio] venir de contra allá dan[do bozes] a Ordian el su enano τ v[io?] y varones como [...] [t]res caualleros del mundo a[rmados τ] [co]nosció luego ..." (And Amadís saw Ordián his dwarf come from there screaming, and he saw men like … three armed knights, and then he recognized …). Amadís subsequently identifies Galaor as one of the combatants: "τ bien cuyda[ba] [...] don Galaor era el un[o] [...]" (And he was realizing … don Galor was the one). There is then a second assertion of Amadís's identification of Galaor in the narrator's indication that Amadís conveys this information to Don Bruneo and instructs him to take up arms to defend Galaor: "e di[xo] a don [Bru]neo que tomase las s[us?] [...][cu]idaba que era don Galaor ..." (And he told Don Bruneo to take up his [?] ... he was realizing that it was don Galaor). It is only after these exchanges that Ardián notices Amadís's arms and repeats information not only that Amadís already knows but also upon which he has already resolved to take action: "ay señor A[madis][...] sea Dios que vos tr[...] buen señor [...]don Galaor [...]" (Oh don Amadís … may God [see] that you … good man … don Galaor …). It is not clear if Ardián's comment in the manuscript initiates Amadís's

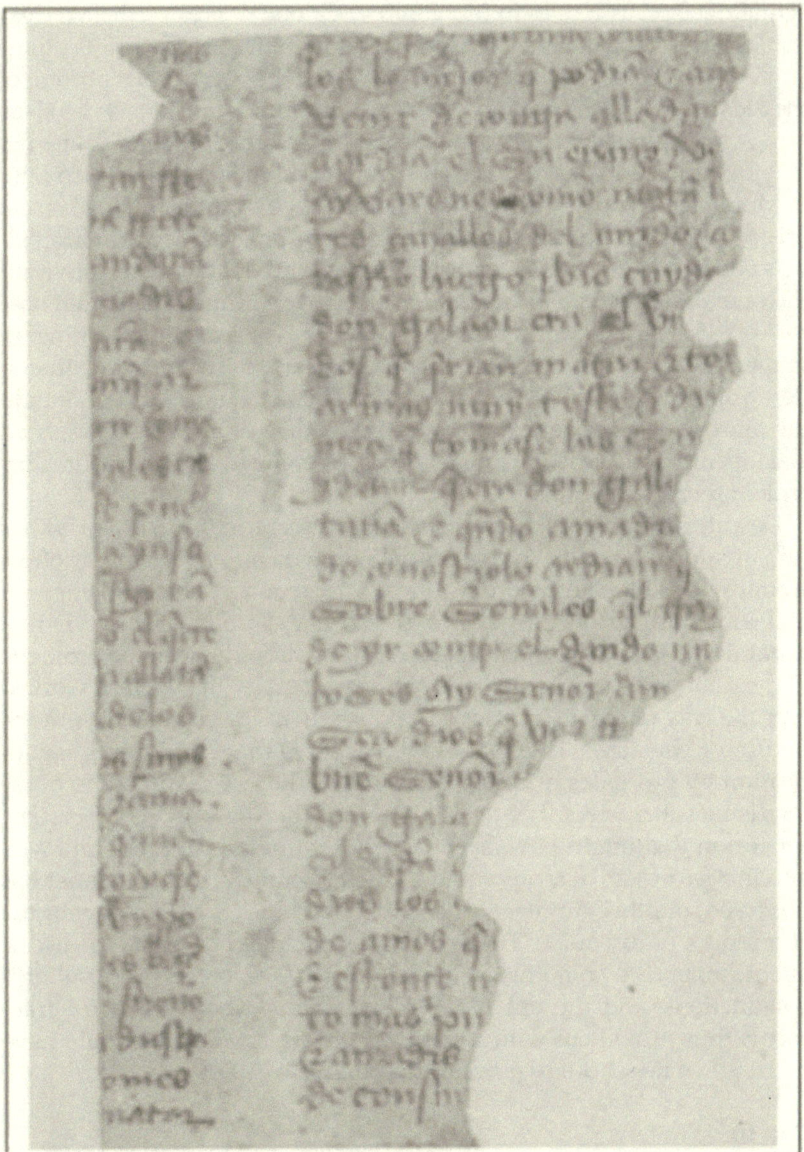

Figure 11 *Amadís de Gaula*, UCB, MS 115, 2v

actual defence, as it does in Montalvo's edition.[47] It is nevertheless clear that as a result of what seems to be a series of unnecessary identifications (Amadís – Ardián; Amadís – combatants) and the narrator's reporting of the combatants' identification ("e dixo a don Bruneo que tomase las s[sus armas que cu]idaba que era don Galaor" ["And he told Don Bruneo to take up arms as it was don Galaor"]), analysed in terms of emblematics in Montaner's study, Amadís's encounter with his brother on the "Ínsola Triste" seems less fortuitous than in the corresponding scene in Montalvo's edition.[48] Chance is thematized throughout Montalvo's chapter, and the unexpected but joyful encounter fuels several subsequent references to Amadís's and Galaor's pleasure at seeing one another, including an immediate reporting of their embraces and tears of joy: "Y desque fueron desarmados, abraçáronse muchas vezes Amadís y don Galaor, llorando del plazer que en se ver avian" (As soon as they disarmed, Amadís and Galaor embraced each other many times, weeping from the pleasure they took in seeing each other).[49]

Despite its highly fragmentary state, this scene in the manuscript has no gaps for the reader to ponder and on which to speculate; it offers a contiguous block of identifications. This repetition is confusing and awkward instead of clarifying. It is also likely a part of the style that Montalvo claims to have corrected, recalling his critique in the prologue of the poor and superfluous style of the originals with which he worked and the way in which he strove to polish them in accordance with the nature of chivalry.[50] The result is a discourse that emphasizes identification by processes of contiguity, such as the use of direct discourse by distinct characters. The text thus evinces needless and cumbersome repetition that might have been less present had its author employed succinct processes of representation such as emblems, as Montaner has observed, or other strategies of abstraction, which would allow for the shortening of discourse. These strategies include inference, the use of subordination to combine several short phrases joined by copulative conjunctions, and the use of collective nouns. The manuscript fragments thus provide us with a window into what Montalvo might have faced when he set out to produce the *Amadís* we read today.

Part for Whole

The early modern disuse of the *Amadís* and *Tristán* manuscripts for hermeneutic purposes, combined with their partial disuse today, reflect the varying needs of users throughout time and the relative popularity and broad availability of printed editions. Despite this disuse, this chapter has shown in a practical manner what was explored theoretically in the first chapter: that fragments can be read and studied in a way that can overcome the shortcomings of being partial and inert, and that they can come to serve as metonymies of their wholes. By locating visual and textual continuities in the extant pieces, these fragments become legitimate objects of study in their own right, serving as a means of hypothesizing about the text of their once-whole manuscripts. The fragments themselves thus temporarily overcome their fragmentariness and become metonyms of those manuscripts. With regard to metonymy and intentionality, it is notable that Lucía Megías follows his list of the extant "instrumental" chivalric fragments with a list of "textual fragments" that were conserved precisely because someone had taken an interest in their text, whether the fragment was conserved in a notebook or a compilation of texts.[51] While the instrumental and textual categories show the diverse ways by which fragments were created, they also highlight how, in both cases, perception makes or breaks fragments.

The textual utility of the *Amadís* fragments has been both implicitly and explicitly placed in doubt since their discovery, and, accordingly, perceptions of them are overwhelmingly positive as artefacts but lukewarm as to their precise function as texts. The present analysis of the *Amadís* and *Tristán* fragments works metonymically and yields modest results. In philological work, the goal is nearly always to produce something specific, but with the *Amadís*, the result might look almost too specific: the history of Amadís's identity, small differences in the way a scene is introduced, and modest observations about the style of the extant manuscript version of the *Amadís*. The majority of the *Tristán* fragment text is similarly closely aligned with the extant printed editions, save the passages discussed briefly above and a few others. This manuscript text, when considered even very briefly from a literary perspective, can nevertheless be used to make some tentative observations about the style of the once-whole manuscript. With the *Tristán* miniatures, the yield of avoiding overly symbolic interpretations and performing instead a philology firmly rooted in the characteristics of these specific pieces and how they function as a group is admittedly small: an explanation of a strange ordering of the miniatures by way of a proposal about the possible function of the miniatures in the once-whole manuscript. This metonymic philology intends only to set the once entombed binding fragments back in motion, moving beyond important yet underused descriptions, transcriptions, and editions by allowing them to come to substitute, even if provisionally and briefly, for their once-whole manuscript by becoming their own whole. The chapter nevertheless also acknowledges their past and partial continued disuse as philological subjects as legitimate uses of the material, uses that testify to the success of their printed editions and to the practical or philological needs of their users.

Chapter Three

Used to Pieces: The Muwashshahas and Their Romance Kharjas from Al-Andalus to Cairo

As the previous two chapters have argued, both what constitutes a fragment and how fragments should be used are often matters of judgment, usually by a critic. In studies of medieval Spanish literature, there are few texts that have produced more critical debate than the Romance kharjas of Andalusian muwashshahas, poems composed primarily in Arabic or Hebrew. While constituting a minority of the total kharja corpus, the Romance kharjas have proven an irresistible philological subject not only for Spanish, British, and American Hispanists who have long coped with a paltry medieval manuscript corpus but also for Arabists.[1]

There was no shortage of contentiousness in the many articles that comprise kharja studies, borne out in the last decades of the twentieth century in the pages of *La corónica* and in the now defunct *Al-Andalus*, much of it derived from debates about the origins of the kharjas and their larger muwashshahas.[2] Spanish and American philologists like Dámaso Alonso, Menéndez Pidal, James Monroe, and Armistead backed Emilio García Gómez's thesis that the muwashshahas followed the rules of Hispano-Romance prosody and were stress syllabic in nature.[3] However, other scholars like Samuel Stern, the first to rediscover the Romance kharjas, along with T.J. Gorton, Jareer Abu Haidar, Alan Jones, J. Derek Latham, and Richard Hitchcock, countered the stress-syllabic thesis.[4] These authors, with important publications in the 1990s and 2000s by Federico Corriente and others, proposed what is now the generally accepted thesis, and the one that I accept here, that the muwashshahas and their kharjas were based on an Andalusí version of Eastern Arabic models, the *tasmit* (pattern of internal rhyme)[5] and the *arud* (prosody of classical Arabic poetry).[6] With this sometimes acrimonious but always stimulating study of the muwashshahas, and especially the Romance kharjas, came a particular sort of intellectual fragmentation, a critical fragmentation, although of a sort only taken seriously by some critics: whether or not studying the Romance kharjas independently (as fragments) of their muwashshahas, with the purpose of deciphering their meaning and determining how much Romance these Romance kharjas contained, was bad practice.

In 1987, Armistead wrote in his "Brief History of *Kharja* Studies" that the issue of whether or not the Romance kharjas can be studied separately from their muwashshahas is an imaginary problem that does not warrant concern or comment, perhaps because he considered it simply an issue of scholarly focus and goals or because there were more pressing issues in kharja studies.[7] Other scholars, however, expressed explicit doubt about the amount of attention the Romance kharjas received. A year after the publication of Armistead's "Brief History," Alan Jones acknowledged the constricted nature of his own work in the introduction of his detailed examination of each of the forty-two Romance kharjas that appear in the extant Andalusian Arabic muwashshahas: "I confess that I have been reluctant to publish a work that concentrates so narrowly on the Romance kharjas. There are two main reasons for this. First, I believe that each kharja, whether Romance or Arabic, needs to be studied as an integral part of the *muwaššaḥ* it rounds off ... Secondly, the study of only a small fraction of a scribe's handwriting is insufficient even for the most skilled paleographer to establish the characteristics, and problems, of that hand."[8] Some seven years later, Antonio Espòsito wrote of this concentration on the Romance kharjas and fragmentation of their corresponding muwashshahas in a metaphoric way, proposing that the Romance kharjas are "foregrounded and amputated, presented to us as poetic islands rather than as the textual peninsulas they are."[9] For Espòsito, this fragmentation of the kharjas from their larger poems is not simply a matter of critical interest but an outcome of how Hispanomedievalism copes with anxieties about ethnic, linguistic, and gender identities. By being dismembered from their muwashshahas and presented in isolation, the kharjas have been purified to become part of the canon of medieval Spanish literature.[10] In 2000, Espòsito reiterated that the fragmentation of the kharja, while constituting an erasure and silencing, allows philology "to rest comfortably in [a] powerful imaginary, secure that neither deviant language nor desire contaminates the nation's linguistic and textual origins."[11] While this point of view may appear somewhat exaggerated, it is noteworthy that some ten years later, in an article centred on Hispanism and Sephardic studies, Michelle Hamilton observed that the Romance kharjas were still presented in anthologies of Spanish literature as peculiar anonymous poems cut from their larger muwashshahas, sometimes cast as women's songs, and accompanied by "a domesticating narrative to explain the inclusion of these seemingly foreign poems in the textbook."[12] Further, Karla Mallette includes a chapter in her 2010 book on the history of kharja scholarship that makes the case for an "engaged" philology that seeks a more global perspective by examining the Arab-European contacts of the Mediterranean, including the poetic ones, and the way in which European and non-European texts interact.[13] Tova Rosen has aptly analysed what is at stake when the kharjas are studied without their muwashshahas, writing that without understanding the function of the kharja within its larger poem, its speech situation cannot be understood.[14] More than pointing out the difficulty in determining the gender of the kharja speakers, Rosen's observation underscores the importance of studying these poems as wholes and from a literary perspective.

In a broader sense, the critical fragmentation of the Romance kharjas is intellectual fragmentation, or fragmentation as a result of conscious mental processes and decisions that involve reflection about the content of the text. An obvious remedy to the critical fragmentation of the Romance kharjas and the setting aside or effective disuse of their corresponding muwashshahas would be to defragment the muwashshahas containing Romance kharjas by reading the Romance kharjas in the context of their larger poems. The issue of reading the Romance kharjas in context arose in late twentieth-century kharja scholarship and earlier, although for purely metrical reasons, in García Gómez's *Las jarchas romances de la serie árabe en su marco*.[15] As I have aimed to show previously, however, it is not always clear what reading the Romance kharjas in context actually entails, with several key theoretical, philological, and editorial questions often left unanswered.[16]

One kharja phenomenon that raises these questions in a particularly explicit way is the use of the same or similar Romance kharjas in two or three different muwashshahas, with one muwashshaha as inspiration or direct model for the others. While it is tempting to call a series of what are at least related kharjas in different poems the same kharja, describing the situation as variations of a kharja, or different but possibly related kharjas, may be more appropriate. Each poem constitutes a unique poetic context, but in attempting to locate commonalities in the kharjas or in an attempt to produce a general edition of "the kharja," we may be undermining these individual contexts and engaging in yet another instance of critically fragmenting the Romance kharjas, only this time ostensibly in context. Further, in producing a general edition or even editions of kharjas as they appear in the different poems, it is not clear that manuscripts of multiple muwashshahas, sometimes in different languages, can be used. Would such a composite edition go against the notion of reading the Romance kharjas in context?

One example that evinces the contextual complexities and multiple fragmentations experienced by a selection of these kharjas, or similar kharjas that appear in multiple muwashshahas, is the Genizah of the Ben Ezra Synagogue in Fustat, Old Cairo. The muwashshahas are quintessentially Andalusian, as Rosen and others have noted, but they travelled east and very successfully so, as attested by Ibn Sana al-Mulk (1155–1212), an Egyptian poet, by Ibn Dihya (b. 1149), an Andalusian poet writing in Baghdad, and by the Genizah fragments.[17] Fustat was the first capital of Egypt under the new Muslim regime and the most important Jewish settlement in Egypt, reaching its height during the Fatimid period (969–1171), when many Jews emigrated from the Holy Land and North Africa. The history of the Ben Ezra Synagogue has several lacunae and ambiguities, including when it was first built and whether it was first a church. That it was demolished around 1012 is certain, for that is when the Shi'ite caliph al-Hakim ordered all Jewish and Christian houses of worship destroyed. Not long after al-Hakim's order, however, the Palestinian Jews of Cairo were allowed to rebuild the synagogue. Mark Glickman proposes that the synagogue may have reopened in 1025, according to medieval reports of an inscription near the doorway, although Stefan Reif suggests its renovations were completed around 1140. The renovated synagogue contained a Genizah about the size of a large walk-in closet, measuring some eight feet long, six and a-half feet wide, and about eighteen feet high.[18]

A genizah typically refers to a depository for worn-out or no longer useful Torah scrolls and other Hebrew documents containing the name of God, but the Cairo Genizah, described by either that term or simply "Genizah" below, was different. In 1896, when scholar and rabbi Solomon Schechter and his friend and patron Charles Taylor began collecting and ordering its contents, they encountered a massive number of fragments. Today these fragments are estimated at some 220,000, ranging in date from the eighth or ninth century to the nineteenth. They are written in many languages in Hebrew characters, including Aramaic, Judeo-Arabic, Greek, Latin, Persian, Yiddish, and Spanish. In addition, there are fragments in Syriac, Arabic, Coptic, and Chinese, as well as palimpsests, especially Hebrew texts copied over Arabic, Latin, and other Hebrew writing, but also Hebrew copied over text in Greek, Christian Aramaic, Georgian, and Coptic.[19] The fragments were diverse in content, consisting of pieces of the Bible, Talmud, Mishnah, contracts and lists, talismans, personal correspondence, medical prescriptions, music, and illuminated pages. The fragments also included poetic texts, including muwashshaha poetry by two of the best-known poets writing in Hebrew in the Iberian Peninsula and elsewhere in the Middle Ages, Yehuda Halevi (1075–141) and Moshe Ibn Ezra (1055–135).

These fragments, including those of the muwashshahas, are the remains of manuscripts and documents that survived in part because they were disused as reading material, whether out of obsolescence, prohibition, or disrepair. This chapter draws on a selection of Cairo Genizah muwashshaha fragments to argue that, rather than having suffered a single, twentieth- and twenty-first-century critical fragmentation, the Romance kharjas have undergone many practical, intellectual, and spiritual fragmentations over time. Some of these fragmentations were accidental and due to textual misunderstandings, others motivated by literary or artistic choices (disuses, rewritings, and erasures of parts of text), and still others by practical or spiritual needs (the fragmentation of muwashshaha manuscripts and their consignment to the Cairo Genizah). The phrase "sacred trash," which Peter Cole and Andina Hoffman apply to the fragments of the Cairo Genizah, perfectly captures the sometimes contradictory nature of the various medieval, early modern, and modern fragmentations of the Romance kharjas.

While a critique of the process of critical fragmentation of the Romance kharjas is neither particularly interesting nor fruitful, this chapter contextualizes this intellectual fragmentation in terms of other fragmentations that the Romance kharjas have experienced over time in response to the changing needs of users. These fragmentations, some literal and some more metaphoric, stem from a variety of spiritual, practical, and intellectual uses of manuscript text, including the practice of genizah, an ongoing negotiation of the relevance of the kharja to its larger composition, and the process of poetic imitation, or *mu'arada*. Studying specific changes in the use of the Romance kharjas in this way reveals that context, a phenomenon that could be seen as a panacea for all that ails the Romance kharjas, is often difficult to grasp and define, and proves more fragmentary and less stable than its topological, religious, and linguistic components suggest, including Andalusian, Egyptian, and Palestinian;

Islamic and Jewish; and Arabic, Hebrew, and Romance components. This chapter begins with the Cairo Genizah and then moves to palaeographic and interpretive issues surrounding a specific kharja contained in the Cairo Genizah and in a muwashshaha in Arabic. The end of the chapter treats the fragmentation of the Romance kharjas in Egyptian imitations of Iberian muwashshahas.

Preservation through Disuse: Genizah Fragments

The practice of genizah has spiritual roots but also served a practical function as a repository for quires, leaves, and fragments that had nowhere else to go. In the books of Esther and Ezra in the Hebrew Bible, the word genizah (possibly from the Persian *ganj*, "treasury or storehouse") refers to a royal archive or royal treasury.[20] The third commandment proscribes the destruction of the name of God, which necessitated the creation of a resting place, though not necessarily a final one, for worn or damaged copies of the Hebrew Bible and eventually other damaged or obsolete Hebrew texts. The Mishnah, the oldest part of the Talmud and first written compendium of Judaism's oral law, prohibited the destruction of items that had been employed for sacred purposes, but not necessarily those that had simply been used to fulfil religious obligations. The Mishnah also suggests that a genizah can hold a wider variety of texts that in practice could be quite distant from the sacred.[21] The genizah is mentioned in the section of the Mishnah explaining the exceptions to the prohibition on lighting or extinguishing fires on the Sabbath, with the issue of kindling and extinguishing fires being one that sharply divides Rabbanites and Karaites. This division rests namely on whether these acts are one of the thirty-nine categories of labour forbidden by rabbinic law on the Sabbath, which did not forbid all secondary actions, such as a candle lit on Friday to continue to burn on the Sabbath, or whether such a Friday lighting would be banned along with all other secondary actions on the Sabbath (the view of the Karaites). In the section on what can be saved in a fire, it is clear that while the main concern is to save the Holy Scriptures from burning, whether they are being put to an active hermeneutic use or not, another more passive sort of protection is also important: the consignment of Hebrew and even non-Hebrew text deemed unfit for intellectual use and not appropriate for practical use to the genizah.[22]

Irrelevant, outdated, dilapidated, or fragmentary books and quires were thus often further fragmented and deposited in the Cairo Genizah because, despite being unfit or unnecessary for reading, they were deserving of protection from profanation. The Cairo Genizah also held documents of another tenor, including those that required concealment because their content had been decreed unfit reading material for the Jewish public, such as the rejected books of the Bible. A genizah thus enabled a two-way protection in some cases: some documents were protected from profanation, and the people were protected from the text of some documents.

The protection of the documents sometimes went even further. Prior to the practice of depositing texts in a genizah, and even after the practice of using a genizah was established, old manuscripts and leaves were buried in cemeteries for their protection or as final resting places, whether buried next to a holy individual or placed on their own in the earth.[23] In the cases of consignment to a genizah and subsequent burial, a genizah thus constituted a liminal ground between disuse as text (with nevertheless the possibility, however unlikely, of being used again) and being permanently given to the earth. In reference to this tradition of burial, Solomon Schechter compared the laying to rest of material in the Cairo Genizah to the burial of bodies whose spirits had departed. Both burial of human bodies and consignment to the Genizah had the same end: "When the spirit is gone, we put the corpse out of sight to protect it from abuse. In a like manner, when the writing is worn out, we hide the book to preserve it from profanation."[24] Schechter further noted that the Hebrew root *g-n-z* was at times used on gravestones, as in, "Here lies hidden (*nignaz*) this man," linking the practice of genizah to human burial.[25]

In addition to the dry climate in Fustat, the Cairo Genizah muwashshaha fragments have thus survived to this day as a result of not having been buried and, most importantly, of a liberal interpretation of the types of documents that a genizah should hold. Hoffman and Cole write that over time the meaning of genizah in Fustat changed to denote the preservation of anything written in Hebrew letters, whether or not it was a religious document or written in the Hebrew language. There are various possibilities as to why this liberal interpretation of the notion of genizah existed, but no single answer stands out:

> Perhaps, as one scholar has proposed, "the very employment of the Hebrew script ... sanctified written material." Another theory holds that Jews of this community may simply have piled up paper in their homes and periodically delivered whole cartfuls to the Geniza without bothering

> to separate sacred from secular writing. Or maybe as another writer has suggested – in an effort to make sense of the hodge-podge of texts that have turned up in the Fustat Genizah – the impulse to guard the written word may have gone beyond piety and evolved into a "generalized aversion toward causally discarding texts of any kind."[26]

It is also known that the Ben Ezra, in addition to being a place of worship, became a central meeting point for the community, serving as a welfare office, soup kitchen, hostel, clerical and bookkeeping headquarters, and the city's court of law.[27] Such a community town-square function could certainly explain the Cairo Genizah's diverse contents. Whatever the reason for this conversion of the Cairo Genizah into a "holy junk heap" for the Jews of Old Cairo, the fragmentation and consignment of text to the Genizah ensured its preservation in at least some form.[28] The Genizah was a place to mark a text's transition from reading material to material that held meaning because its meaning once derived from content written in Hebrew letters. It also saved texts from some of the late-medieval and early modern practices discussed in the previous chapter, including the use of manuscript material as binding strips, endpapers, and book covers.

Critical Fragmentation

Like most of the Cairo Genizah fragments, the muwashshahas are leaves or partial leaves torn from quires, which have themselves been ripped from larger manuscripts, and as a consequence, have a definitively damaged appearance.[29] Apart from looking ragged, however, the lucky consignment of these poetic and sometimes very explicitly profane texts to the Cairo Genizah also reflects a liberal interpretation of what sort of partial, unsightly, or irrelevant texts merited consignment to this holy storage room. These muwashshahas are written in Hebrew characters, which helped grant them a place in the Cairo Genizah but also makes them a minority within a minority: the Romance kharjas in Hebrew letters total about twenty, compared with the forty-six Romance kharjas in Arabic characters that Jones studies in *Romance "Kharjas"*; Romance kharjas as a whole constitute approximately 10 percent of all known kharjas.

The ragged appearance of the Genizah muwashshahas evinces the problems of readability that the large majority of the Romance kharjas pose as a group, whether written in Arabic or Hebrew characters. These difficulties are such that all of the reconstructions cited here are speculative, no matter how meticulous the edition. In terms of the Romance kharjas in Arabic characters, in the most important extant anthology of Arabic muwashshahas, Ali Ibn Bishri's *Uddat al-jalis* (The courtier's equipment), in Maghribi script and most likely a Morrocan manuscript, five different scribes were involved in copying the muwashshahas containing Romance material, at times with vocalization and in other moments without.[30] Jones notes that it is likely that, in at least one case, a scribe having misunderstood the final word of the kharja purposefully left the word incomplete, such that a trained reader might be able to fill in what he could not. The manuscript of the *Uddat al-jalis* also provides many opportunities for modern-day misunderstandings due to differences, for instance, in the use of the Arabic letters *alif* and *ya*, which are used interchangeably for the letter *alif maqsura* and an irregular presentation of *hamza*. Neither is the Hebrew manuscript situation a simple one, in that we preserve muwashshahas in several kinds of manuscripts and from multiple geographic regions, including in the diwans (poetry collections) of individual poets, at the end of *tiklals* (prayer books), and in the Genizah fragments. Benabu and Yahalom have argued for the privileging of readings from the Genizah fragments because some might date back to the twelfth century. We can compare this date, for instance, with that of the oldest extant complete copy of a later version of Halevi's diwan, the thirteenth century, and the extant copy of his definitive diwan, which is a seventeenth-century Yemeni copy, though Benabu and Yahalom report having found a partial twelfth-century copy of this diwan in the Genizah material. Whether the Genizah readings are preferred or not, they provide material, poetic evidence that the muwashshahas circulated in the East in the twelfth century.

The Cairo Genizah muwashshaha fragments contain several Romance kharjas that are found in no other manuscripts, including those in fragmentary anonymous muwashahas ("'Go away, you rogue, get out of here, you are not devoted to me!'"), and in complete muwashahas by known poets, including Ibn Ezra ("'She is a poor woman, you can see it, made jealous by her own kin. Sell your love to others, you harlot who is not paid on the spot!'").[31] The Genizah fragments are of particular interest for the study of the Romance kharjas that appear in the muwashshahas of two of the most important eleventh- and twelfth-century poets writing in Iberia and elsewhere: Yehuda Halevi, whose poems include eleven of the known Romance kharjas, and Moshe Ibn Ezra, whose muwashshahas contain five. Both composed poetry in al-Andalus and parts of Christian Spain, though Halevi spent the last years of his life in Egypt en route to Palestine. While in Egypt, Halevi wrote just one muwashshaha ("The golden bell and the pomegranate tree"), but in a syllabic metre specific to Hebrew poetry as opposed to the quantitative metres common in al-Andalus. Despite their metrical peculiarities, Iberian-style muwashshahas were nevertheless popular among Halevi's Jewish Egyptian hosts and poets, inspiring the latter to write imitations. Ibn Ezra, for instance, composed a muwashshaha in honour of Halevi that was later imitated by an anonymous Egyptian poet.[32]

The phenomena that fall under the category of imitation are actually quite diverse. In addition to revealing processes of replication and borrowing, which constituted public displays of brilliance rather than plagiarism, they also evince erasures and difficulties in interpretation that constitute fragmentation. There are cases in which two different kharjas appear in different copies of a single muwashshaha, as with a poem copied in both the *Uddat al-jalis* and the *Gays al-tawsih* (Army of muwashshaha poetry) but containing different kharjas. More commonly, however, a single kharja inspired more than one muwashshaha. The repurposing of kharjas is in fact normative for the kharja corpus. Among the muwashshahas with Romance kharjas, there are some eleven in which fairly or very similar kharjas appear in two or more muwashshahas, and in four cases of those eleven, the kharjas cross languages, appearing in both Arabic and Hebrew muwashshahas. Some of these imitations are formal imitations, known as *mu'arada*s, a fairly common phenomenon in classical Arabic poetry but one that is particularly well represented in muwashshaha poetry. The basis for the *mu'arada* is the kharja, whose metre and rhyme serve as template for a new or at least newish muwashshaha. In other poems, a single kharja or group of closely related kharjas gave rise to both *mu'arada*s and poems that are perhaps better labelled simply as inspired poems. There are poems by Ibn Ruhaym from the Almoravid era and by the twelfth-century Ibn Baqi, containing a very similar kharja that also appears with some differences in a Hebrew poem by Halevi. The two Arabic muwashshahas in the *Uddat al-jalis*, with the second one also found in the *Gays al-tawsih*, have a very similar metrical and rhyme structure, and clearly contain a highly similar kharja; but the kharjas are different enough that Jones decided to edit them in two different chapters of his *Romance "Kharjas,"* explicitly recognizing that they belong to two different poetic contexts. In the Ibn Baqi muwashshaha, the second section is scarcely legible in some parts. Below I cite Jones's reading, followed by Corriente's most recent edition and translation:

> nun mi-mərdəš yā ḥabībī lā nu-qaru dənīšu
> al-gilālah ... ə ṭrṭr m?rətīšu.[33]
>
> ---
>
> NON ME MÓRDAŚ, ya ḥabíbi, KÉ + N LÓQRAD EN + ÉŚŚO
> alghilála rákhṣa BÍSTO E(D) ṬÓṬA ME REVÉŚŚO.
>
> ---
>
> Do not bite me, my darling; what does he achieve by this? I wear such a fine garment that makes my flesh shiver.[34]

The kharja in the Ibn Ruhaym poem comes through more clearly, however, with a few emendations to the text in the Colin manuscript of the *Uddat al-jalīs*. Halevi's kharja, while similar in meaning and also appearing in an amorous context like the Arabic poems, is sectioned differently; it is in four parts instead of two. Neither is Halevi's poem a true *mu'arada,* as it has a different structure. Despite the known differences in Halevi's kharja, it was the one used to produce an edition of the kharja, a common practice that is logical but not entirely unproblematic.[35]

The Cairo Genizah fragments also reflect a variety of types of incompleteness, some of which privilege the kharja and others that do not. With regard to the latter, for instance, the Cairo Genizah copy of one of Halevi's muwashshahas that contains the Romance kharja "Foreign boy, may you soon sleep on my bosom" is fragmentary and does not conserve the kharja.[36] In other cases of the Cairo Genizah fragments, however, only the last parts of the poems, including the kharjas, are preserved, as with two cases of anonymous muwashshahas with Romance kharjas, in one of which only the transition to the kharja and the kharja itself are extant: "If I could get wings, I would go flying after you; if you wanted my heart, I would know how to give it to you."[37]

In yet other cases, a muwashshaha may be technically complete, in addition to being a *mu'arada* and even relatively clear to transcribe, but nevertheless pose issues of fragmentation due to the difficulties of interpretation of the meaning of the kharja. These muwashshahas in particular raise questions as to whether there really is such a thing as *one* kharja that appears in multiple muwashshahas, or multiple kharjas that appear in a single muwashshaha, questions raised primarily because a relatively unproblematic transcribed text does not always mean that the meaning of the kharja is clear. A case in point among the Genizah fragments is a muwashshaha by Halevi that is a *mu'arada* of a muwashshaha by Ibn Baqi. Jones proposes that a *mu'arada* can be complete, in which the rhymes and metre are copied or partial, in which the metre is maintained but not the rhyme, or vice versa. In the event that any material of the original poem is quoted in the *mu'arada*, it is the kharja, which in many cases served as a sort of public knowledge for poets, that is quoted either completely or partially, that is, as a kharja or an opening line (*matla*).[38] In Halevi's poem, Ibn Baqi's kharja is at least partially quoted, but with some possible differences in text and meaning. Apart from the Genizah copy, there are three other manuscripts or fragments that contain Halevi's poem and only one manuscript that contains Ibn Baqi's, the Colin manuscript mentioned above. As transcribed, edited, and translated by Benabu and Yahalom, the Genizah fragment (MS Cambridge T-S H15.46) reads:

> bnyd lbškh 'dywn šn'lh / km knd myw qwrgwn pwr 'lh.[39]
> venid la pasca ed yo sin elu / com caned meu corajon por elu.[40]
>
> Passover comes and I am without him. How my heart burns for him![41]

While the interpretation of the individual Romance kharjas is contentious, few would dispute that they are characteristically difficult to interpret. The kharja above is not especially problematic as Romance kharjas go, but interpretations have changed significantly throughout the nineteenth and twentieth centuries. Along with the corresponding transcriptions, we can compare, for instance, Solà-Solé's rendering of the kharja in modern Spanish in the 1970s with Corriente's most recent published Spanish version (2008):

> Viene la Pascua y yo aún sin él *perdido (o: decepcionado) (está) mi corazón por ello.[42]
>
> (Pascua arrives, and I am still without him, my heart is lost – or disappointed – because of it.)
>
> Sin él resulta la Pascua como ayuno, como si hubiera dedicado mi corazón a él.[43]

(Without him Pascua is like fasting, as if my heart had dedicated itself to him.)

As is common in working with Arabic and Hebrew muwashshahas that contain very similar kharjas, Solà-Solé's and Corriente's editions draw on both Arabic and Hebrew manuscripts to render a kharja in modern Spanish, substituting readings from the Hebrew manuscripts for any damaged sections in the Arabic manuscripts and vice versa. In Corriente's case, however, he specifically aims to produce an edition of the Arabic-series version of the kharja (A12), rather than framing the kharja as a composite one, but he still relies on the Hebrew-series kharja to complete the Arabic.

In the case of Ibn Baqi's kharja, it becomes clear that the Hebrew manuscripts of Halevi's kharja, including the Cairo Genizah fragment, can prove useful for resolving oddities in the sole extant manuscript of Ibn Baqi's kharja, but that Ibn Baqi's kharja does not resolve the problem sections of Halevi's. When dividing Ibn Baqi's kharja into two main parts with four subsections and reading Jones's facsimile of the Colin manuscript, the first section of part one reads *nun, ba, dal.* This section could be the pattern of Arabic *nabada* (to fling, cast off, neglect) if it were not for the series of letters that follows, *lam, ya, shin, qaf, ha,* which can be read as *li–yashuqqahu* (so that he might split it): *nbd lyshqh əywn shnl.*[44] Because the Arabic reading of "to cast off so that he might split it" works in neither syllables nor meaning, readings from the manuscripts of Halevi's kharja are typically substituted, all of which read *bnyd,* except for the Schocken manuscript (*'g'm*). The second section of Baqi's kharja reads *lyshqh,* a reading that is typically discarded in favour of readings from Halevi's kharja that differ from *lyshqh* by just one letter, again except for the Schocken manuscript (Schocken: *bnyd;* other Hebrew manuscripts: *lpshkh* or *lbshkh*).[45] The third and fourth subsections of the first part read similarly in Baqi's and Halevi's versions, *əywn shnl* (Colin) and *'ywn shn'lw,* the most common reading in the Hebrew manuscripts cited above.

In the second part of Ibn Baqi's kharja, the first cluster is *ha, sad, ra* in the Colin manuscript, which in the end Jones proposes is better left in its manuscript form, after having first proposed a hybrid Arabic and Romance form (*hasrandu*).[46] Halevi's version is typically consulted in attempts to resolve this enigmatic section of the Baqi kharja, but without much conclusive aid. Two of the copies of Halevi's kharja read *km knd*: the Cairo Genizah fragment and Oxford

1971. The two other Hebrew manuscripts cited above present what Benabu and Yahalom read as scribal errors that prevented the *km knd* reading.[47] Following Francisco Cantera, Benabu and Yahalom resolve *km knd* to *caned* (how [my heart] burns), a reading to which I return below.[48]

The next sections of Ibn Baqi's kharja mostly agree with Halevi's versions, with a minor emendation to the Colin manuscript. In summary, reading Ibn Baqi's version of the kharja from the Colin manuscript side by side with the Genizah fragment, which reflects general trends in the other Hebrew manuscripts of Halevi's version, yields the following texts:

Ibn Baqi
nbd̲ lyṣqh əywn šnl
ḥṣry mw qrhwn brl.[49]

Bairam without him turns into something like fasting, as if I had restricted (the joys of) my heart to him.[50]

Halevi
bnyd lbškh 'dywn šn 'lh
km knd myw qwrgwn pwr 'lh.[51]

Passover comes and I am without him. How my heart burns for him![52]

Pashkah

Due to problems of legibility in the Colin manuscript, the production of a readable and publishable version of Ibn Baqi's kharja has typically depended on borrowing pieces from the manuscripts of Halevi's later kharja, including the case of the word *pashkah*, rendered as Spanish *Pascua*. This weaving together of fragments results in the edition of the kharja in a limbo space in which the kharja is fully attached to neither Halevi's nor Baqi's composition, nor to any one manuscript. In the present case, borrowing between manuscripts of an older Arabic kharja and a more recent Hebrew one is not necessarily bad practice, but it does raise important interpretive questions. One of these questions is the interpretation of the word *pashkah*, while another is the more general but also thorny question of how the poems are related thematically.

The muwashshahas often treat love and longing with the kharja in the voice of a woman lamenting the absence of her beloved,[53] but some are panegyrics that praise men, including patrons, contemporary poets, and late family members. The themes of the muwashshahas are generally consistent with a predominantly Muslim society and fall within the range of themes present in both classical Arabic poetry and popular forms, such as the Egyptian *mawwal* (colloquial poetry). Save some differences in the rhyme in the returns, Halevi's poem imitates the metre and rhyme of Ibn Baqi's poem. Ibn Baqi's muwashshaha featuring the above kharja is an amatory composition on love and longing. The muwashshaha begins by referring to the beloved's immaterial substitute, a breeze. She cannot be held in place, escaping him, and makes her bodily absence known to her lover. The poet asks what crime he has committed against his beloved and if he has any clever means by which he might assuage his plight. He recalls the appearance of the beloved's locks of hair as they protect her face and their resemblance to three curved phenomena: the Arabic letter *nun* (ن), a curved mallet, and a cobra. In the last stanza, a young maiden suffering from the absence of her beloved and a figurative hunger enters to sing the kharja:

0
From where the beloved lives comes
a breeze that imposes warnings of ignominy.

1
The storm of powerlessness raged in my body
and awakened the grievances within,
parting a greeting from my tormentor
like an enormous thirst in my sickly heart.
Oh absence, if you would have never existed!

2
What can I do with this passion I have stirred,
since I have been rejected by that which I love,
even though I love no one but him?
How do I have patience? He has refused to meet me.
Is there a ruse that I might use against him?

3
Return to him, breeze, return,
and send to the land of the beloved

a desperate greeting of the lover in distress,
place in his hands a kiss
on my behalf, with customary humility.

4
It is a flirting like the darkness of night, a curl
drawn on a sheet of roses,
like the curve of the *nun* above the cheek
or a curved mallet or a cobra
whose steely blades protect his domain.

5
Many a young girl has been mistreated by love,
and has been emaciated by separation and distance,
and has proclaimed that separation is harsh:
[Pascua] without him turns into something like fasting, as if I had restricted [the joys of] my heart to him.[54]

In terms of motifs and tropes, Ibn Baqi's poem is consistent with other amatory muwashshahas. The poetic voice asks questions of himself and of his beloved. His apostrophic complaints about the pain of being separated from his beloved are directed to intangible entities, including to his own feelings, the sensation of absence, and the wind. Ibn Baqi's beloved and the different manifestations of her are in part antagonistic to the poetic voice and his pursuit. While the poet requests the aid of the soft wind mentioned in the prelude, the wind also recalls his old anxieties and the absence he bemoans. Similar to the sweet but painful wind, the curls of the beloved's hair draw the poet in but do not allow him to connect with her. More than showing the bittersweet character of love, the poem slowly builds the complexities of the interrelated phenomena that allow one to know love exists: wind, anxiety, absence, and physical aspects of the beloved.

Apart from the change in register from classical Arabic to Andalusí Romance, the transition to the kharja above brings about a thematic change, from the lovely, sophistically constructed resistant beloved to a lovesick and suffering maiden.

Many a young girl has been mistreated by love,
and has been emaciated by separation and distance,
and has proclaimed that separation is harsh.

In several interpretations of the kharja for Ibn Baqi's poem, the words that Benabu and Yahalom read as *ed yo* (and I) in the Cairo Genizah fragment and other Hebrew manuscripts – a reading that Menéndez Pidal had previously proposed for the kharja – are read either as *ay, aun* (oh, still; García Gómez) or *ayuno* (fasting; Corriente).[55] Considering the verses cited above that precede and make the transition to the kharja, this last reading (*ayuno*, "fasting") is most appropriate thematically, due to its continuity with the hunger motif ("emaciated").

If the reading of *ayuno* for *əywn* is accepted, recalling that *'ywn* is the most common reading in copies of Halevi's kharja, then *pashkah* contrasts with *ayuno* to allegorize the inability of the beloved to be fulfilled without her lover. *Pashkah*, likely with the connotation of the Eid al-Fitr, which breaks the fast of Ramadan, occurs in the last stanza of *zajal* number 50 of the Andalusian poet Ibn Quzman (1078–1160), with *zajal* referring to a strophic form in colloquial language similar to the muwashshaha.[56] *Pashkah* conveys the state that would result from a rare lightening up of the beloved's iron heart:

> law ra'áyt ḥabíbak mayyít bihawák,
> las yaḥíbbi qálbu f_addúnya siwák!
> MANYÁNA DE PÁŠKA, law_ánni narák,
> walaw_ánna qálbak yakún min ḥadíd.[57]
>
> (If you could only see your lover dying of love
> his heart loving nothing in the world but you!
> To see you tomorrow would be pashkah
> though your heart be iron.)[58]

Similarly, in two Arabic muwashshahas by poets who likely composed in the Almohad period (1121–1269), *Id*, likely short for the Ramadan-ending Eid al-Fitr, expresses the impact of the physical loving presence of the beloved. The stanzas by the poets Ibn al-Habbaz and Ibn Nizar read as follows respectively:

> Quien está en Pascua [*fi l'id*] lejos de su amado,
> aunque venga con sus galas y perfumes,
> muestra en su cantar lo que sufre;
> la Pascua no consiste en túnica, bonete y oler perfume;
> Pascua es tan sólo el encuentro con el amado.[59]
>
> (Whoever is in Pascua far from her beloved,
> though she comes with finery and perfumes,

shows what she suffers in her song;
Pascua does not consist of robe, bonnet, and the smell of perfume;
Pascua is only the encounter with the beloved.)

He agotado en el pulido brillo mis palabras;
señora de apariencia hermosa, cede,
pues sólo tú eres mi anhelo,
por el Profeta, que en tu fausto rostro vi mi Pascua [ssa'idi].[60]

(I have exhausted my words on shiny splendour;
woman of beauty, yield,
since you alone are my yearning,
for the Prophet, that in your auspicious face I saw my Pascua.)

The *Id* in the first stanza, which could connote any lively festival, conveys something that has arrived whose joy is marred by the yearning and suffering of unrequited love, a phenomenon consistent with the sacrifice required during Ramadan. In the second poetic fragment, the deprivation implied by a longing for the beloved and the Prophet suggests Eid al-Fitr. "Festivity of original nature," the literal translation of Eid al-Fitr, is thus elicited in both stanzas, as the presence of the beloved removes suffering from the poet and restores him to his ideal condition.

The stanzas that precede Halevi's version of this kharja do not contain an explicit fasting metaphor, but they do convey a psychological anguish. Halevi's muwashshaha is directed to another muwashshaha poet represented in the Cairo Genizah fragments, Moshe Ibn Ezra, in sympathy for the death of Moshe's brother Yehuda Ibn Ezra, who had died some time before 1121.[61] Halevi laments Yehuda's passing and calls for relief from his own pain, which he states cannot be remedied not only because Yehuda is gone, but also because Yehuda's brother Yosef Ibn Ezra (d. 1128), an official in the Castilian administration whom Halevi chides for being absent in another poem, is away.[62] The verses that immediately precede the kharja are not a transition to the kharja but are so intimately connected to the plight of the Ibn Ezra brothers that it is difficult to determine whether a woman or one of the bereft Ibn Ezra brothers, most likely Moshe, pronounces the kharja:

0
Greetings for the man whose pleasure has been exiled;
he is without the one who can console him, oh, he does not have him.

1
Yosef's leaving turned my heart into an oven;
further, the passing of Yehuda pains me to the core,
and the pain of the third brother worsens my burden
because his sorrows weigh upon my soul;
like his, my heart has been pierced through.

2
Moshe, my dear, I would give my soul for you;
neither have I quieted my sobbing
since the tragedy arrived in a harsh vision:
one day, like an eagle, it was swift, it did not cease,
until it consumed my soul, that loves you,

3
For the first our hearts have despaired,
the image of the second I see only in dreams;
one I remember, the other I lack.
My eyes, to what height should they be raised?
It is there where Elohim is revealed to me.

4
Oh, of the beloved man entombed in the earth,
he who had been withheld among thc luminaries!
The favours will cease, as if
the generous rains were restrained and stopped flowing
upon seeing that their lights no longer shined.

5
The song of the separated brother is a flame in my heart;
he sings like a young woman with an unquiet heart,
because it is her time and her beloved does not arrive.
Bairam without him is like fasting; how my heart is burning for his sake!
Passover comes, and I am without him. How my heart burns for him! [63]

Returning to the question of the interpretation of *pashkah* and examining what this word might mean raises several provocative questions about the meaning of context. It is useful to review Benabu and Yahalom's interpretation of Halevi's kharja as it appears in the Cairo Genizah fragment and in other Hebrew manuscripts quoted above. Their interpretation of *pashkah* as "Passover" seems like a logical choice, if not the only one. Yet, apart from the fact that Halevi was Jewish, is there other evidence, especially in the poem itself, that justifies this reading? Georg

Bossong notes that while Halevi clearly uses popular, orally transmitted material as inspiration for his poetry, in his kharjas, most of which Bossong argues are of Halevi's own creation, we find an undoubtedly personal touch.[64] But in this borrowed kharja, could *pashkah* mean something else? Specifically, despite the lack of an explicit fasting metaphor in Halevi's muwashshaha, could *pashkah* mean "Eid," as it appears to in Ibn Baqi's kharja?

Halevi's diwan, including his poems represented among the Genizah fragments, evinces the variety of ways in which a poet can imitate. With regard to *mu'arada*, Bossong recently examined one of Halevi's panegyric muwashshahas containing a Romance kharja that was inspired by three different amorous Arabic muwashshahas containing Arabic kharjas, with one of these Arabic muwashshahas extant in two fairly different versions. There is also a spiritual-religious imitation by Halevi himself, amounting to five poems of the same tradition that span the many themes of Iberian muwashshaha poetry (eroticism, both simple and panegyric, religion, and asceticism), as well as its many languages.[65] The two muwashshahas by Halevi reveal both his interest in imitation and his unique treatment of his models, in both linguistic and thematic terms. In contrast to the muwashshaha containing *pashkah* analysed above, in Halevi's imitation of the Arabic compositions, he replaced the Arabic kharja with kharjas of his choosing. His panegyric imitation ends with the well-known Romance kharja typically transcribed and vocalized as *ben sidi bene* (Come, my Lord, come), and the other, with a spiritual theme, ends with a Hebrew kharja. Apart from showing Halevi's willingness to use existing muwashshahas as inspiration but to insert his own kharjas, *ben sidi bene* reveals how a single kharja, studied in context, can be read alternatively as containing Arabic or Romance concepts and vocabulary.

Drawing on a unique presentation of the *ben sidi bene* kharja in the twelfth-century Cairo Genizah fragment (*byn syry byny*, as opposed to the more common readings of *b'n sydy b'n* or *b'n sydy b'ny*), Benabu and Yahalom interpret the *ben sidi bene* as the entirely Romance *venceray beni* (*venceré*, "I will overcome"), eliminating the dialectal Arabic *sidi*, citing thematic elements of the poem as support for their reading, specifically the notion of a fight (*lucha*).[66] The frequent difficulty in distinguishing between the between Hebrew *dalet* (ד, in *sidi*) and *resh* (ר, in the interpretation *venceray*) makes Benabu and Yahalom's interpretation possible, at least in palaeographic terms, as Bossong and the authors themselves note.[67] Further, as Bossong observes, the reading resolves the peculiarity of two different manifestations of the same word, *ben* and *beni* (come).[68] Benabu and Yahalom's interpretation of the Genizah fragment is generally not accepted as a plausible reading, however, for reasons of metre and rhyme, as recently analysed by Bossong.[69] The reading is nevertheless important in that it shows how thematic consistencies between the muwashshaha and its kharja are not necessarily the strongest basis for arguments for or against certain meanings of the kharja or parts of the kharja.

In another instance in Halevi's diwan, Halevi composed a muwashshaha based on an existing kharja from an anonymous Arabic poem extant in the Colin manuscript, "Como si fuese muchachito forastero, a quien ya no apretase más contra mi seno" (As if he were a foreign boy, whom I would not hold to my bosom), but with important changes to the kharja.[70] Due to the use of a different metrical structure, Halevi's version of the kharja omits the first two words of the Arabic kharja and also has an opposite meaning: "Muchachito forastero, pronto duermas en mi seno" (Foreign boy, may you soon sleep on my bosom).[71] There are also several cases in which Halevi inserts his kharjas into definitively Jewish contexts, including mentioning the following Jewish friends in three different Romance kharjas, each among the Genizah fragments: Ibn Dayyan (in the final section of the *ben sidi bene* kharja discussed above), Abraham Abu Ishaq Ibn Muhajir, and the doctor of Alfonso VI of Castile, Yosef Ibn Ferruziel (Cidello), with Yosef appearing in a kharja that also mentions Guadalajara, an important Jewish community.[72]

Nothing definitive can be drawn from Halevi's willingness to add new kharjas to muwashshahas that inspired him or, rather, to modify an existing kharja in form and meaning to suit his own purpose. It is nevertheless clear that the kharjas had the potential for mobility and change. While providing the foundation, or what twelfth-century writer Ibn Bassam called the *markaz* (base) for the muwashshaha, the kharjas had an open-ended, fragment-like character in practice.[73] Returning to the kharja containing *pashkah,* it does reveal at least one probable innovation that suggests that Halevi broke free of certain Arabic or Islamic motifs present in Ibn Baqi's poem. If Cantera's interpretation of the first section of the last verse of the kharja as *caned* ("How [my heart] burns") is accepted, then the kharja continues the theme of a burning heart that occurs in the first stanza ("trocó mi corazón en horno" [turned my heart into an oven]) and continues with the mention of a flame in the transition to the kharja: "El canto del hermano separado es en mi corazón llama" (The song of the separated brother is a flame in my heart).[74] Considering Halevi's possible innovation of *km knd*, it is reasonable to posit that *pashkah* could have shifted meaning in Halevi's poem, perhaps meaning "Passover" (*Pesach*), as Benabu and Yahalom have interpreted above, or a non-specific festivity, as is possible in the case of Eid, cited in regard to the Ibn al-Habbaz fragment quoted above. If an interpretation of *pashkah* as Passover is accepted, a reading of *dywn* or *əywn* as *aún* could be considered or Corriente's *ayuno* read in a more general sense of exodus or suffering.

Imitations and Reorientations

The Genizah kharja and its movement, from Ibn Baqi to Halevi, from al-Andalus to Egypt, and finally to the Cairo Genizah, show the editing of the Romance kharjas, along with the concepts of *mu'arada* and poetic context, to be fluid phenomena. These phenomena involve the appreciation and use of some elements, such as metre, rhyme, or theme, and the discarding of others, a practice like the narrowing function of textual criticism and especially the controversial critical fragmentation of the kharjas. In terms of the kharjas discussed above, while it is common practice to adopt readings from Halevi's more recent kharja to resolve problematic sections of Ibn Baqi's (in this case the first two sections of the first verse), this practice effectively constitutes editing Ibn Baqi's kharja out of its poetic context and engaging in a sort of critical fragmentation or, at a minimum, borrowing. On the other hand, the thematic consistency between *pashkah* and *ayuno*, coupled with the fact that *pashkah* requires only a minor emendation to become present in Ibn Baqi's kharja, could make such a borrowing acceptable. More problematic, however, is resolving the *hsry* section at the start of the second verse of Ibn Baqi's kharja using the *km knd* reading in the Genizah fragment, Oxford 1971, and with a minor emendation in Schocken 37. Corriente's most recent English and Spanish interpretations of Baqi's kharja reflect a reluctance to omit the burning element, even if proposals for *hsry* remain up for debate. *Hsry* is either explained as a hybrid Arabic-Romance verb meaning *dedicar (especialmente)* (*ḥṣ(ṣ)* + *ÁR*; to dedicate, especially) that could be compared with the unique reading of *bsr nd* in MS Oxford 1970 of Halevi's kharja, whose phasing out due to incomprehensibility is reflected in the other Hebrew manuscripts or simply noted as a difference between the Arabic and Hebrew versions:

> **Ibn Baqi:** Bairam without him turns into something like fasting, as if I had restricted [the joys of] my heart to him.[75]

> **Halevi:** Bairam without him is like fasting; how my heart is burning for his sake![76]

> **Ibn Baqi:** BÉNED LA PÁŚQA AYÚN ŚIN ÉLLE: xaṣREYA MEW QORAČÓN POR ÉLLE.[77]

> **Halevi:** BÉNED LA PAŚKA AYÚN ŚIN ÉLLO: KÓM KÁNDE(D) MEW QORAČÓN POR ÉLLO.[78]

In this case, the question of whether amending an older Arabic kharja with the more plentiful manuscripts of a more recent Hebrew kharja is methodologically sound depends on the goals of the critic. The same is true for editing the kharja independently from its individual poetic contexts. One conclusion that could be reached is that while these practices may not be ideal, they are difficult to resist in specific cases. The modern practice of the consultation of multiple poetic contexts of a single or similar kharja may be an inauthentic way to experience the Romance kharjas. There are uses of the muwashshahas, however, that do not privilege or even retain the Romance kharjas. The muwashshaha fragment that contains Halevi's kharja containing the word *pashkah* dates from the twelfth century, a period in which the use of secular muwashshahas was popular in the East.[79] As mentioned above, Halevi's Iberian muwashshahas inspired Egyptian imitations, both before and after his death around 1141.[80] Rather than secular poems, however, these imitations were generally *piyyutim* (liturgical compositions), but unlike typical *piyyutim*, they were scanned according to the rules of the Andalusian quantitative system. As Ezra Fleisher notes, the presence of *piyyutim* in quantitative metres is surprising in some respects, since the pure syllabic metric system seems to have been more in vogue in the second half of the twelfth century.[81] At the same time, seeing as the *piyyutim* were imitations of, in some cases, easily identifiable muwashshahas and bearing in mind the practice of *mu'arada*, their presence in quantitative metres may be simply logical.

While citation of the kharja in full or in part can occur in the process of *mu'arada*, some Egyptian imitations eliminate the Romance kharjas and repurpose existing metres and rhymes, going from the secular to the liturgical. Among the Cairo Genizah fragments are Egyptian imitations produced by the poet R. El'azar ben Chalfon, one of the earliest Eastern Hebrew poets to implement Andalusian prosody and poetic customs and a poet who wrote panegyrics in honour of Halevi's patron, Samuel ben Hananya.[82] Nearly all of R. El'azar ben Chalfon's poems are *piyyutim*. Some of the strophic compositions are direct imitations of Halevi's muwashshahas, with the Cairo Genizah fragments indicating the model melodies (*lahn*) to which they should be sung.[83] For instance, R. El'azar imitates the metre and rhyme and the opening words of Halevi's amorous muwashshah about a fair-haired young woman referred to as a *hammah* (sun), which contains the Romance kharja: "Como prenda tenedme el collar, madre, en depósito a mi disposición; cuello blanco quiere ver mi señor, no quiere joyas" (Keep my necklace for me, mother, as a deposit, as an overdue pawn; my lord wants to see my [bare] white neck; he does not want jewellery).[84] In addition to eliminating the Romance kharja, R. El'azar's composition substitutes Halevi's sun, whose beauty radiates light throughout the secular model, for a *nefesh hakhama* (wise soul).[85]

In another case, R. El'azar imitates a muwashshaha titled "You Have Done Enough, My Adversaries."[86] In one case, the muwashshaha contains an Arabic kharja, and in another, the Romance kharja "Se me va el corazón, Díos mío, ¿si me volverá? ¡Tan mal me hace sufrir el amado! Está enfermo: ¿cuándo sanará?" (My heart is leaving me. Oh God! Will he ever come back? My darling is hurting me so badly! [My heart] is ill: when will it be cured?), which occurs in a slightly different form in a muwashshaha by Todros Abul'afiya.[87] Maintaining the metre and rhyme scheme of the muwashshaha, R. El'azar eliminated the Romance kharja and created a divine love poem (*ahava*), replacing the censorship of the *raqib* (spy, censor) with the enemies of Israel who try to keep a woman from God and the profane kharja verses with a pledge to commit to God's love: "When I hope for your compassion and to be sheltered by your salvation, your words are clear to me and with your love I shall be awakened." There are three other liturgical imitations of this particular muwashshaha by Halevi, including two by R. Abraham Ibn

Ezra and a third by another poet possibly of North African origin, none of which contain Halevi's Romance kharja.[88]

The Egyptian imitations of Halevi's muwashshahas, which so clearly admired their model's metre, rhyme, and skill in Hebrew poetry, put them to a liturgical use that suited their needs and that necessarily, due to the religious content of their compositions, involved a replacement of the Romance kharjas. Whereas the metre and rhyme that accompanied the kharjas survived, the kharjas themselves did not.[89] The reorientation of existing metre and rhyme for a new purpose combined with changes in the interest in or feasibility of using Romance kharjas, as well as the modern-day practice of editing related Romance kharjas, comprise some of the shifts and fragmentations of the muwashshahas over time.

Halevi himself went through significant changes in his lifetime. Before his death and before the Egyptian imitations were composed, Halevi made a physical and spiritual departure from the Iberian Peninsula for Palestine and publicly rejected muwashshaha poetry. Around 1140, Halevi wrote the *Book of the Khazars* (the *Kuzari*). The *Kuzari* is known for the polemical views expressed by one of the main interlocutors, a rabbi who speaks with the king of the Khazars, a Turkish people, about the conversion of the Khazars to Judaism in the eighth century. The *Kuzari* presents proofs for the superiority of Judaism and also harshly criticizes panegyric and Andalusian metrical poems, arguing for the need to recover authentic Jewish heritage by separating what was Jewish from the Arab-Islamic culture of al-Andalus. As Raymond Scheindlin has noted, modern critics have mined the *Kuzari* for answers as to why Halevi wanted to isolate Jewish from the Andalusian culture, wondering whether Halevi rejected Andalusian poetry because it was too Arabic, rejected panegyric poetry because it was too secular, or simply stopped dealing in poetry altogether because he came to see it as frivolous.[90] As testament to the presence of contradictions among the contradictions, however, Ross Brann cautions that one should not assume a priori that the work represents Halevi's view on Andalusian poetry and poetics, citing the author's words in the introduction about identifying the character known as the Scholar's views with his own: "I found *some* of the Scholar's arguments convincing and in accord with my own beliefs."[91] With regard to the interpretation of the word *pashkah*, Halevi's spiritual and geographic moves do not provide any definitive evidence as to whether he intended to refer to Passover, Eid al-Fitr, or a festival in general;

his change of heart about muwashshaha poetry is equally unhelpful on that issue.

Halevi's rejection of the Andalusian muwashshaha and his move to demarcate Jewish culture by differentiating it from Andalusian culture underscores the Abrahamic tangle that is Andalusian culture and the limits of poetic context as a solution to what Andreas Schönle called in another situation the muwashshaha's "palimpsest of construction, use, and decay."[92] Returning to the question of *pashkah,* while it is a limited approach to assume that Halevi's and Ibn Baqi's kharjas are the same, because such an assumption obscures difference by reading across poetic contexts without caution, elements of Halevi's poetic context, such as the use of Hebrew instead of Arabic or the use of biblical references, should not overdetermine the reading of Halevi's kharja, which began its life outside of any specifically Jewish context.

One use of the Genizah muwashshaha fragments containing Romance kharjas today is their employment in the production of more legible texts of some of the Romance kharjas that appear in Arabic muwashshahas. More interestingly, however, these physical fragments elucidate the variety of ways in which the Romance kharjas and their muwashshahas have been moved, fragmented, and re-evaluated, whether intentionally or accidentally, over a period spanning some nine hundred years. While one can lament that the Romance kharjas were artificially created fragments, and that they are the victims of critical fragmentation or fragmentations, reading these kharjas in the context of their muwashshahas is not an easy means of making them whole again, as a problematization of the notion of context and the practice of borrowing across different muwashshahas clearly shows. The kharjas were adapted and moved, sometimes even eliminated. As we have seen here and in many other examples not cited in this chapter, the practice of repurposing existing kharjas is normative for the muwashshaha corpus.

In reading fragment theorist Maurice Blanchot, Leslie Hill writes that the fragment need not be a "codicil or belated homage to totality" but rather can serve as a "demand, a requirement or an imperative, an exigency (from the Latin *ex-agere,* to force out or extract) that draws writing and thinking beyond the shelter of philosophy, culture, or art towards something still without name."[93] Despite sometimes being set aside or forgotten, as we saw in the previous chapter with the chivalric fragments, there is something urgent about the fragment. Its incompleteness spurs efforts at reconstruction, which can lead to a setting aside of the fragment because piecing it back together is too difficult or not considered worth the effort, or creating a transcription and an edition only to set the fragments aside shortly afterwards. As discussed here, however, attempts at reconstruction can also lead to very intense study.

My aim here has been to open the kharjas, to extract some of the history and movement of these pieces. I will end here by returning to Halevi's poetry. It is clear that towards the end of his life he had the clear goal of Zion, which nevertheless remained difficult to reach due to a series of spiritual and practical impediments. It is clear that he took part in creating a masterful Andalusian poetry, but it is also apparent that he wanted to separate himself from Andalusian culture towards the end of his life:

> My heart is in the East and I am at the edge of the West.
> How can I savor what I eat, how find it sweet?
> How can I fulfill my vows and pledges while
> Zion is in Christendom's fetter, and I am in Islam's shackle?
> It would be easy for me to leave behind the opulence of Spain;
> It would be glorious to see the dust of the ruined Shrine![94]

Halevi's road to Zion was complex, not unlike the path of some of his poems. Viewing the Genizah fragments as an opportunity to open up some of the pieces of their often unsung pasts, exemplified here by the brief investigation of *pashkah* and the Egyptian experience of an Andalusian poem, allows for these pieces to pass through different times and places. As in the case of the chivalric fragments, the history of the kharja fragments is composed of individual users and their sometimes contradictory demands, some of which are visible today on their weathered pages.

Chapter Four

Faith in Fragments

In the late 1990s, workers restoring the eleventh-century Aljafería Palace in Saragossa, Spain found folios of two different fourteenth-century Qur'ans placed in one of the ceiling coffers.[1] The palace was built as the residence of the Banu Hud, an Arab dynasty that ruled the Muslim-ruled principality of Saragossa, Spain, from 1039 to 1110. The discovery of the folios was particularly noteworthy because they were not found in a room used during Muslim control of the palace, which lasted until 1118, but in one constructed by Muslims working for Pedro IV in the fourteenth century. In 1492, the year in which Granada fell, the Jews were expelled, and Columbus arrived in the Americas, Ferdinand and Isabella took up residence in the same palace. From 1485 to 1706, the Aljafería served as the seat of the Spanish Inqusition.

In the same room of the palace where the Qur'an folios were found, another surprising discovery was made: nondecorative, carefully written inscriptions of some sixty-one one-word or partial phrase inscriptions in Arabic inspired by the Qur'an. The inscriptions are painted on planks in the ceiling and are visible only from the vantage point of the ceiling itself. The planks contain decoration, but only on their visible sides. The inscriptions focus on God as opposed to the Prophet and include some of the Ninety-nine Beautiful Names of God (the Adored, the Sustainer, the Greatest, the Benevolent) and phrases from suras on the greatness and oneness of God (20/6–8, 57/3, and 59/22–4), such as parts of the *Shahada*, the Muslim profession of faith, *la ilaha illa Huwa* (There is no god but He), as well as *Huwa al-Awwalu waal-Akhiru* (the First, the Last).[2] The inscriptions are written in different directions and in places on the ceiling in which it would have been impossible to write after construction was completed. María José Cervera Fras has thus suggested that the words must have been written after Christian workers decorated the planks and before they were placed in the ceiling in a different order than the one in which they were written.[3] She proposes that the inscriptions comprise part of an ejaculatory prayer inspired by Qur'anic text, but that the inscriptions are neither quotations from the Qur'an nor a prayer that can be precisely identified.

Some forty years before the Qur'an folios were found, another strange discovery was made in Burgos, a different city in Northern Spain, in a house that sat near a Roman-era hermitage dedicated to Saint Marina of Antioch.[4] A man by the name of Ángel Ruiz Sainz was renovating his house in the province of Villamartín de Sotoscueva when he found a medieval fragment. Under the kitchen floor in a hole covered with a stone, Sainz found a 14″ x 8″ red clay shingle inscribed with text in a fourteenth- or fifteenth-century Gothic cursive and some strange images (figure 12).[5] Today the shingle is known for what several scholars have identified as a fragment of the thirteenth-century *mester de clerecía* Castilian epic, the *Poema de Fernán González* (*PFG*).[6] The poem tells of the tenth-century Castilian count Fernán González's defence of Castile against the Muslims, his wars against the Kingdom of Navarre, his debates with the king of León, and his protection of the San Pedro of Arlanza Benedictine Monastery. The shingle is said to feature verses from four different stanzas of this epic, with two stanzas comprising part of a prayer that appears frequently in Spanish and French medieval epic and didactic works, the *Ordo commendationis animae*, a prayer commending the souls of the dying and those in grave peril unto God.[7] The tile is also physically fragmentary; it has lost its upper right corner, so the first words of the first three lines of text are missing. Furthermore, the very first line that appears on the tile, which José Hernando Pérez and Isabel Velázquez have ascribed to another thirteenth-century *mester de clerecía* work, the *Libro de Apolonio* (Book of Apollonius), is crossed out ("de fuera s(o) rayda" [rough on the outside]).[8] The right side of the tile is also incomplete, cutting off the final word of most of the tile's lines, including the last word of a signature that concludes the tile that reads, "En testimonio de verdat philosopho sure+ [–]" (In witness of the truth philosopher sure+ [–]). The tile has holes covering its surface, but none that extends through to its reverse that could have been used to hang the piece on a wall, though there may have been holes in the tile's missing corners.

What, then, do the Qur'anic and shingle fragments have in common, the first Islam's central text and the second a certainly Christian

Figure 12 La teja de Villamartín

and perhaps literary text? Both the Qur'anic and shingle fragments are outlier cases that do not fit neatly into the categories of amulets, votive offerings, literature, popular culture, religious doctrine, and magic. This chapter argues that these fragments are also similar in the use for which they were created: they served a spiritual or more specifically an apotropaic purpose, a means of protection for the workers or visitors to the buildings in which or by which they were found. Drawing on Islamic and Christian practices and the intersection of magic in these two religions, and building on the practice of genizah discussed in the previous chapter, I propose that the Aljafería and shingle fragments evince a use of fragments for protective purposes in the Iberian Peninsula in the medieval and early modern periods. These protective fragments are an important but underexplored part of manuscript culture. Their power derives not necessarily from reading the text or from that text's accuracy but from knowledge of the text's physical presence in the area in which it was intended to have its effect. Drawing on theories of presence, where presence refers to the effects of proximate people or things on bodies and consciousness or to a persistence or survival of the past, this chapter argues that the physical presence of the fragment is similarly important in the uses of medieval and early modern manuscripts in the present.[9] As in the medieval and early modern periods, today reading is not always the reason given for why fragments are important to communities and institutions.

Aljafería Fragments

The Qur'an folios include six complete parchment folios that had been folded, presumably to hide them from view, and two highly fragmentary paper folios. The folios convey basic tenets of Islamic monotheism, including the Oneness of the Lordship of Allah, the Oneness of the Worship of Allah, and the Oneness of the Names and Qualities of God, in addition to the peace that will be bestowed in the afterlife on faithful Muslims who honour and fear only God. The nearly complete parchment folios contain Sura 21, on the prophets prior to Muhammad, and Sura 22, on pilgrimage, along with two highly fragmentary paper folios containing verses 62, 63, and 69 of Sura 8, on the spoils of war, and verses 40–5 of Sura 9, on repentance. While it is possible that two complete Qur'ans were left in the ceiling and that the folios are simply what survives after years of loss to pests and the environment, the fact that the parchment folios are preserved as well as they are makes it unlikely that they would be all that remains of a once complete Qur'an.[10]

Even if it is assumed that selections of the Qur'ans, rather than complete Qur'ans, were left in the ceiling, at least in the case of the parchment folios, it is impossible to know why these particular suras were chosen. As in the case of the *Carmen Campidoctoris*, it is nevertheless difficult not to look to the text of the fragments to propose a motivation for their specific presence. Suras 8 and 9 are both Madinan suras and form a pair, with Sura 9 containing the famous sword verse (*ayat al-sayf*), which has been decontextualized and used to support the notion that Islam aims to exterminate all infidels. Sura 8 was completed at the time of the Battle of Badr, a key battle in the early days of Islam in which divine intervention in Islamic history is asserted. Sura 9 was completed after the battle or military expedition of Tabuk, which, if historical, would be the start of the Byzantine-Arab wars. The part of Sura 8 contained on the folios urges believers to maintain their faith in Allah and to enjoy what they have won, while the extant verses of Sura 9 differentiate between believers and unbelievers, referencing the Prophet Muhammad and his companion and father-in-law Abu Bakr's seeking refuge in a cave from the Meccan search party sent after them during the Hijra (or Hegira, Muhammad's departure from Mecca to Medina). Finally, Sura 21 treats the prophets who preached Islam, and Sura 22 warns of the judgment day that awaits the Meccans who reject God and deny Muslims access to Mecca for pilgrimage.

The Qur'an folios and inscriptions in the Aljafería date from the fourteenth century and were found in Pedro IV's hall. Though Pedro IV ruled Aragon from 1319 to 1387, before the era of forced conversion in Spain, the folios and inscriptions are typically considered a case of protest or manuscript hiding, a frequent practice among the Moriscos who lived some two centuries later. Though the content of the folios could be read as supporting the protest or concealment thesis, it is implausible on two fronts, since the fourteenth century was one without widespread persecution of the Mudejars, Muslims living in relative peace under Christian rule, as well as one without the Spanish Inquisition. I propose that the folios and inscriptions were used apotropaically, serving as a means to protect the carpenters working in Pedro IVs hall and possibly to protect the hall itself.

Islamic dogma is generally against magic, primarily due to its link with associationism (*sirk*). As in Renaissance treatises on magic by Christian writers and theologians, including Pedro Sánchez Ciruelo

(1470–1548), Francisco de Vitoria (ca. 1483–1546), Benito Pereira (1536–1610), and Martín Del Río (1551–1608), there was nevertheless a distinction in the Islamic world between beneficial, licit magic – "magia benéfica," as Yvette Cardaillac-Hermosilla has called it, which drew on both supernatural and natural phenomena but did not challenge the oneness of God – and illicit magic, which aimed to cause harm and relied on demonic forces.[11] Even Muhammad used techniques of protective and healing magic (*ruqya*) to ward off the evil eye and to cure certain illnesses.[12] After the tenth century, verses of the Qur'an, abbreviated versions of the Qur'an, letters of the alphabet, and the names of God, some of which are included in the Aljafería rafter inscriptions, were ascribed supernatural and symbolic powers. These texts were used in conjunction with a variety of symbols drawn from other cultures as a sort of supercharged prayer to cure ailments and problems in the home or family life.[13] Many different suras of the Qur'an were employed for protective purposes in medieval and early modern Islamic works, but the suras contained in the rafters (8, 9, 21, and 22) are not those most commonly so used.[14] The messages of the suras are consistent, however, with fundamental concepts of Islam in general, including God as omnipresent, one, omnipotent, and protector.[15] The large majority of extant Morisco texts containing magic include beneficial, licit, and pragmatic magic that primarily grew out of the urgent need to protect themselves and their property. As Ana Labarta has noted, Morisco magic texts are surprisingly free of greed, unlike many of the recipes connected to Christians, such as those to find treasure.[16]

We know that the Moriscos made magical use of verses of the Qur'an in divination, potions, talismans, aromatic substances, and spells, including Suras 8, 9, 21, and 22, but not especially these four. The Qur'an's powers are unlocked in several ways, including through the use of verses written on paper, hide, or cloth as talismans and through the simple reading of Qur'anic verses. The power of the Qur'an was also realized, however, through such means as the mixture of rose water and saffron, and the wetting and drinking of scraps containing religious formulas. Apart from the frequent inclusion of magic remedies and magic squares in Morisco miscellanies, we conserve Morisco works such as the *El fablamiento del Alcoran y del bien que se haze con el* (The discussion of the Qur'an and of the good that is done with it), in which fragments or complete versions of Suras 2–72 are used to various ends, most of them positive and corresponding to one of the categories that Pablo Roza has identified for Morisco talismans (health, universal talismans useful for all problems, love, farming, domestic issues, and the dead).[17] *El fablamiento del Alcoran* uses verses of the Qur'an to ease pain and cure illness, especially in issues relating to women's reproductive health, as protection against Satan, demons, earthly creatures such as scorpions and lions, to repress erotic dreams, for success in commerce and hunting, and protection from poverty and death.[18] In each case, the user also finds instructions on how to make his or her own talismans (which most often contain a Qur'anic element) and potions. Like the *Fablamiento del Alcoran,* the divinatory text the *Libro de las suertes* (Book of fate) is similarly rooted in the Islamic faith. The future is predicted based on a professional seer's or sorcerer's use of a magic square on which the Arabic letters *alif, ba, gim,* and *da* are written, in conjunction with the four elements of fire, air, water, and earth. The combination of letters shown and their correspondence with verses of the Qur'an provides the user with answers about the future. The *Libro de los dichos maravillosos* (Book of marvellous sayings), on the other hand, is extant in a miscellaneous manuscript in which a copy of the *Libro de las suertes* is copied, along with many fragments. In some cases, the same or very similar recipes and talismans are copied three different times. The *Libro de los dichos maravillosos* contains talismans and highly varied prescriptions as in *El fablamiento del Alcoran,* from how to cure a toothache to how to make oneself invisible, making use in some cases, as Luce López Baralt has noted, of the hoopoe bird, a species well represented in Spain and known for its crown of feathers.[19] In addition to magic texts and many religious texts, the manuscript containing the *Libro de los dichos maravillosos* offers a variety of other fragments that are not explicitly religious or magic, including those on astrology and one on the properties of animals.[20]

If the Qur'an fragments in the rafters of the Aljafería were meant to provide general rather than specific protection and were not produced by a specialized process but simply left in the ceiling without modification, they would have the qualities of what Labarta calls an amulet rather than a talisman.[21] The Aljafería Qur'an folios certainly differ from the most common type of talisman present in Morisco manuscripts, those carried on one's person and consisting of two parts: instructions regarding the contents of the talisman and its preparation, and the magic content of the talisman itself. There is a record, however, of Morisco talismans being placed in the general vicinity of the person who was to be protected when the impossibility of direct contact necessitated the use of symbolic action.[22] Qur'ans were buried under the floors of homes such that every time the inhabitants passed in or out they had to step over fragments for health and safety. In other cases, those protected were not even among the living. As Miguel Asín Palacios notes, al-Ghazali writes of a practice in other Islamic cultures in which the dead were buried with a copy of the Qur'an or with certain Qur'anic verses in their hands.[23] A Christian corollary is Alfonso X's desire that all copies of the *Cantigas de Santa María* be stored in the church where he was entombed.[24] Symbolic action could also be antagonistic. Roza cites a recipe in a Morisco manuscript in the BNM that stymies love for an enemy by breaking a cane inscribed with text in the house in which the enemy and his lover have intercourse.[25]

Several centuries before the Moriscos, however, there is a record of architectural inscriptions that were likely undertaken for an apotropaic purpose. There is a Latin version of a Greek inscription dedicated to the gods and goddesses with the interpretation of an oracle of Apollo Klarios that is often inscribed on plaques. These plaques, found in La Coruña, Italy, and elsewhere, were designed to fit into walls on buildings. Christopher Jones has proposed that the plaques served as a means to ward off the plague that began in 165 CE.[26] Scholars of the Byzantine periods have documented early Christian use of the special abbreviated writing of *nomina sacra* (sacred names), crosses, and other inscriptions on houses as blessings.[27] Maria Paz de Hoz has proposed that a small second- to fourth-century lapidary found near Astorga in the province of León, possibly of Syrian origin, had apotropaic value and may have been placed on the door of a house, akin to the Syrian custom of placing Christian inscriptions on lintels.[28] The lapidary consists of a picture of a temple or pavilion and upstretched palm containing three lines of text, the henotheistic and syncretic acclamatory *Heis Zeus Sarapis* (Zeus and Serapis are only one), common on Syrian amulets, rings, and papyri used in incantations with the name Iao, the deity in Gnosticism, Greek mystery cults, and magic that appears frequently on second- to fifth-century amulets.[29]

Perhaps the best-known example of placing sacred fragments in buildings is the Jewish practice of mezuzah, the placement of an encased piece of horizontally written parchment with verses of the Torah (Deut. 6:4–9 and 11:13–21) on the upper right portion of the door, in the right door jamb, or on the doorpost to protect the inhabitants of the household. Upon entering the house, pious Jews touch or kiss the mezuzah, speaking a benediction or asking for God's protection. As Maimonides writes in the *Mishneh Torah* (1170–80), it is critical that the mezuzah be prepared and used correctly; certainly, it is not to be modified and used as an amulet for personal gain.[30]

As Maimonides indicates, the mezuzah, along with tefillin containing verses of the Torah, were obligations according to the Old Testament and Jewish practice, but some Jews chose to modify them with additional names and other text in hopes of fulfilling personal desires. As Joshua Trachtenber has noted, the mezuzah was widely used as an amulet and in some cases a talisman in Labarta's terminology (involving a specialized process of creation) in the Middle Ages, and the instructions for preparing mezuzot often resembled those for preparing talismans.[31] There is evidence that some Christians respected the talismanic properties of the mezuzah and that some Jews thought that non-Jews could benefit from them as well. The fourteenth-century king of Salzburg asked a Jew to give him a mezuzah to place on the gate of his castle but was eventually denied.[32] There is a story in the Talmud (Yerushalmi, Massekhet Peah) in which Rabbi ha-Nasi (d. 188 or 219 CE), who codified the Mishnah, gave a mezuzah to Arteban, the third-century king of Persia, as a gift after the king had given him an exotic pearl. When the king complained about the seemingly worthless gift he had received, after having explicitly asked for a gift of equal value, the rabbi replied: "The two objects we have exchanged cannot be compared in value. You sent me something which I must guard, and I sent you something which, even while you sleep, keeps watch over you. As it is written: 'When you walk, it shall lead you; when you rest, it shall keep you'" (*Tehillim* 6:22). The rabbi's mezuzah clearly aims to have a protective function, but it has another key characteristic, one related to a fundamental principle of magic, which can be summarized by Frazer's "law of contact" or "contagion":

> If we analyze the principles of thought on which magic is based, they will probably be found to resolve themselves into two: first, that like produces like, or that an effect resembles its cause; and, second, that things which have once been in contact with each other continue to act on each other at a distance after the physical contact has been severed. The former principle may be called the Law of Similarity, the latter the Law of Contact or Contagion. From the first of these principles, namely the Law of Similarity, the magician infers that he can produce any effect he desires merely by imitating it: from the second he infers that whatever he does to a material object will affect equally the person with whom the object was once in contact, whether it formed part of his body or not.[33]

Frazer's notions regarding an object's continuing to act after contact has been broken and the idea of a person with whom an object "was once in contact" recall the situation of the Aljafería inscriptions and Qur'an folios containing text that need not be actively read or in some cases seen to have an impact. In fact, there is evidence that some users of textual amulets thought that they maintained their effectiveness only if they were *not* read. Don Skemer cites Ciruelo's observation that in the 1530s "most people were loath to read their amulets for fear that the brief prayers, divine names, and other textual elements would lose their potency after the amulet was opened."[34] In the case of the fragments studied here, what was important is that those seeking protection or to make a statement of faith had knowledge of the text's physical presence in the area in which it was intended to have an effect or to make that statement, or where the intended beneficiaries of the text were present, even if asleep. The Aljafería inscriptions were written on boards that had been previously decorated by Christian painters, but the inscriptions themselves were clearly not decorative and, once placed in the ceiling, did not receive meaning as a result of reading or by what Gumbrecht has called "meaning effects," referring to those produced via a hermeneutic process.[35] Instead, the inscriptions and the Qur'an folios were important because they were a part of the structure that would endure, provided they remained unseen, regardless of the ownership and function of the room. Like the mezuzah, their effect derived not from being read by a person desiring protection but from a belief in the power of the simple physical presence of the text, in addition to knowledge, whether direct or indirect, of the text's content.

Villamartín Shingle

The diffuse nature of context, as well as doubts as to the principal place of reading in the early modern function and use of certain objects containing text are equally present in the Villamartín shingle, the other fragment considered here. Modern approaches to the shingle, including aspects of the approaches in this chapter, have focused on reading the tile, particularly on the identification of the text as part of the *PFG*. The challenge of defining the shingle's context has yielded a wide range of critical results.[36]

Velázquez begins her study of the shingle with an inscription, though not one that necessarily hung in a building. The inscription to which Velázquez refers is conserved in the Museo Histórico de Priego de Córdoba and features a Christian inscription contemporary with the later amulets containing the name "Iao" mentioned above.

Some scholars refer to the inscription explicitly as a *tabella defixionis* (curse tablet), and it may well have been. It is certain, however, that the fourth- or fifth-century lead inscription is definitively Christian. It also invokes saints mentioned in the *Commendatio animae* prayer present in the *PFG*, including Saint Susanna, with a similar formulation in the inscription: "bindicasti san[c]ta[m] Sosan<I>na[m]" ("Tú que libreste a Susana" [You that freed Susana] in the *PFG*). Velázquez proposes that the lead inscription may reveal a utilization of part of the *Commendatio animae* for an amuletic purpose. Although some parts of the inscription are illegible and others notoriously difficult to decipher, it is worth citing its interpretation simply to show its highly fragmentary nature:

> ADEIS qui bindicasti san(c)ta(m) Sosan{I}na(m]) de falso crimene / ADEIS qui bendecasti san(c)ti IMASI spe labur et de / TRISLAMINUS ardes et ADOSSISTILVRAT gratia / IISPROVBIGA factores et libera inn(o)centes / Leopardus super isto bisto latronatu fui / ITVILODEM ostendis [- - -]diculus magus ISITI // MAR[-]TERETRAVSEMVNDAV[-]R[-] fe[s]tina qui biceris E[-]T / ibi AVBE et qui tu biceris fuerunt IDI pro / BALVS firmum / ANOS / IOC qui ibi curriat I verum INPERI quibus OS / Martis die ut quinto die A ET.[37]

In proposing that the inscription is a primitive version of the *Ordo*, Velázquez suggests that the third line of the inscription transcribed as "TRISLAMINUS ardes" might evoke "tres pueros de camino ignis ardentis" (three boys from the furnace of burning fire), a phrase found in the earliest definitive extant version of the *Commendatio animae*, an eighth-century copy of the second-oldest extant Western liturgical text, the *Gelasian Sacramentary* (Biblioteca Apostolica Vaticana, MS Reginensis 316) and in the *Rituale romanum*.[38]

While the connection between the *Commendatio animae* and the fifth-century inscription is not definitive, the inscription's mention of God's deliverance of the Old Testament's Susanna from *falso crimene* recalls the medieval *Commendatio animae.* More generally, the *Commendatio animae*'s enumeration of acts of divine assistance make it a logical amuletic or talismanic text. A closer correlate to the Villamartín tile than Velázquez's inscription is a late fourteenth- or early fifteenth-century amulet roll containing a fragment of the *Commendatio animae*. This roll, possibly of Burgundian origin, consists of eighty-seven lines of text and was probably created for a noblewoman of childbearing age. Like other extant birthing amulets and the shingle, the amulet roll is the work of a professional scribe. The *Commendatio animae* appears in lines 31–7:

> nocebit super egros manus imponent et bene habebunt Do-
> mine liberasti tres pueros de camino ignis ardentis sydrac
> misac et abdenago danielem de lacu leonum Jonam de ventre ceti
> teclam de bestis susannam de falso crimine petrum de mari et vinculis
> et cathenis paulum de carcere libera me de isto langore et omni
> crimine et a presenti tribulatione in quo sum miserere mei Exaudi me
> sicut exaudisti mariam et martham deprecor sancte petre.[39]

> (It will [not] harm [them]. They will lay the hands upon the sick, and they will recover. Lord, you released three boys from the furnace of burning fire, Sidrac, Misac, and Abdenago; [released] Daniel from the lions' den; [released] Jonah from the belly of the whale; [released] Thecla from the beasts; [released] Susanna from a false accusation; [released] Peter from the sea, links, and chains; [released] Paul from prison; release me from this weakness and from all accusation and tribulation in which I find myself. Take pity on me, and listen to me as you listened to Mary and Martha, I pray, holy stone.)

The amulet's version of the *Commendatio* is generally consistent with versions thought to have served as inspiration for the version that appears in epic and *mester de clerecía* works, with mention of the Old Testament figures of Daniel, Jonah, and Susanna, the Hebrew children delivered from the fiery furnace. One notable difference between the amulet and the *Commendatio animae* in the *PFG*, in the *Libro de buen amor*, and on the tile is the amulet's mention of a different saint associated with Antioch: Thecla in place of Marina. Recalling that the main text of the shingle comprises verses that Hernando Pérez, Ángel Gómez Moreno, and Velazquéz have identified as versions of stanzas 180, 107, 106, and 108 of the *PFG*, the verses read:

> ... sieste q*ue* fues la tu mesurra q*ue* tornase la rrueda q*ue* ...
> ... castelanos pasado grant rrencura co*n* las gentes paganas fu ...
> [Se]ñor tu q*ue* libreste a Dauid d*el* leo*n* mateste al fillisteo un soberbioso ...
> [quitaste] allos judios de*l* rrey de Babillon saca a nos e libra desta
> tribulacio*n*
> Señor q*ue* entre los sabios valiste a Catalina e de muerte libreste a
> E<s>t[er la rreyna]

<al> drago*n* destruxiste d*e*la virge*n* Marina tu da a n*ues*tras plagas la s*an*ta melecyna
Tu libreste a Danj[el] d*e* entre los leones libreste sa*n* Mateo *de*los fieros dragones tu saca a nos.[40]

(... if it were for your benevolence to turn the wheel that ...
... Castilians have suffered great dishonour with the pagan people ...
... Lord, you freed David from the lion, you killed the Philistine, an arrogant man ...
... You removed the Jews from the king of Babylon, remove us and free us from this tribulation.
Lord, that among the wise assisted Catalina and from death liberated Esther ...
You destroyed the virgin Marina's dragon, give our wounds holy medicine,
you freed Daniel from the lions, you freed Matthew from the fierce dragons, remove us ...)

Joseph Gwara has rightly proposed that the formulaic nature of *mester de clerecía* text in general, the highly derivative nature of the *PFG*, and the frequent use of the *Commendatio*-inspired topos in *mester de clerecía* text make it possible that the tile text does not derive from the *PFG* at all and that it is logical to ask, "Why would a notary copy stanza 180 of the *PFG* and then skip back to 107–108?"[41] Gómez Moreno, on the other hand, accounts for variations between the *PFG* manuscript and the tile by suggesting that the scribe copied imperfectly memorized portions of the poem, rather than using a manuscript, as Hernando Pérez suggests.[42]

The considerations of variants between the *PFG* and tile, and the reasons for those particular variants, as well as more generally the quantity of repetition in cuaderna vía verse, are part of two interrelated theoretical problems that surround fragments in general: the questions of which textual contents and which social contexts elucidate a fragment's conditions of use. With regard to textual contexts for the shingle, one provocative proposal from Gwara is that the presence of the formulation *Señor, (tú, que, ya)* in stanza 105, at the start of stanzas 106 and 107 (the *Commendatio* section), and stanzas 180 and 181 (Fernán González's first speech) of the *PFG* could suggest that these stanzas may have once formed a single unit. This prayer may have been a pre-existing cuaderna vía prayer or a prayer in circulation at the time of the shingle's composition.[43] If this possibility is to be considered, however, two more questions must be asked. First, if the stanzas comprised a pre-existing prayer, should the *PFG* still be considered the immediate if loose inspiration for the shingle text? Second, if the *PFG* is indeed considered the immediate inspiration, did the person who determined the shingle's content consider the poetic (*PFG*) contexts of the sets of stanzas in a specific way or simply in the general sense that they both ask for divine aid?

In terms of the second question and with regard to the more specific consideration of the poetic contexts in conceptualizing the tile, if stanza 105 is considered the exposition of the problem for which the *Commendatio* is invoked, and if stanza 179 is considered an introduction for the suffering described in 180 and 181, then both sets of stanzas begin with an indication of *coita* (disorder, disgrace, misfortune). In stanzas 104–5, the Christians in general suffer from *coita*, while in stanza 180, as Julian Weiss has noted, a defiant Fernán González equates *coita* with Fortune and challenges God to put a spoke in Fortune's wheel.[44] If one admits that the shingle's text is inspired by a version of certain stanzas of the *PFG* and somehow takes into account the poetic context of those stanzas, then the tile inverts stanzas 106–7 and 179–80, and voices them with a single speaker who conceives of Fortune as *coita*, generating the problem for which the *Commendatio* is invoked. Citing stanzas 179 and 105 in italics to reveal the presence of *coita* in each set of stanzas, the *PFG* context for the shingle text would read:

Cuando iba el mozo las cosas entendiendo, 179
oyo commo a Castilla moros la iban corriendo;
Valas me dijo. Cristo, yo a ti me encomiendo;
en coita es Castilla según que yo entiendo.

Señor ya tienpo era sy fuese tu mesura 180
que mudases la rrueda que anda a la ventura
asas an castellanos pasada mucha rrencura
gentes nunca pasaron atan malla ventura.

Duro les esta coita muy fiera temporada 105
los cristianos mesquinos, conpaña muy lazrada,
dezien: "Señor, nos vala la tu merçed sagrada,
ca valiste a San Pedro dentro en la mar irada.

Señor que con los sabyos valiste a Catalina 106
e de muerte libreste a Este la rreyna
e del dragon libreste a la virgin Marina
tu da a nuestras llagas conorte e medeçina.

Señor tu que libreste a Davyt del leom 107
mateste a Filisteo un sovervio varon
quiteste a los jodios del rreyno de Vavilom
saqua nos e libra nos de tan cruel presyom.

Tu que libreste a Susaña de los falsos varones 108
saqueste a Daniel de entre dos leones
libreste a San Matheo de los fieros drragones
Señor libranos destas tentaciones."[45]

(As the boy came gradually to see how matters stood, 179
he heard of how the Moors were bringing ruin on Castile.
"Help me, Christ," he said; "I commend myself to You.
A troubled time had fallen on Castile, as I have learned.

The time has come, Lord, if You should so judge it, 180
for You to spin the wheel that turns at random;
bitterness enough have the Castilians endured;
no people ever suffered such misfortune as them."

This time of misfortune endured a bitter age 105
for those wretched Christians, a sorely-treated band:
"Lord," they cried, "may Your holy mercy protect us,
for You protected Saint Peter in the angry main.

Lord, who with the sages gave Catherine protection, 106
saved Esther the queen from the threat of death,
and freed the chaste Marina from the clutches of the dragon,
may You grant us comfort and healing to our wounds.

You, Lord, who delivered David from the lion, 107
brought death to the Philistine, a man of haughty pride,
and freedom to the Jews from the king of Babylon,
free us and deliver us from so cruel a prison.

You rescued Susanna from the slanderous men 108
and Daniel You delivered from within the lions' den;
You freed Saint Matthew from the ferocious dragons;
so may You free us, Lord, from these temptations.")[46]

Several of the arguments used to support or critique the tile's link to the *PFG*, namely that the variants between the tile and *PFG* result from imperfect memorization of the *PFG*, and the shingle text may have been a pre-existing cuaderna vía prayer, gain new meaning when the fragment is considered as having been conceived and used for a spiritual purpose. Part of the perceived uniqueness of the Teja de Villamartín derives from the difficulty of identifying historical and generic contexts by which to understand its purpose. As discussed in part in chapter 3 in regards to the kharjas, the notion of context is often left undefined and taken as phenomenologically uncomplicated. The context invoked here for the shingle nevertheless shows just how constructed and diverse in chronology, form, and content that context can be, ranging from the Qur'anic fragments and ceiling inscriptions to the Qur'an folios buried in the floor, to the mezuzah, Roman inscriptions, birthing amulets, and both religious and magic practices and texts like the *Commendatio* prayer and the *PFG*. It is clear that the tile was not a personal handheld amulet like the birthing roll, but the shingle's text does bear similarity to some amulets. Discussing textual amulets, especially those like the birthing amulet described above, Skemer proposes that while some amulets are composed of single and brief religious texts, others were a bricolage of fragments, seemingly composed by centonization or patchwork of pre-existing material.[47] Whereas it was essential that amulets that relayed a single religious text, like those consisting of Qur'anic verses mentioned above in conjunction with the Aljafería discoveries, or that relayed a religious text and constituted a commandment, like the mezuzah, convey a specific text accurately, others could present a unique text or a text with no significance at all.[48]

The Villamartín shingle itself contains a piece of seemingly insignificant text and two images that appear to be doodles. With regard to the former, the shingle begins with the end of a verse or sentence whose first words have been lost with the rest of the upper left corner of the shingle and that has been partially struck through by part of the lines that demarcate the verses below. Hernando Pérez's and Velázquez's identification of the text as a fragment of a verse of the *Libro de Apolonio* is provocative, in that it supports the hypothesis that the shingle's scribe wrote versions of cuaderna vía literary works that he had memorized on the tile.[49] As Gwara notes, however, such a hypothesis ignores the fact that the tile is notarized, complete with *siglum* (sign) and testimonial, "En testimonio de verdat philosopho sure+ [–]," leaving the

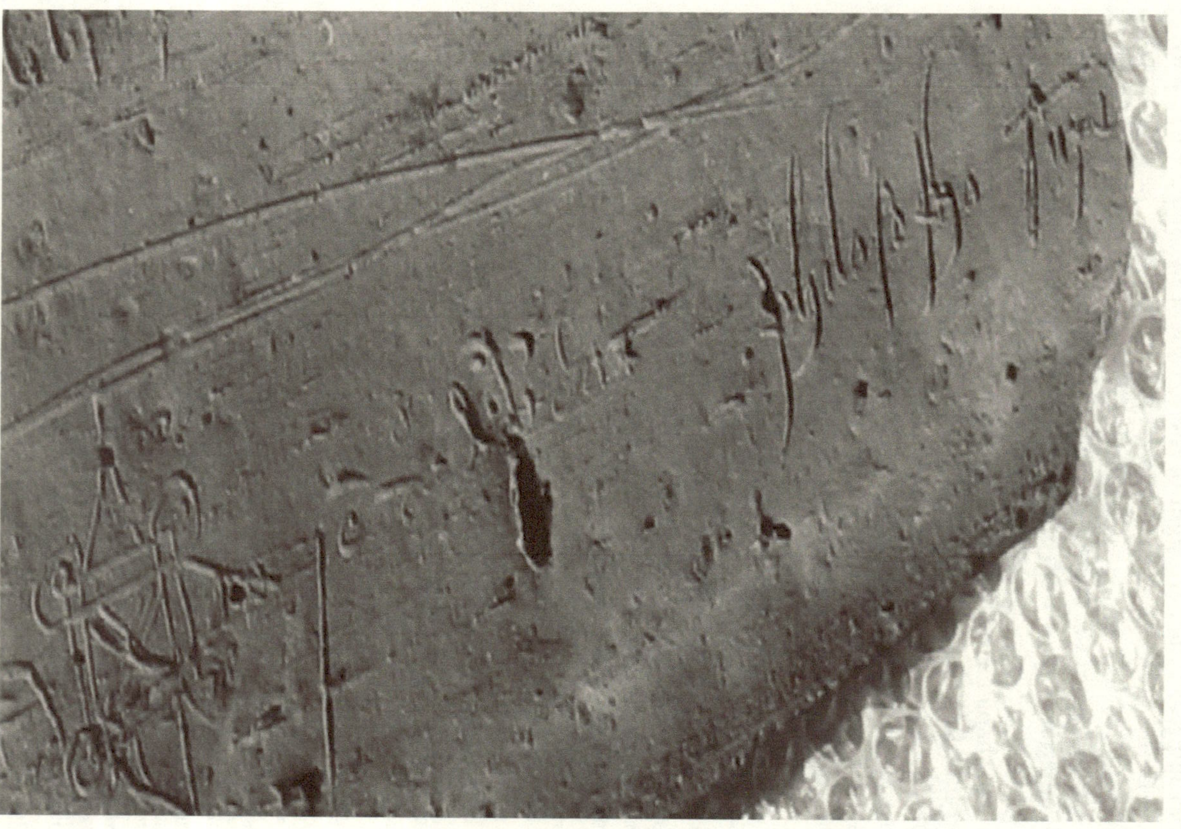

Figure 13 La teja de Villamartín, "En testimonio de verdat philosopho sure+ [–]"

question of why a scribe would copy such a group of verses unanswered (figure 13). In challenging the thesis that the shingle text is a version of the *PFG*, Gwara argues for the medieval use of cuaderna vía verse as a vehicle for prayers and hymns, proposing that the shingle prayer, along with the prayer in the *PFG* and those in other cuaderna vía works, may actually be versions of cuaderna vía devotional literature and that the prayer had a votive function, since Marina was a known protector of Camino de Santiago pilgrims and the hermitage was near that route.[50] Gwara further argues that the curious crossed-out line, "de fuera s(o) rayda," is not then from the *Libro de Apolonio* but is part of the prayer, either referring to the story of Jacob, who impersonates his hairy brother Esau and steals his father's blessing, or to the tile's physical appearance, with one rough and one smooth side.[51]

There are other explanations for the "de fuera s(o) rayda" line, however, including one that could support its link to the *Libro de Apolonio* and one that could support Gwara's claims. In terms of the shingle's connection to the *Libro de Apolonio*, the link certainly does not derive from an explicit connection between the line's context in the *Libro* and the *Commendatio* prayer. For Hernando Pérez and Velázquez, "de fuera s(o) rayda" recalls the stanza of the *Libro de Apolonio* in which Tarsiana and Antinágora present Apolonio with a series of riddles, this one resolving to *pelota* (ball):

> -"De dentro só vellosa e de fuera raída,
> "siempre trayo en seno mi crin bien escondida;
> "ando de man' en mano, tráenme escarnida,
> "cuando van a yant ar nengún me convida." (518)[52]
>
> ("I am downy on the inside and rough on the outside,
> I always carry my mane well hidden on my breast;
> I go from hand to hand, they treat me roughly;
> when I go to eat no one invites me.")

These lines spoken by Tarsiana are not particularly remarkable in themselves; they evoke a ball, possibly like the very one that enabled penniless Apolonio, thanks to his skilful play, to ingratiate himself with Architrastes when he fortuitously lands at Pentapolin:

> -"Cuando en Pentápolin entré desbaratado,
> "si non fuese por ésa andaría lazdrado;
> "fui del rey Architrastres por ella honrado,
> "si no, non me hobiera a yantar convidado." (519)

("When I entered Pentápolin, I entered in rough condition,
if it weren't for this, I would be damaged.
Because of this I left King Archistrastres honoured;
if not, no one would have invited me to eat.")

The common thread between these passages referencing balls and eating (*ésa* referring to *pelota* in the second verse of stanza 519) is the ability of positive change to come from even the shabbiest exterior.[53] The ball serves as a literal and figurative conduit of exchange and sustenance, as well as a location of hermeneutic activity, which manifests itself in Tarsiana's and Apolonio's poetic exchange of riddles and answers, and also in the image of peeling back the worn or vile outside (*raída, escarnida, desbaratado, lazdrado* [*lacerado*]) such as to reach an inner truth or a renewed state.[54] While a search for change and truth is certainly consistent with the *Commendatio* prayer, the *Apolonio* context bears little more than this very general connection to it. A more obvious and more plausible connection between *Libro de Apolonio* and the shingle is that the shingle's creator, in wanting to produce an object to protect visitors to the hermitage dedicated to Saint Marina or as an offering to the hermitage itself, recalled a work contemporary with the *PFG*, belonging to the same genre as the *PFG*, and that centred on Antioch, the region in which the hermitage's saint was born.

The possibility that the shingle had an apotropaic function – using the *Commendatio* in an amuletic way like the birthing amulet above and perhaps having an architectural location like the inscriptions and mezuzah to protect visitors – could also explain the presence of the "de fuera s(o) rayda" line. Writing in the context of the birthing amulet, Skemer notes that some amulet texts were copied from manuscripts, while others were quoted or paraphrased from memory. Further, amulets could be scrupulously crafted or, more often, not meant to last:

> Like other varieties of medieval ephemera unsystematically produced in odd physical formats (lacking the stout wooden boards that encased and protected the text block of Western codices), written amulets rarely survived and thus have been little explored for want of physical evidence. Distinctive forms of presentation and physical use led to an extremely high rate of attrition. The meager number of common examples that actually do survive are sometimes so crude in appearance that they have not always been recognized for what they were, meriting at most a passing reference. At the same time, written amulets could be so elegant that their amuletic function has seemed marginal next to their potential interest for art

> historians or students of vernacular literature. Many late-medieval prayer rolls, despite their professional production and illumination, functioned as written amulets to protect the bearer from menacing demons, sudden death (including in childbirth), and a host of specific misfortunes.[55]

It is clear that the shingle is no birthing amulet, but a patchwork mode of composition that is characteristic of protective texts could explain the variants between the shingle's text and the extant *PFG* manuscript or the quotation of a circulating cuaderna vía prayer, along with the presence of the "de fuera s(o) rayda" line. The *Commendatio animae* prayer was likely a recognizable text to the person who composed the shingle or the person who ordered the shingle composed; perhaps he also remembered that it formed part of the *PFG* or was related to the story. Working from memory or thinking in terms of conveying a story rather than a precise fragment of a work, the shingle scribe created a unique composition that honoured Saint Marina and asked for God's protection. "De fuera s(o) rayda," then, as Gwara has suggested, could be a reference to the physical appearance of the shingle itself, recalling Skemer's comment that some amulets or talismans were "crude in appearance." Another option that speaks to Skemer's proposal that some amulet texts were composed or paraphrased from memory is that the shingle's creator was thinking of Saint Marina, the patron saint of the hermitage by which it was found, when he created the tile and first recalled a line from a work that centred on her place of birth, the *Libro de Apolonio*. In this case, "de fuera s(o) rayda" could be a sort of a false start that is still inspired by the overall apotropaic use of the piece.

Considering Skemer's observation of the amuletic use of professionally prepared late-medieval prayer rolls, and hence the combination of not only religion and magic but also professional scribes and magic uses, the fact that that the shingle is notarized is perhaps not as curious as it might appear. Writing of Italy, Skemer notes that while social critics tended to focus on amulet production by those on the fringes of society, clerical, professional, and domestic amulet production was common in the late Middle Ages.[56] Thus, what might now seem like textual imperfections unbecoming of a notary – the shingle's deviations from the *PFG* manuscript text and its inclusion of a seemingly random half hemistich from the *Libro de Apolonio* – might not have had any importance at all given an apotropaic function. Curt Bühler has proposed that even the same text can vary from amulet to amulet, depending on "the date of writing and nationality of the scribe or patron who commissioned the amulet."[57] In this vein, what might have been notarized was not that the text fit together perfectly or corresponded with a particular existing text, but that the piece as a whole was a suitable object to protect its users or to honour Marina.

Modern Belief in Medieval Fragments

Anthropocentric paradigms, while constituting an important theoretical turn, in part tell us something we already knew about the powers of nonhuman subjects, including, perhaps paradoxically, their ability to inspire very powerful human emotions. Medieval and early modern manuscripts, whether complete or fragmentary, present problems of readability for all but an infinitesimal subset of the public. Due to textual incompleteness and problems of context, including questions surrounding the whole from which they came and the reasons why they were separated from those wholes, fragmentary manuscripts take these readability problems to the extreme.

I have argued in this chapter that the Aljafería and shingle fragments were not necessarily valued only or even primarily as reading material, or because they conveyed a perfectly cohesive or the best version of a text or oral prayer in circulation. Rather, a belief in the shingle as a means to honour Marina and the hermitage dedicated to her, or a belief in the Aljafería fragments as an effective statement of faith and protection on behalf of the Mudejar workers in the construction of Pedro IV's hall also gave these fragments meaning. The shingle's text was likely important to its creator at least to the extent that it was notarized, but the text, with its unusual support and unique combination of verses, partial verses, and drawings, is clearly not a daily-use reading copy. Further, as I have argued above, what was notarized was likely not that the text conformed exactly to some model, but that its verses comprised an effective honour to Marina. The Aljafería folios and inscriptions were clearly not intended for daily or even occasional reading. In their case, while the fragments transmitted an official text, direct or indirect knowledge of those texts' presence is what most likely gave them meaning.

Today, medieval and early modern writing still has a charismatic appeal that does not always derive from the text that it conveys. A modern corollary to this medieval and early modern faith in texts for more than reading purposes occurs in the exhibition of manuscripts. In the display of manuscripts, one obvious technical problem that has rich theoretical implications is that manuscripts can only be open to two folio sides (one verso, one recto) at a time. If reading were actually desired, the displayed pages would be difficult to decipher for all but a very few visitors to an exhibit, even fewer in the case of Aljamiado, Arabic, or Hebrew.

In a manuscript exhibit, though, the manuscripts are not there to be read in detail. They are presented as cultural heritage, as a means to conjure a sense of the past or to establish some sort of contact with a nonspecific past. This avoidance of specificity comes through in the description of an exhibit to remember the expulsion of the Moriscos ordered by Philip III in 1609, which lasted until 1614, the *Memoria de los Moriscos: Escritos y relatos de una diáspora cultural* (BNM, 2010). The physical exhibit displayed some sixty-five manuscripts with text written primarily in Arabic and Aljamiado. Darío Álvarez, the exhibit designer, writes that the twelve pillars that organize the groups of manuscripts simultaneously evoke a house, a mosque, and a garden. They do not, however, convey any specific context or time. Álvarez calls for a direct sensory experience and memory exercise that avoids reproduction: "Ninguna concesión a la imagen, solo un ejercicio de memoria y una experiencia espacio-temporal" (No concession to the image, just a memory exercise and a spatial-temporal experience).[58] This same move towards conjuring a nonspecific feeling of the past is part of what Beth Lord describes as the goal of exhibiting like objects in groups. The aim is not to reproduce a particular point in the past but to allow users to engage in tourism, to discover what the objects might mean to them, engaging in the "general history":

> The museum object is not the inert trace of a fixed past with which we can only connect through memory or empathy ... We no longer treat the past as a total object that is other than us, but as that which is contained in multiple, changing ways in what we are ... The twenty-first century museum can give power to both objects and visitors, avoiding the heavily didactic displays of the past. It can do this in a way that avoids aestheticism by arranging objects in groups that encourage the visitor to practice "general history": developing them into multiple discontinuous series.[59]

The family that owns the Villamartín shingle undoubtedly has a personal connection to the piece. Except for a few exhibitions and scheduled viewings, it is kept in a safe deposit box in Medina de Pomar, Burgos. It is clear that the owners are deeply protective of the shingle and cautious regarding its exhibition, but it is unlikely that the owners' faith in the shingle and the value that they ascribe to it is one produced solely by reading its text. When Sainz discovered the shingle, the quality that motivated him bring it to the attention of bibliophiles and scholars was the possibility that it might contain history or a record relating to Villamartín de Sotoscueva, not because he recognized the text as the *Ordo commendationis animae* or a possible fragment of the *PFG*.[60]

At its most basic, the use of fragments for a protective purpose is a faith in the power of the handwritten word, even if this faith is not derived solely or at all from a reading of the actual words. The tone of Álvarez's description of the Morisco exhibit and the spirit of the curatorial techniques and user reception that Lord describes at times approximate principles of magic, especially the importance of believing in magic. Georg Luck invokes the soul as a source of powers essential to magic, writing that magic is "a technique grounded in a belief in powers located in the human soul and in the universe outside ourselves, a technique that aims at imposing the human will on nature or on human beings by using supersensual powers. Ultimately, it may be a belief in the unlimited powers of the soul."[61] Social anthropologist Bronislaw Malinowski wrote of magic as a source of hope, desire, and optimism. Magic structures and energizes optimism the way religion does for a belief in God: "Magic [is founded] on the belief that hope cannot fail nor desire deceive ... The function of magic is to ritualize man's optimism, to enhance his faith in the victory of hope over fear. Magic expresses the greater value for man of confidence over doubt, of steadfastness over vacillation, of optimism over pessimism."[62] Magic has thus never simply been a spell, sorcery, or enchantment but is at its initiation the organization of something favourable or even good, at least from the perspective of the user. Magic dispels some of the cowardice in a fearful user, moves forward the encumbered one, and creates a sanctuary for the wearied pilgrim.

Fragments like the Aljafería Qur'an folios and shingle help fill in the gap, serving as a bridge between what is and what could have been or what we wish would be. I have argued here that fragments are not simply texts but also objects whose presence was believed to protect their creators and other believers. When the Muslim workers placed the Qur'an folios and inscriptions in the Aljafería, they knew that they would not be read with any frequency or likely at all. The creator of the shingle aimed to transmit a text to others. It was neither purely epic nor simply a prayer, but a bricolage of useful pieces of text and one other that was perhaps not so useful: a crossed-out text reading "de so fuera rayda." The tile and Aljafería fragments evince a faith in fragments, showing us how manuscript culture was not and is not driven solely by practices that fall under what we might typically consider reading. The tile text shows us that text beyond what we traditionally conceive of as manuscript text can also be fluid, even when placed on a very durable foundation. Finally, the Qur'an fragments, inscriptions, and the shingle evince how manuscript culture was and is partially driven by a faith in fragments and the power of their presence.

Chapter Five

The Fragment among the Moriscos: Mohanmad de Vera's Culture of Compilation

At the beginning of the seventeenth century, Mohanmad de Vera, a Morisco from the town of Gea de Albarracín in Aragón and perhaps an *alfaquí*, compiled an Islamic treatise in Spanish using Latin characters.[1] The colophon of the manuscript confirms this general dating, without the certainty of the particular year due to a tear in the paper: "Acabose d'escrevir el presente alquiteb por la mano [d]el menor siervo de Dios y más neçesitado de su perdón. [...] çalei [...] del año mil seisç[...]n[...] de Yza, alei" (244v–245r; I just finished writing the present book by the hand of the most wretched servant and the most in need of his forgiveness. [...] may God bless and save him [...] of the year one thousand six [hundred] in the year of Jesus, peace be upon him). Little is known about De Vera apart from what can be inferred from the prologue of his treatise. We do know that until the expulsion of the Moriscos from Aragón in 1610, Gea de Albarracín had a population of over two thousand Moriscos, which had grown steadily throughout the sixteenth century. As in many Morisco texts, De Vera makes clear that his compilation of a text in Spanish is a reflection of his community's loss of Arabic rather than faith, the burden of living among enemies, and the order to convert.[2] De Vera further affirms the faith of his community by noting that he undertakes the compilation of his treatise at the suggestion of others. The intent is to preserve and diffuse the Islamic faith as much as possible, in an accessible form:

> ynbió su escojido y bienaventurado profeta Mohanmad, çalei, con su santa ley e onrado Alcorán, [...] conbiene a saber, de su çiençia y buenos juiçios de que oy careçen nuestros deçendientes, no por falta de fe, sino por aver perdido el lenguaje ára[bigo], por la grande oprisión

y apretura que siempre ave[mos] tenido en bivir entre nuestros enemigos y forca[...] guardásemos otra ley. Y a pedimiento y súplica [de] algunos amigos de obligaçión, tubiendo buen zelo, me pidieron a mí, Mohanmad de Vera, natural de la villa de Xea de Albarraçín del reyno de Aragón, sacase a luz algunos de los capítulos que tratan lo que Dios adebdeçió a su santo profeta Mohanmad, çalei, y a su aluma, para que siempre que se les ofreçiere pidir o saber alguna cosa de los deudos o çuna, lo allen en lengua que lo entiendan para podello cumplir. (Suárez García, *El tratado,* 1r)

(He sent his chosen and blessed Prophet Mohammad, may God bless and save him, with his holy law and honoured Qur'an ... it is good to know about his science and good judgment of which our descendants lack today, not because of a lack of faith, but for having lost the Arabic language, because of the great oppression and pressure that we have always had to live among our enemies and forced (?)[...] to observe another law. And at the request [of] some very close friends, who asked me, Mohanmad de Vera, native of the town of Xea de Albarraçín, in the Kingdom of Aragon, to bring to light some of the chapters regarding what God uttered to his holy Prophet Mohammad, may God bless and save him, and his nation so that whenever they needed to ask for or to know anything about their duties or the Sunna may find it in a language that they can understand, such that they may obey.)

The Mancebo de Arévalo (b. ca. 1500), author of three lengthy doctrinal works and other shorter texts, described the time in which he lived and wrote as far from pleasurable, and one in which it was impossible to write joking or insulting things ("para decir donaires y cosas desaguisadas").[3] De Vera expresses similar sentiments, explaining the precariousness of the bodily and spiritual life of his fellow Moriscos in the years just before the expulsion. De Vera's words are indeed not unique, in that they echo Yça Gidelli's prologue to his fifteenth-century *Breviario Çunni,* a work containing the tenets of Islam, Islamic cosmology, and Muslim ceremonies. In addition to explaining the choice of Spanish over Arabic, something present in many Morisco texts, and the note that the treatise was undertaken at the suggestion of friends, the *Breviario Çunni* and De Vera's prologue both affirm the derivative nature of their texts. While the *Breviario* suggests that it is a compilation and translation of Islamic law and Sunna useful for any good Muslim, De Vera, who relies heavily on selections of three well-known Aljamiado works, including the *Breviario* itself, writes that he has brought to light some of the chapters that God had bequeathed to Muhammad and his community of believers.

The literature of the Moriscos is generally regarded as derivative and not especially literary, as it consists primarily of translations of Islamic works in Arabic, including pieces of the Qur'an, legends of pre-Islamic and Islamic prophets, and eschatological texts.[4] Morisco literature is also a literature of fragments. The majority of the some two hundred extant Morisco manuscripts are miscellanies of varying degrees of thematic coherence containing intellectual fragments of longer works, with an intellectual fragment referring to pieces of text extracted from a whole or relatively whole text for an intellectual use. Nuria Martínez de Castillo describes miscellanies as manuscripts that result from an intentional act of compilation or series of compilations: "el producto resultante de la selección y reunión de una serie de piezas – capítulos completos o extractos de obras más amplias – que un compilador hace con una voluntad concreta: bien como respuesta a un encargo, o bien por voluntad personal" (the product that results from the selection and gathering of a series of pieces – complete chapters or extracts of longer works – that a compiler creates with a specific purpose, whether in response to the request of another or for personal benefit).[5] Those manuscripts that are not miscellanies could be called factitious, differing from miscellanies in their method of production, in that they are accumulations of documents copied by multiple scribes at different moments, each with his own intentions, and brought together by a user or users with more intentions still.

De Vera's manuscript does stand out in that it contains fragments of just three works, but he is certainly not the only Morisco to adapt and sometimes misattribute existing texts, and to create compilations that easily comprise works. As is well known, the Mancebo de Arévalo drew not only on Muslim authorities but also on authors writing in Greek and Latin – even if he did not read them in the original – and, most notably, adapted both Jewish and Christian sources. As Gregorio Fonseca has shown, the Mancebo reworked Thomas à Kempis's *The Imitation of Christ* in his *Sumario de la relación y ejercicio spiritual* (Summary of the description and spiritual exercise), attributing the thought to various Muslim authorities, including to the Qur'an itself, though notably, as Gerard Wiegers notes, there are few to no citations or paraphrases of the Qur'an in the Mancebo's works.[6] In some cases, the Mancebo took entire chapters from *The Imitation of Christ*, while in others, he partially rephrased, abbreviated, or expanded Thomas à Kempis's ideas such that the teachings align with key principles of Islam. In another occasion, he copied a fragment of the prologue of the *Celestina*.[7] The Mancebo or his collaborator, the Aragonese *faqih* (Islamic jurist) Ibrahim de Reminjo, adapted parts of the *Breviario Çunni* to form part of their *Breve compendio de la santa ley i sunna* (Brief summary of the holy law and sunna). At the same time, the Mancebo is thought to have added text to existing, important Islamic works, including a chapter to the Toledan lawyer al-Tulaytuli's tenth-century legal treatise, the *Muhtasar* (Compendium).

Using De Vera's treatise as a point of departure, this chapter examines intellectual fragmentation through aspects of the fragmentariness of Aljamiado literature, with a focus on De Vera's use of intellectual fragments. De Vera's manuscript is perhaps a strange example with which to start, in that it is unusually cohesive for a Morisco manuscript, though consistent in several aspects with the Mancebo's compilations, for instance. De Vera's treatise is written in a single hand, likely that of De Vera himself, and as Raquel Suárez García has shown, primarily composed of extensive selections of three easily identifiable works or traditions of significant diffusion among the Moriscos: Iça Gidelli's *Breviario*; the advice (*wasiyya*) of Muhammad to Ali Ibn Abi Talib, Muhammad's cousin and son-in-law, known as the *Encomiendas de Mohanmad a Alí* (*Encomiendas*; Muhammad's advice to Ali); and fragments from a Morisco version of the tenth-century jurist and ascetic (d. 983) Abu al-Layth al-Samarqandi's *Tanbih al Ghafilin*, a work of ethics, hadith, and moral tales known among the Moriscos, with modifications, as the *Libro de Samarqandi*. One of these sections, the *Encomiendas*, while composed of fragments of advice, is not even a fragment itself, since it is as complete as or more complete than any of the other extant versions. De Vera's treatise is further a strange codex with which to start, in that it is one of the fourteen Aljamiado manuscripts in Spanish in Latin characters as opposed to Arabic script, constituting roughly 7.5 percent of all extant Morisco manuscripts.[8]

Despite the apparent cohesiveness and even simplicity of De Vera's treatise in comparison to other Morisco manuscripts, which often contain a variety of different texts and several different hands, this manuscript, when studied in conjunction with codices containing fragments of De Vera's source texts, reveals a key but little-acknowledged aspect of intellectual fragments: that they always both refer to and undermine the source text or referent. This undermining can take various forms, including excessive compilation, liberal editing at the level of the sentence, or lengthy but incomplete citation of the work that convincingly stands for its referent. While De Vera's sections appear to be complete units that together compose De Vera's complete work, these sections consist partly of fragments. In using the notion of fragment as a measure to evaluate the similarity or dissimilarity of De Vera's text to copies of his immediate or near-immediate sources, and in analysing De Vera's compilation practices at the chapter level, it becomes clear that De Vera produces his own sort of novelty. In an effort to understand De Vera's intellectual fragments and those related to them, this chapter turns directly to the Moriscos discussed briefly in the previous chapter, examining four main questions: What is the meaning of source in De Vera's treatise? What sorts of fragments compose it? How does he conceptualize his role of compiler? Further, through an analysis of De Vera's selections and their presence in other forms in other Morisco codices, are intellectual fragments particularly useful to a clandestine manuscript culture?

Source

In his prologue, De Vera first describes the texts that constitute his treatise as chapters that God bequeathed to Muhammad. While he employs one main text at a time, he uses the organizing principle of *tratado* (treatise) to structure his work. The first tratado, which contains seven chapters, is composed of chapters taken from the *Breviario* on the principal commandments and duties specified by the Qur'an, articles of faith, and the way in which general ablution and the ritual purification of certain parts of the body should be carried out and under what conditions. The second tratado, chapters 8–13, includes information on salat (ritual prayer), fasting, tribute, the hajj (pilgrimage), sacrifices, and holy war taken from some seventeen chapters of the *Breviario*, along with other texts. De Vera identifies the third treatise as discussing the signs of the end of the world and the ways in which the world is governed, drawing on the corresponding chapters of the *Breviario*, in addition to treating the subject of repentance as presented in the *Breviario*. Tratado 4, then, consists of chapter 17, the *Encomiendas de Alí*, and the final tratado is that of "Çamarcandil" (Samarqandi). In summary, tratados 1–3 include selections from the *Breviario*, while tratados 4 and 5 contain pieces of the *Encomiendas de Alí* and the *Libro de Samarqandi* respectively.

The materials that constitute De Vera's work clearly come from three easily identifiable works or traditions, but in only one case does he refer to a source by title. In describing his sources, he names only Samarqandi, while in terms of texts he mentions only the Qur'an, apart from referring to his fragments from the *Libro de Samarqandi* as a treatise of "Çamarqandil." The lack of an explicit reference to the *Breviario Sunni* is unusual, as numerous Morisco manuscripts that contain fragments of the *Breviario Sunni* refer to it by title.[9] It is nevertheless notably absent as well in the Mancebo and Ibrahim de Reminjo's *Breve compendio*.[10]

De Vera claims not to have eliminated text or to have added to any of his selections, citing God as witness to his fidelity to his models. He further notes that it is nothing less than a sin to amend or delete from God's law:

> No é puesto nada de mío, como Dios bien sabe, a quien dexo por testigo; ni tanpoco é quitado de aquello que é allado escripto por sabios doctos del açihaba de nuestro santo annabi por no caer en el pecado de los que quitan y ponen en la ley de Dios. É andado bigilante por escribir verdades y por ponello todo como se debe poner. (2r)

> (I have not included anything of mine, as God well knows and as my witness; neither have I removed anything from what I found written by learned wise men whose testimonies form the basis of the Sunna of our Prophet such as not to fall into the sin of those who remove and add to God's law. I have tried to be vigilant to write truths and to write everything as it should be written.)

While a faithful copy is his stated intent, he does concede that it is possible that his ignorance, working conditions, poor style, and the custom of leaving known errors in the copy so as to avoid erasures might produce errors. After explaining why he cannot be certain that his copy is as it should be ("no puedo asigurar es ansí"), he explains his purification of his source texts:

> No puedo asigurar es ansí [todo como se debe poner] porque soy ombre y en los ombres suçeden los yerros e innorançias, mayormente aviendo ruido de niños, cosa contraria al qu'escrive. Por ser la lectura qu'es, mereçía estar más purificada de una lengua más cortada que la mía, aunqu'es verdad é procurado muçhos vocablos purificallos y ponellos de modo que agraden a todos, no quitándoles sustançia ninguna; pero an sido tantos y tan diferentes, que forçadamente abré escripto algunos d'ellos no de mío,

antes bien biniendo a la lectura, escrivillos, después echallos de ver y, por no azer borrones, dexallos. Por lo qual ruego al lector y oyentes, si acaso allaren en mi escriptura algunos yerros o descuidos, suplan mis grandes faltas como a prudentes [por] que los descuidos y yerros se allan en las criaturas, y en los discretos, disimularlos. (2r)

(I can't ensure it is so [that everything is as it should be], because I am but a man, and since errors and ineptness occur in men, especially when surrounded by noisy children, something which is not favourable for a writer. Being the reading that it is, it deserved to be more purified in a more correct language than mine; and although I've truly intended that many terms be purified and put in a way that please everyone, not altering their meaning in any way, they have been so many and so different that I must have written some that were not mine mistakenly; and when reviewing the text to avoid smudging, I just left them there. This is why I ask the reader and listeners that, if they find any mistakes or carelessness in my writing, they correct my significant errors as they see fit, because carelessness and errors are found in all creatures, and that they ignore the small ones.)

Appealing to the sympathies of his readers and listeners, De Vera asks that they forgive him his errors, citing the general human propensity for error and also more personal impediments to accuracy and the conveyance of truth, including noisy children ("ruido de niños"). Related to possible errors is his assertion that due to the nature of the reading ("lectura") that constitutes his treatise, the text deserves to be "purified" by one with a more correct ("cortada") vocabulary and expression than his.[11] De Vera's comments about purified works and text extend into other realms, however. He admits that because he has procured so many purified words, it is possible that he included some that were not his own ("algunos de'ellos no de mío") but rather from his source texts. De Vera expresses clear concern that his text is properly purified; he attributes the inclusion of nonpurified words from the source texts to carelessness and designates the words themselves as errors, imploring readers to remedy the most significant mistakes and to ignore the rest.

De Vera's Fragments: *Breviario Sunni*

Setting aside De Vera's own assessment of his editing practices and fidelity to his sources, I turn directly to the nature of his fragments, first those in the *Breviario Sunni* section. De Vera draws his fragments and, as I describe below, text that does not quite qualify as fragments from what Wiegers calls the "adapted" version of the *Breviario Sunni*, a modernized version in which archaic words were eliminated, the linguistic influence of Arabic often removed, and certain content elements changed.[12] The Mancebo and his collaborator used this version as well. This version is extant in S3 of the Real Academia de la Historia, the base manuscript for Pascual de Gayangos's edition (which I will cite throughout); BNM, MS 6016; and CSIC (Consejo Superior de Investigación Científica), Junta 60.[13] The more archaic version of the *Breviario* appears in BNM 2076 and Junta 1, with this last manuscript being the only extant copy of the *Breviario* in Aljamiado.

De Vera's *Breviario* section is unique in the context of his treatise as a whole in that it is the only one in which De Vera combines fragments of multiple chapters of his source to form new chapters, specifically in eight out of seventeen cases. For instance, the first seven chapters of De Vera's treatise draw on eleven chapters of the *Breviario*. He combines chapters 6 and 7 of the *Breviario* into one (his chapter 6) and interpolates fragments in five of the *Breviario* chapters from which he draws. In De Vera's chapter 6, for example, he reproduces the *Breviario's* text on the importance of clean water for ablution and *tayammum*, performing ablution with dust or sand when no clean water is available. In this text, De Vera introduces three substantial interpolations: a lengthy section on how to circumvent dead animals in bodies of water used for ablution; a text linking the origin of *tayammum* to the prophet Joseph; and another detailing an alternate method of *tayammum* that involves only the hands and face. His chapter 9 draws on five mostly discontinuous chapters of the *Breviario* (11, 14, 17, 18, and 22), some of which he reproduces in their entirety and others only fragments, with one case in which he presents a fragment while also interpolating text. De Vera's chapters 9 and 10 contain fragments of nine chapters of the *Breviario*. His chapter 13 combines fragments of three *Breviario* chapters with interpolations, whereas his chapters 12, 14, 15, and 16 reproduce *Breviario* chapters in their entirety.

Reading on in De Vera's treatise, the meaning of referent and fidelity to a source become muddied. Chapters 9, 10, and 13 are representative of the scope of De Vera's compilation work, in that each combines multiple chapters of the *Breviario*, with interpolations in several cases, engaging in levels of borrowing that range from direct citation to vague reference. Chapter 9, "Trata con quántas cosas se cumple el açala adebdeçido y agraçiado, y qué açalaes son los que son deudos y los que son çuna" (On what things should be done to complete obligatory prayer and optional prayer, and which prayers are those that are mandatory and those that are Sunna [optional]), compiles four or possibly five *Breviario* chapters to create a chapter not present in that work. In the first paragraph and a half on the twelve requirements for completing daily prayer (*açala*) properly, De Vera follows the *Breviario* chapter 11 on requirements for completing mandatory and optional prayer closely but corrects an aberration in the manuscript that Gayangos cites: there are twelve conditions for fulfilling prayer, but the *Breviario* mentions only eleven.[14] One notable difference between the passages is De Vera's use of *ennia* instead of *yntençion* (intention) in the first requirement. As Luís Bernabé Pons has recently observed, *ennia* refers not only to spiritual dedication but also to a rational commitment to the correct realization of acts of adoration such that they be considered valid in an Islamic sense.[15] Drawing on this meaning, De Vera establishes *ennia* as the "precondition" to the performance of the eleven other obligations in the list. *Ennia* appears elsewhere in the *Breviario*, but not in the passage from which De Vera draws. Correspondences appear in bold:

Breviario Sunni:
Con doçe cosas se cumple el açala, asi el de deudo como el de çunna. La primera es la yntençion; la segunda bestidos linpios, que estando el honbre abaxado, cubra sus bergueças, y la mugger que cubra todas sus carnes; la tercera, **el atahor; la quarta l'alguado; la quinta estar en pied tubiendo salud; la sesta deçir Allah ua acbar; la setima es haçer de cara alquibla; la otaba es deçir al hamdu lillehi** y mas donde deube; **la nobena es arraquear; la decimal es açaxdar;** la onçena **es dar açalem.**[16]

(The salat [prayer] is accomplished by following twelve things, both the compulsory and the Sunna [optional]. The first is with intention; and the second with clean clothing, so that the man can hide his genitals and the woman can cover her entire body; the third is with ablution; the fourth, with washing; the fifth, by standing up if in good health; the sixth, by saying, *Allahu akbar* [God is greatest]; the seventh, by facing Mecca [Qibla]; the eighth, by saying, *Alhamdulillah* [Praise be to God] and even more, where it is necessary; the ninth, by completing the movements involved in prayer; the tenth, by prostrating yourself; the eleventh, by greeting.)

De Vera:
Con doze cosas se cumple el açala, assí el qu'es deudo como el qu'es çuna, y son éstas: **la primera es la ennia; la sigunda, un vestido limpio;**

la terçera, el tahor; la quarta, el alguado; la quinta, estar en pie tubiendo salud; la sesta, dezir "Allahu aquebar"; la séptima, azer cara alquibla; la octava, dezir "alhamdu lila" donde se deve dezir; la novena es araquear; la dézima, açajedar; la onzena, estar sentado; la dozena, **dar açalem.** (23r)

(The salat is accomplished by following twelve things, both the compulsory and the Sunna, and they are these: The first is ennia [intention]; the second with clean clothing; the third is with ablution; the fourth, with washing; the fifth, by standing if healthy; the sixth, by saying, *Allahu akbar*; the seventh, by facing Mecca; the eighth, by saying, *Alhamdulillah*, where it is necessary; the ninth, by performing the movements of prayer; the tenth, by prostrating yourself; the eleventh, by greeting.)

Midway through the second paragraph, however, De Vera changes course, using fragments of four *Breviario* chapters to create a chapter whose focus is to clarify which prayers are obligatory and which are Sunna, those following the customs of Muhammad. Following the requirements for completing salat, De Vera inserts a hadith on the importance of midday prayer that serves as an end to the topic of obligatory prayers before turning directly to those that are Sunna, creating a pastiche of portions of *Breviario* chapters 17 (prayer at sunset), 18 (prayer for water), 22 (bathing, prayer, and burial of the dead), and a small piece of 14 (voluntary prayers between obligatory prayers). In treating practices pertaining to the dead, for instance, while following the main points of the content closely, De Vera occasionally abbreviates or adds details that clarify the purpose, method, and duration of prayer rituals. The section De Vera borrows from the *Breviario* on bathing, prayer, and burial of the dead occurs midparagraph in the second half of chapter 22. Eliminating the first part of chapter 22 on bathing the dead, the passage from which De Vera extracts consists primarily of the words of the actual prayers (see appendix 1).

De Vera adds an introduction, clarifies what should be said and when, and modifies the final instructions, noting that a lengthy closing, perhaps like that included in the *Breviario*, is not required in prayers for the dead: "Y dirá el aljamaa las vezes que dixere el alimen 'All hu aquebar,' porque en el açala del muerto no ay deudo más de las ataquebiras, qu'es dezir 'Allahu aquebar'" (And the community will say, "Allah is greater," the number of times the imam says, because in the prayer of the dead there is no more important obligation than the saying of the *ataquebiras*, which is to say, "God is greater"). While De Vera does abbreviate some sections, he is cautious not to overabbreviate, preserving a lengthy paragraph on specific praises to be offered to Allah. Save for some changes at the end of the passage and his process of purification (a change from *Chihanam* to *infierno* [hell], for instance), as with the text at the beginning of *Breviario* chapter 11, De Vera's borrowed passage from *Breviario* chapter 22 is similar enough to be considered a fragment.

This is not the case, however, with the last part of De Vera's chapter 9. De Vera ends with a topic treated in *Breviario* chapter 14 on another Sunna prayer, *algüitri*, a voluntary prayer individually performed between evening prayer and dawn. Apart from treating the topic and noting that *algüitri* serves as the *sello* (seal) of daily prayer, it is difficult to identify from which part of the *Breviario* text De Vera draws. The correspondence between De Vera's writing on *algüitri* (the last two paragraphs of De Vera's chapter 9) and that in the *Breviario* (last paragraphs of chapter 14) is rough at best, making De Vera's writing very difficult to call a "fragment" of the *algüitri* section in the *Breviario* (see appendix 2, in which possible correspondences appear in bold) or, rather, to call a specific part of the *Breviario* his source. De Vera is less interested in speaking generally of voluntary prayer than Iça de Gebir, but he does more or less follow the *Breviario's* content. Unlike in the previous examples, though, he never cites the *Breviario* exactly, apart from referring to *algüitri* as the *sello* of daily prayer.

A similar variety of borrowing strategies, both close and distant from the source text, occurs in chapter 10 ("Trata de la manera que se an de azer los çinco açalaes adebdeçidos, y los yerros e inmiendas que tienen, y las annafilas se pueden hazer entre cada uno d'ellos" [On how the five obligatory prayers should be done, and the possible errors and modifications, and the voluntary prayers that can be done between each one of them]), composed in part of text from five different *Breviario* chapters (11, 12, 14, 15, and 16). In this case, De Vera begins with information on prayer at dawn and midday prayers taken from *Breviario* chapter 11, following the text exactly on how to perform the prayer. He then treats topics found in other *Breviario* chapters, quoting directly in some cases and simply treating content contained in the *Breviario* in others, which is perhaps the case in the example above. At times, De Vera does both. For example, in the middle of the chapter, De Vera addresses four ways in which daily prayer is confused or modified. In the *Breviario*, the topic composes its own chapter, 12, "De las imiendas del açala" (On modifications of ritual prayer). De Vera begins similarly to the *Breviario*, but certainly does not follow it, then inserts a hadith, as in chapter 9. In chapter 10, however, the hadith contains information dispersed in various paragraphs of *Breviario* chapter 12, rather than appearing somewhat out of place. As in the case in chapter 9, De Vera's treatment of errors and emendations of daily prayer is hardly a fragment of the *Breviario*; in fact, it is difficult to find a pair of corresponding phrases. De Vera provides a concise summary of the information in *Breviario* chapter 12 and due to his previous borrowings, it is likely that the *Breviario* is De Vera's source. It is highly debatable, though, whether this sort of borrowing could be said to yield fragments, even less likely than in the case in De Vera's chapter 9 cited above (see appendix 3). De Vera does end chapter 10 with a clear fragment, albeit one introduced by text that is not found in the *Breviario*. He continues on with the theme of transgressions of salat but draws on a chapter treating a related but separate topic in the *Breviario* (chapter 11, what is required for completion of daily prayer and how to prostrate oneself in prayer) from which he had already drawn. The first sentences could be his own words, but the rest come directly from the *Breviario Sunni* (see appendix 4).

De Vera's use of textual fragments from the *Breviario* thus spans a range of borrowing techniques. While at times he uses direct citations of his source, in other cases he strays so far from his referent that he can only really be said to treat topics covered in the work or to create near fragments or simply text inspired by the *Breviario*. This inspired text, while failing to correspond enough to specific parts of the *Breviario* to qualify as intellectual fragments, is nevertheless similar enough not to be labelled as text coming from another source entirely – as in the case of one of De Vera's interpolations – or as original thought. De Vera shows how a diluting of the referent can nearly erase it, whether that diluting is produced by excessive compilation or movement of pieces of text or editing at the level of the sentence.

Encomiendas

The concept of referent becomes increasingly muddy in the next section of De Vera's treatise, the *Encomiendas de Alí,* which comprises chapter 17 and consists of twenty folios (48r–68v). De Vera's *Encomiendas* section is not a proper fragment, in that none of the seven versions in Spain could be considered its source, despite its corresponding fairly closely with at least four of these versions: a relatively brief Arabic-character version in 11/9410 (T-13) of the Real Academia de la Historia (dated to 1589); 11/9393 (S-1) of the Real Academia de la Historia (late sixteenth/early seventeenth century), acephalous and in Latin characters; Junta 4 of the CSIC (late fifteenth to early sixteenth century), fairly extensive and in Arabic characters; and two manuscripts found among others in Ocaña in 1969, one a manuscript dated to 1428 and the other a group of loose leaves.[17]

While not properly a fragment itself, De Vera's *Encomiendas* chapter is composed of pieces of advice, some of which has been ascribed to Samarqandi, but all of which have become subsumed under the category of advice that Ali received from Muhammad. Unlike the *Breviario* section and the final part of De Vera's compilation (the Samarqandi section), in the *Encomiendas* section it is difficult to evaluate the completeness of De Vera's version. In comparison with the other extant versions, De Vera's is as or more extensive, but not exactly more "complete," since the extant versions prove quite variable. Further, any text that could be called "referent," if De Vera's section were indeed so considered, is multiple.

The versions of the *Encomiendas* display variation in style, in vocabulary, and at times in the compilation of the fragments of advice or the fragments included. For instance, on the theme of the importance that all works be dedicated to Allah alone, De Vera most closely corresponds with S-1 and Ocaña 1, when comparing T-13, S-1, and Ocaña 1:

De Vera

Ya Ali, quando yzieres alguna buena obra, óbrala en Dios y por Dios; y si gastares algún gasto estraordinario, gástalo por Dios, porque lo que hizieres por grandía es como el fuego en la leña, que la consume y acaba.

Ya Ali, si obrares obra, sea purificada a Dios, porque Dios no reçibe sino aquello que se aze sólo por él y en serviçio suyo, y no a otro fin.

Ya Ali, la grandía en la lei de mis sequaçes es más secreta qu'el ruido de los pies de la hormiga en la tierra blanda y suave en la escura noçhe, y es la descreençia menor, como Dios dixo en su lei. (52v)

(Oh, Ali!, when you do a good work, do it in the name of God, and for God's sake; and if you expend for some extraordinary expense, spend it for God, since what you do for pretentiousness is like the fire that consumes and extinguishes the firewood.

Oh, Ali!, if you do some work, may it be purified to God, because God doesn't receive but that which is done in his service, and not for any other reason.

Oh, Ali!, boastfulness in the law of my followers is more secret than the noise caused by the feet of an ant on soft and smooth land in the dark night; and it is the lesser unbelief, as God said in his Law.)

T-13

Ya Ali, kuwando obrarás, obrarás por amor de Allah, y kuwando espendarás, espendarás por amor de Allah, ke las garandias en ll-din son komo el fuwego en la leña. (232v)

(Oh, Ali!, when you act, you will act for the sake of Allah, and when you expend, you will expend for the love of Allah, since pretentiousness is like fire on the firewood.)

S-1

Ye Ali!, quando querrás hazer algun bien, hazlo en serviçio de Allah y no por la uffana, ni grandia, porque ad Allah no le plaze con la uffana, ni con la grandia, porque es como la leña será en el fuego.

¡Ye Ali!, obra enta Allah obra buena, porque no rreçibe Allah sino las buenas obras.

¡Ye Ali!, quien tiene esperança del encuentro de Allah, haga buenas obras y no mete aparçero a ninguno con Allah en su serviçio. (181v–182r)

(Oh, Ali!, when you want to do some good, do it to serve Allah and not for boastfulness nor pretentiousness, since Allah is not pleased with boastfulness nor pretentiousness, because it will be like the firewood to the fire.

Oh, Ali!, do towards Allah good acts, because Allah doesn't receive [any] but good acts.

Oh, Ali!, he who has hope of meeting with Allah, may he do good works, and not set an intermediary between Allah and his service.)

Ocaña, vol. 1

quando fizieres bien, fazlo por de Allah, e cuando gastares, gasta por amor de Allah e guarte de la hazalegería que la hazalegería es como el fuego en la leña, e la hazalegería en la ley es más escondida sobre mi aluma que el monimiento de la formiga en el cuero […] en la noche escura e la hazalegería es una excrecencia menor porque dixo a Allah: el [...] tiene fuzía de parecer ante a Allah faga buenas obras e non ponga aparçero en el serviçio de su señor. (19v)

(When you do good, do it for Allah, and when you expend, expend for the love of Allah, and avoid ostentation, since ostentation is like fire to firewood, and ostentation is more concealed to my community of believers than the movement of an ant on leather [...] in the dark night, and ostentation is a lesser excrescence, because Allah said: the [...] has confidence in appearing before Allah may he do good acts and never set an intermediary at his master's service.)

De Vera's version reflects a general tendency to clarify his source or to further purify an already clarified source. For instance, he glosses the simile "fuego en la leña (que la consume y acaba)" (fire that consumes and extinguishes the firewood) present in all the cited versions and modernizes it throughout. He includes the line about good works in the service of God present in S-1 and Ocaña 1, but does not include "aparçero" (counterpart, fellow participant), emphasizing that works be done in favour of Allah alone; instead of noting explicitly that no other individuals share (*aparçero*) in the worship due unto Allah, the latter being more consistent with the final verse of Sura 18, El Kaf (The Cave): "Say, 'I am only a human being, like you, to whom it has been revealed that your god is One. Anyone who fears to meet his Lord should do good deeds and give no one a share in the worship due to his Lord.'"[18] It is also noteworthy that De Vera follows the *Encomiendas* tradition that invokes the movement of the *hormiga* (ant) in the dark night, present only in Ocaña 1.

While we might expect De Vera to follow the version in Ocaña 1 elsewhere, in the section of the fates of children conceived on certain days – a passage that appears in the majority of the manuscripts – De Vera more closely follows S-1 and T-13. It is also noteworthy that De Vera's version is some 150 words longer than S-1, nearly twice as long as T-13, and almost four times longer than the versions found in Ocaña volumes 1 and 2 combined. Part of De Vera's relative verbosity comes from his clarification of several of the situations of conception and other sexual practices. For instance, De Vera elaborates on why a couple should not clean their genitals with the same cloth after sex. Compare De Vera with S-1:

De Vera

Y no os limpiés los dos, después del acto, aquellas partes con un paño, sino cada uno con el suyo, porque d'ello pende rencor y enamistad entre ti y tu muger; y si lo aréis, os dividiréis i apartaréis los dos. (63v–64r)

(And after the act, both should not clean those parts with a single cloth, but each with his own, because from this resentment and enmity will come between you and your wife; and if you do it, you will become divided and grow apart.)

S-1

Y no os limpiéis las vergüenças tú y tu muger con un paño, que de aquello creçe enemigança entre marido y mugger. (198r)

(And you and your wife should not clean your private parts with a single cloth, since from this enmity grows between husband and wife.)

On the other hand, S-1 offers three additional situations in which one should avoid intercourse that are not present in De Vera, including when a woman is menstruating; when one desires another woman; and on the terrace of one's home. The circumstances or settings that would surround the sex and the undesirable outcomes of the sexual act are menacing, as unlikely as some of those outcomes might appear:

Ye Ali, no te acuestes con tu mujer teniendo de sus cuentos, que, si se engendra criatura, será leproso y tiñoso. Y no te acuestes con tu muger por sabor de otra, que, si se engendra criatura, será de poco alholoque. Dixo el annebi: "el hombre con su buen alholoque llega a dreça del dayunante.

Ye Ali, no te acuestes con tu muger encima del terrado de la cassa, que, si se engendra criatura, será ladrón y fuidor. (198r–v)

(Oh, Ali!, do not sleep with your wife while she is menstruating, since if a child is conceived, it will be leprous and mangy. And do not sleep with your wife out of lust for another, since, if a child is conceived, it will have few moral qualities. The Prophet Muhammad said: "The man with his good moral qualities arrives at the state of purification [?] of he who fasts.

Oh, Ali!, do not sleep with your wife on the roof of your house, since if a child is conceived, he will be a thief and a fugitive.)

De Vera's *Encomiendas* is as whole or more so than the extant versions cited above; it could be called one of several wholes. De Vera's version can indeed serve as a whole for the fragmentary versions of the *Encomiendas* in T-13 and the Ocaña manuscripts, but it is not a fragment itself, primarily because we cannot determine what it lacks, since passages like those in S-1 cited above are not additional but rather pieces of that particular version. From De Vera's *Encomiendas* we learn that a referent must be singular enough to yield strong intellectual fragments that successfully refer to their whole. Paradoxically, only a strong referent or, more importantly, a convincing image of this referent, whether the exact details of the text are clear or not, can produce the dialectic that is essential to fragments. A convincing notion of the whole text is necessary for the creation of intellectual fragments, but the fragments can undermine their whole, whether through excessive compilation, editing, or the rearrangement of chapters and creation of a convincing surrogate whole, as is clear in the next section, taken from Samarqandi.

Samarqandi

Unlike the *Encomiendas*, the *Libro de Samarqandi* is a strong referent for the corresponding text in De Vera's treatise, because of which his selections should be clear intellectual fragments. Samarqandi is the only author that De Vera names in his prologue, noting that he includes "un tratado [treatise] de Çamarcandil," thus supporting L.P. Harvey's theory that Samarqandi had become a watchword for the Moriscos, or at least was more known to De Vera or perceived by him as more important to credit than Iça de Gebir and the *Breviario*, perhaps because Iça's text was so well known.[19] Further, unlike the *Breviario* section, De Vera preserves the thematic integrity of Samarqandi's chapters (though not always the order of content), avoiding the practice of combining multiple chapters into one or the addition of interpolated text from other sources.

De Vera nevertheless introduces his share of variation in the Samarqandi section, so much so that Suárez García argues that it is only possible to compare two or three specific chapters of De Vera's work with those in the two extensive extant versions of the *Libro de Samarqandi*: one chapter on alms and one on faith in God. The chapter on alms begins one of the two lengthy extant versions of the work, a fragmentary copy in Junta 6, copied by Mohamed Escribano Mayor and dated to 1601; this copy is De Vera's closest surviving referent and corresponds with chapter 38 in the other extant extensive version, a complete copy in BNM 4871 that dates to the middle or end of the sixteenth century.[20] Suárez García analyses these chapters with attention to abbreviation, amplification, and variation, showing that while De Vera's aim generally appears to be the clarification and reduction of his sources, he sometimes introduces significant changes to the text, ranging from those that reduce the Arabic-influenced syntax of his sources, such as reducing the paratactic style, to the addition of clarifying and concluding sentences, the insertion of more modern phrases, and even misreading the text and completely altering its meaning.[21]

This variation can be seen in other De Vera chapters based on the *Libro de Samarqandi*, each of which, I argue, can be compared with De Vera's proximal referents, including BNM 4781, which features a more archaic text than Junta 6. For instance, the amplification, abbreviation, and variation to which Suárez García refers is quite clear in De Vera's chapter 44, "Trata la istoria de Muça, alei, y quándo le tomó Dios por annabi, y la destruiçión de Firaon i su conpaña" (On the story of Moses, peace be with him, and when he took God as prophet, and the destruction of Pharaoh and his company), which corresponds to and can be compared with chapter 89 in BNM 4871, a chapter not extant in the Arabic *Tanbih al Ghafilin* but added by the Moriscos. At the end of the chapter is a hadith that tells the story of a servant of God who believed himself God's most faithful servant until God himself informed him that a butcher was actually more faithful. In the conversation with the butcher, it is evident that the two passages are clearly comparable despite some differences (see appendix 5; differences highlighted).

De Vera definitely edits, but not so much that he produces near fragments or inspired text as in the case of the *Breviario*. He alters the *isnad*, interpreting Abdu el Malik as Abdulmelique, eliminating Ibn Wahb, and excising the last part of Abdu Rahman's name. He then proceeds to abbreviate, augment, and vary several parts of the passage. For instance, he adds a line about the "siervo de Dios" (servant of God; *ermitaño* [hermit] in BNM 4871, 291v) that further casts a negative light on the *siervo* and anticipates the lesson at the end of the paragraph: "y tubo por çierto era él el que más sirvía a Dios y el que mejores obras azía" (De Vera, 232v; And he was certain that it was he who most served God and did the best works). He abbreviates several other lines but also adds text, most of which dramatizes the story. For instance, in asking God who exceeds him in service, De Vera indicates Allah's words, "deçendió del çielo" (De Vera, 232v; came down from the sky); he adds an additional question as to why the *siervo* descends from his tower ("¿I por qué as deçendido de tu açumua?" [De Vera, 232v; And why have you descended from your tower?]); adds the emphasis that the *siervo* descends from the tower out of respect for the butcher; indicates that the economic and physical well-being of the butcher's mother and father is wanting ("viejos y pobres" [De Vera, 233r; old and poor]); and inserts a short Arabic phrase that indicates that the butcher gives alms "for God's cause" ("fi çabirila" [De Vera, 235v]). The butcher shows his selflessness in the way in which he divides his earnings, leaving just a third for his own family. De Vera eliminates a line in BNM 4871 that emphasizes this characteristic of the butcher.[22]

While in many respects De Vera certainly plays the editor, in other chapters De Vera proves quite faithful to his source with regard to content and even to expression, such that his editing does little that obviously undermines his referent. This is clear in De Vera's chapter 18, a chapter, not extant in Junta 6, which begins with what corresponds to chapter 38 in BNM 4871. The chapter cautions against performing works out of conceit (*ufana*) and as a show of faith to others ("Trata en el apuramiento de la ufana, qu'es contra aquellos que sirven a Dios con grandía y sobervia, y por ganar fama entre las gentes" [On being free of conceit, this is against those who serve God with arrogance and pride, and through gaining fame among people]), rather than serving God alone; it begins with a piece of advice that closely resembles the one in the *Encomiendas* examined above on the dangers of failing to dedicate one's works solely to God. Aside from De Vera's process of purification and changes to the *isnad*, which is very common in the successive redactions of the *Libro de Samarqandi*, De Vera's version strays little from BNM 4871, even from that manuscript's archaisms, in all sections of the chapter (see appendix 6).

An analysis of three passages from the beginning, middle, and end of the chapter shows small changes that, with the exception of one deletion, are not significant abbreviations, amplifications, or variations. Further, these changes, unlike cases in the *Breviario* section, in no way compromise the pieces as fragments of the *Libro de Samarqandi*. In the first passage, the only significant change is a slight alteration of the *isnad*, not by reducing or augmenting it but by introducing the error of *hijo* (son) by contamination between Omar and Abdulmelique Elmuzniyu, likely to make the name fit the pattern of the other authorities that begin and end the *isnad* (for example, *Mohanmad hijo de Çhafar Elcuyasio*). A reduction in the *isnad* does appear in the second passage, however, with a simplification of BNM 4871's "Abi Hurayra" to "un sabio" (a wise man). The third passage shows an inclusion but misreading of the initial authority mentioned in BNM 4871 ("Çilmen Alfaraçiyu" for "Çilman al-Fariçi"). The only other significant change in the third passage is De Vera's deletion of a useful clarifying line midparagraph that emphasizes the error in performing obligations simply as a show of faith for others – as a hypocrite – and says that this practice is clearly unbelieving: "Pues este es munafiqe claramente."[23]

In another chapter, there are similar small changes, most particularly with the *isnad*, but also more significant modifications that primarily reflect De Vera's tendency to simplify his referent. In De Vera's chapter 31, "Trata del dreçho del vezino y lo que se deve onrrar" (On the right of the neighbour and what should be honoured), which treats duties towards neighbours, he modifies the *isnad* and eliminates an exchange that clarifies, if cryptically, what is meant by a neighbour's *estorbo* (impediment). A man is not safe from harm unless his neighbour is also free from his own impediment, which in BNM 4871, is his *encubrimiento* (concealment) and *escuredad* (darkness, ignorance):

> **BNM 4871**
> **Fue recontado por 'Abdu el-lahi ibnu maçud, que el diso: Diso el mensajero de Allah, sala Allahu alayhi wa çalem,** por aquel que mi persona es en su poder: No está salvo el siervo fasta que es salvo su coraçón i su lengua i no está seguro el siervo fasta que está seguro su vezino de su **estorbo. Disimos: ¡Ya mensajero de Allajh! ¿qué es su estorbo? Diso: Su encubrimiento i su escuredad.** (58v)
>
> (It was recounted by **'Abdu el-lahi ibnu maçud,** who said: "The messenger of Allah – peace be upon him – said through him my person is in his power: the servant will not be safe until his heart and tongue are safe; and the servant will not be safe until his neighbour is free of his impediment." We said: "Oh messenger of Allah!, what is his impediment?" He said: "His concealment and ignorance.")
>
> **De Vera**
> **Después dixo, çalei:**
> –Por aquel que mi persona es en su poder, no está salvo el siervo asta qu'es salvo su coraçón y su lengua. Y no está siguro el siervo asta qu'está siguro su vezino d'él. (156r)
>
> (After that he said, God bless and save him:
> "For him, in whose power is my person, the servant will not be safe until his heart and his tongue are safe. And the servant is not be safe until his neighbour is safe.")

De Vera employs a variety of editing practices, including the deletion of lines that he may have considered redundant or did not understand. He does not, however, make changes that produce the near fragments or the inspired text of the *Breviario*. The difference between this last section and the *Breviario* section is the nature of De Vera's compilation. As noted above, while introducing some abbreviation, amplification, variation, and even deletion, De Vera respects the structure within the chapters in the Samarqandi section by not combining multiple, sometimes discontiguous, chapters into one. As in the *Breviario* section, in the Samarqandi section he *does* modify the arrangement of some of the chapters. De Vera respects the order of the *Libro de Samarqandi* for the first twenty-five chapters of his section, save two chapters on gluttony and greed, and then picks, chooses, and reorders among the *Libro de Samarqandi*'s remaining fifty-nine chapters. He eliminates chapters on a wide variety of subjects, ranging from those on ritual practices (prayer, fasting) and spiritual concepts (piety, goodwill, cleanliness, fear of God, wisdom) to the treatment of certain groups of people (servants, orphans, wives, husbands), choosing to end his treatise with the following: a chapter on the importance of trusting in God; the chapter on Moses described above; a chapter on alms; and finally and very appropriately, a chapter on misfortune.

The reason why De Vera chose these four nonconsecutive chapters and reordered them cannot be known for certain. Writing in the years before the expulsion, it is difficult to interpret his ending of his treatise with a chapter on misfortune as accidental. This is particularly true since the chapters that precede the final one relate the importance of trusting in God, the importance of charity, and a chapter unique to the Morisco version and edition of the *Tanbih al Ghafilin*. A tear in the paper obscures some of the final pieces of advice, but it is worth examining what remains of the last lengthy lesson in the misfortune chapter, one on patience from Samarqandi (here called Abu Laizi). The lesson relates the importance of patience during times of great need and conflict through the story of a woman who has more faith and hope in God after having lost her children, home, and slaves. Because she has been patient in times of adversity, she is now more certain that she will be rewarded in the afterlife (see appendix 7).

When read in the context of tumultuous years prior to the expulsion, the series of last chapters, rearranged from the order in which they appear in the *Libro de Samarqandi* and preceded by chapters that primarily offer advice on ensuring entry into the next life, bring cohesion to the section and a definitive end to the treatise as a whole. They also give purpose to De Vera's compilation of fragments. The Samarqandi section thus does not challenge its referent significantly in its difference at the level of the sentence, as in the case of the *Breviario*, nor is the referent multiple, as in the case of the *Encomiendas*, which exists in several versions. Rather, the Samarqandi section in its cohesion, extensive citation of its referent, and relatively small but important change in the arrangement of the chapters challenges its referent by its very similarity. De Vera's "tratado de Çamarcandil" can perfectly substitute for its source, constituting an ideal *Libro de Samarqandi* for his own moment in history.

De Vera as Compiler

Having examined the way in which De Vera manages his sources and creates fragments, it is useful to return to the prologue to read how he himself conceived his role, at least in writing. We recall that in his prologue, De Vera claims that he neither adds to nor deletes from his sources, saying that it would be a sin to do so. Specifically, he notes that he adds nothing of his own to his sources ("No é puesto nada de mío"). He suggests that the presence of additions or rather deletions would mean that he had fallen prey to the sin of those who remove and add to God's law: "el pecado de los que quitan y ponen en la ley de Dios."

Setting aside for a moment the question of whether De Vera follows his statement in practice or not, his note about adding nothing of his own corresponds perfectly with the difference between compiler and commentator. In some medieval definitions of compiler, and in modern assessments of the medieval compiler, what separates compiler from commentator is not the addition of just any text to a main source but the inclusion of one's own writing in the copy. Malcolm Parkes wrote that the compiler of the Middle Ages is one who "adds no matter of his own by way of exposition (unlike the commentator), but compared with the scribe ... is free to re-arrange (*mutando*). His function is to impose a new *ordinatio* on the materials he extracted from others."[24] The addition of one's own material as the difference between compiler and commentator is also present in Saint Bonaventure's commentary on Peter Lombard's *Sententiae*. Compiler and commentator are two of four methods that can be used to make (*facere*) a book:

> The way of making a book is fourfold. For one man writes down others' works, adding or changing nothing, and he is simply to be called a scribe (*scriptor*). Another writes others' works, adding material, but not of his own confection; and he is called a compiler (*compilator*). Another writes both the works of others and his own, but in such a way that the works of others are in principal place, and his own are added for purposes of clarification; and he is called a commentator (*commentator*), not an author (*auctor*). Another writes both his own works and those of others, but in such

> a way that his own are in principal place and the others are added for the sake of confirmation; and such a man should be called author (*auctor*).[25]

De Vera is a compiler who employs various techniques to "impose a new *ordinatio*" on his fragments, whether by taking pieces from various chapters to form new chapters or by reordering chapters. He is also an editor and perhaps, in the case of the *Breviario*, can be seen as composing inspired text that is of his own confection in stylistic terms, though not in content. De Vera adds material that does not circulate with the lengthy extant versions of the *Breviario*, including additional hadith. It is unlikely, though, that any of this added material could be considered entirely or even mostly of his own confection. Thus, while De Vera is not properly a commentator according to Lombard's typology, he reveals the creativity possible in compilation. Provided that De Vera was speaking in earnest in his prologue about not having put anything of his own in his treatise, he also reveals that fairly significant editing and compilation did not fall under the rubric of adding something of his own to his sources or rather deleting from them. We can compare De Vera's description of his treatment of sources with the Mancebo's description of his reasons for writing a religious compendium (the *Breve compendio*).[26] Like De Vera, the Mancebo suggests that his content is borrowed, claiming that the majority of his text is taken from the Qur'an. He also offers explanations for any aberrations, including that his is the first such compilation and that it incorporates words from many regions that may not have blended together seamlessly, but nothing that would explain the level of variation found in the work and perhaps even more notably in the *Sumario*. As Bernabé Pons has noted, the Mancebo most often cites the Qur'an in Spanish and with great liberty and originality, both in the sense that his commentary of the Qur'an is the only known commentary of the Qur'an by a Morisco that did not draw on existing glosses and interpretation of the Qur'an (practice of *tafsir*) and in the liberal nature of the citations themselves.[27]

My analysis here of the three main parts of De Vera's treatise yields several theses about intellectual fragments and their relationship with their referents. The first is fairly straightforward but essential: that excessive compilation can distance a piece of text so far from its referent that it ceases to be a fragment proper and instead becomes what we might call near fragment or inspired text. On the other hand, as the Samarqandi section shows, if the referent is strong enough and the compilation less invasive, a fragment can remain a textual fragment even with significant modifications, whether these modifications be abbreviations, amplifications, or variations. Lastly, from the *Encomiendas* section, it is clear that a referent must be strong enough to produce intellectual fragments: it must clearly be a whole by which the user can divine what text or at least the type of text the extant piece or pieces lack.

While De Vera is not a commentator per se, there is one part of Bonaventure's conception of commentator that is useful for understanding De Vera's intellectual fragments and the notion that an intellectual fragment always refers to and undermines its referent: the idea of "principal place." For an intellectual fragment to exist, there must always be a known whole or one that we can fairly clearly see or convincingly imagine. The fragment must be subordinate, at least in terms of completeness; we recall that the existence of multiple states of incompleteness is an issue in De Vera's *Encomiendas* section. The intellectual fragment or group of intellectual fragments thus always threatens to take "principal place." The intellectual fragment threatens to usurp its referent, whether by convenience or, as I argued in the case of De Vera's rearrangement of the Samarqandi chapters, in its appropriateness to the moment.[28]

Pieces of De Vera's Sources in Other Contexts

As mentioned above, De Vera was not alone in generating intellectual fragments of varying degrees of fidelity to the *Breviario Sunni* and the *Libro de Samarqandi*: nor is the fragment foreign to other Morisco manuscripts. In addition to the Mancebo's use of the *Breviario,* and a possible reference to it in the title of his *Breve compendio,* there are other fragments of De Vera's sources. Of the *Breviario,* in addition to the four main manuscripts (CSIC, Junta 1 and Junta 60; Real Academia de la Historia S-3; and BNM 6016) and De Vera's fragment, there are at least four other fragments of different degrees of similarity to MS S3. As in De Vera's case, one of these fragments forms part of a compilation (Junta 12, fols. 192–232). While not as lengthy as De Vera's text from the *Breviario,* it is fairly substantial and is composed of *Breviario* text in Aljamiado on prayer, alms, and fasting. The other fragments are brief and contrast with De Vera's treatise and the compilation just mentioned by being individual excerpts of *Breviario* text or supposedly inspired by the *Breviario.* Another Junta manuscript (13) includes "dichos of the Segovian" (sayings of the Segovian), while on BNM 5223, 191v, there is a prayer ("rrogarya"), "sacada del libro segovyano" (taken from the Segovian book). More generally, as Suárez García observes by drawing on Wiegers, the text that later became the *Breviario* chapter on the thirteen articles of faith (chapter 3 in Gayangos's edition) first circulated independently before it was incorporated into the *Breviario*.[29]

As in parts of De Vera's treatise, some of these fragments are perhaps better labelled near fragments or even inspired text. For instance, regarding the *rrogarya* in BNM 5223, it appears that fidelity to the *Breviario* was less important than the inclusion of some text in the codex that was attributed to the Segovian book. The prayer reads:

> ¡Señor Allah!, contigo amameçko i anocheçko i vivo i muero, i a ti tornaré. ¡Señor!, ponme de los más servidores en ti en kantidad i parte en que alkiere bien ke rrepartas en este dia i despues de el; en luz que guies o piedad que apiades, o rresplandor que rresplandeçkas, o arrizque que tiendas o daño que quites o yerro que perdones o trabajo que desvies, o tención que desvies o misarkordia que glorifiques por tu piedad que tu eres sobre toda cosa poderoso. ¡Señor Allah!, pídote que me hagas que sea virtuoso y buen creyente i de buena espernaza y piadoso sabio tenparado y justo y humil i paciente, temeroso y amador del bien, limosnero y aunador con buena rrepintencia oracionero contento, palativo con honestad y verquenza y castidad porque yo alcance mi verdadera gloria. Amen. (191v)
>
> (Oh, Lord, Allah! With you I rise and set, and live and die, and to you I will turn. Oh, Lord! Set me as one of the most bountiful servers of yours, and as part of those who want nothing but you to spare in this day and after it. In light with which you guide, or mercy with which you pity, or brilliance with which you shine, or manna that you bestow, or harm that you prevent, or error that you forgive, or work that you lighten, or strain that you relieve, or compassion that you glorify with your mercy, since you are almighty. Oh, Lord, Allah! I beg you to make me virtuous and a good believer, and aspiring, pious, tempered, wise and fair, and humble and patient, God-fearing and good-hearted, charitable and conciliatory with repentance, a willing supplicant, helpful with honesty and a sense of shame and chastity so that I can reach my true glory. Amen.)

There is some similarity with the *Breviario* in the use of Allah as a vocative and some correspondences in words and phrases (for example, "tu eres sobre toda cosa poderoso" [You are Almighty]), but there is little other overlap; instead, we see the inclusion of a series of noun-verb combinations that would not likely be found in the *Breviario*: "piedad que apiades ... resplandor que rresplandezcas, o arrizque tiendas o danño que quites, o yerro que perdones ..." (piety with which you pity

... splendour with which you shine ... or manna that you bestow, or harm that you prevent, or error that you forgive ...). In this vein, what appears to be most important is to convey to readers that the prayer is "sacada del libro segovyano." Considering that the prayer is introduced by the information that it is indeed "taken," it is clear that such a small fragment of such a lengthy work, with "fragment" loosely applied here, cannot substitute its whole. In the context of the codex, however, it does serve as an effective surrogate for Iça de Gebir's book.

The *Libro de Samarqandi* was also transmitted fragmentarily among the Moriscos, at times presented as clear fragments and at others in the form of near fragments or inspired text, as in the prayer just cited. There are two fairly lengthy fragments in BNM manuscripts, including a series of summarized and freely copied chapters on prayer in MS 5267 and five chapters in MS 4908: those on controlling anger, holding one's tongue, greed, the advantage of poverty, and renouncing the world, which is unfinished. Real Academia de la Historia, MS T-19 also contains several chapters on marriage and parents and the chapter on the five daily prayers. There is also a series of manuscripts that contain one chapter or less, including a copy on the five daily prayers just mentioned in BnF 774; another copy, similar to that in T-19, of the chapter on the five daily prayers in Aix-en-Provence; a text inspired by a chapter on the *ataçbihar* (pronunciation of the formula "God be praised") in Junta 4; and a significant portion of a chapter on the punishment that a healthy person neglectful of prayer receives from God in Junta 8. Junta 53 incorporates multiple fragments of the *Libro de Samarqandi* over the course of some 350 folios, with some passages interpreted quite liberally, including *Alhhadiz del al'abid y la mengrana* (*al'abid*, "devout one, ascetic"; *mengrana*, "pomegrante"), as well as a full copy of the chapter containing the hadith of Almaçih Addaçhel (the false messiah to appear before the end of the world) over the course of over three hundred folios. Further, Juan Carlos Busto Cortina notes that there are instances in which the *Libro de Samarqandi* was transmitted even more indirectly. Such is the case in BNM 5223, the manuscript containing the prayer discussed above, which contains summarized passages of the work within the story of the young necrophiliac, the "Relato del mancebo necrófilo" (242r–244r). Busto Cortina suggests that due to the summarized and newly redacted nature of the passages, while one can identify them as having been inspired by the *Libro de Samarqandi*, it is impossible to tell from what copy they were produced, or if they were copied from an Arabic or Aljamiado version.[30]

The degree of difference between a fragment and its source can vary widely, and some fragments are much more convincing fragments of their sources than others. Morisco manuscripts in and of themselves are already quite diverse, not so much in the type of texts they include (which are primarily Islamic) but, as noted above, in the manner in which they are pieced together and the specific excerpts from each text. In many cases, the originality is thus in the arrangement of existing texts or, as in the case with the Mancebo, in the manner in which the texts are attributed. Through an analysis of the meaning of referent and De Vera's compilation practices, this chapter has aimed to show that imposing a "new *ordinatio*" and creating fragments is its own breed of creativity. At least one important, two-part question remains, however: why are there so many miscellaneous Morisco manuscripts, and is the fragment particularly useful to a clandestine manuscript culture?

López Baralt has called the Moriscos' unique experience a Spain lived upside down ("al revés").[31] While accepting this thesis and the awful reality in which the Moriscos lived, there are notable instances of borrowing or even exchange between Muslim and Christian cultures. Vincent Barletta, in his analysis of the use of cuaderna vía and related language ideologies in the Mudéjar-era *Poema de Yuçuf* (Poem of Joseph), has proposed that rather than serving as a means of creating opposition between Christians and Moriscos, the composition or copying of text in cuaderna vía tells us more about the Morisco communities themselves, including the social hierarchy of those communities, as opposed to their relationship with Christians.[32] Another instance of exchange that served to mark difference is Iça de Gebir's creation of a now lost trilingual edition of the Qur'an at the request of Juan de Segovia (d. 1458), who recognized the need for a good translation of the Qur'an as an important aid in the peaceful conversion of Muslims to Christianity.[33]

A set of manuscripts that sheds light on the role of fragments in a clandestine manuscript are those containing magic texts, especially grimoires, or textbooks of magic. As discussed briefly in the previous chapter, Moriscos clearly possessed and were interested in magic texts, with the most famous texts conserved being the *Misceláneo de Salomón* (Miscellany of Solomon), the *Libro de los dichos maravillosos*, and the *Libro de las suertes*.[34] Apart from the written amulets, talismans, spells, potions, seals, recipes, Kufic signs, and Qur'anic material contained in these works, the Moriscos also used verbal magic, with both written and verbal forms used to very diverse ends – from help with loans to curing muscle cramps, and remedies for controlling crying, evidence of the suffering of the Moriscos.[35] Moriscos were nevertheless no more interested in magic than Christians, as Roberto Morales Estévez has shown.[36]

In this vein, there are several points of contact between Morisco manuscripts and magic manuscripts as a whole, both in terms of their individual contents and organization, and their forbidden status. Like many of the Morisco codices mentioned in this chapter, magic manuscripts are generally greatly diverse in content, containing astrological tables, invocations, lists of angels and demons, curative potions and prescriptions, demonic pacts and magic circles, and both learned and popular magic.[37] Writing of magic manuscripts in Latin or a vernacular and often with the inclusion of evocations in Hebrew, Morales observed that despite the circulation of printed grimoires in the early modern period, in practice there was no single book of magic formulas.[38] The presence of the Inquisition stunted the growth of a robust industry of printed grimoires and fostered the creation and clandestine circulation of handwritten books of magic.[39] As Morales notes, many of these books were copies or recreations of codices from France, which were, in turn, copies of other grimoires still. Beyond the practical, another reason that grimoires went unprinted, however, was due to the belief in the power of the handwritten word. For a magician's magic to be most successful, he needed a handwritten textbook, most especially in his own hand if possible and adapted to his needs. There is thus a significant degree of variation among manuscript copies of the *Clavícula* (*Key of Solomon*) and the *Libro de san Cipriano* (Book of Saint Cyprian), each tailored to the magician or aspiring magician that used it, such that some scholars argue that there were as many different grimoires as users of the same, and some copies of text that was supposed to be that of the *Clavícula* could barely be recognized as such. This piecemeal compilation of magic text yields a personalized manuscript culture and challenges for any editor. In this way, we conserve some highly personalized fragmentary notebooks of magic, fragmentary in terms of lacking pieces and also in that they are comprised of excerpts of texts, short texts, and separate quires cobbled together according to the needs of their compilers.

Many of those forbidden and customized manuscripts have not survived to the present.[40] As Skemer notes in writing of amulets, the parchment and paper amulets of the Middle Ages were in most cases never intended to be preserved, let alone in libraries and museums. Even in the case in which a library did come to possess an amulet, oftentimes they are not properly identified. The threat of loss of manuscript books was not something the Moriscos could control. Given that so much has been lost, the conservation of some two hundred Morisco manuscripts, some from the Mudejar period, is no small feat, even in the modern age. We need only remember, for instance, how the children of Almonacid de la Sierra (Saragossa) in the 1880s amused themselves by setting fires with Aljamiado manuscripts that were uncovered under a floorboard of a house. Recovery efforts in the twentieth and twenty-first centuries have been undertaken by those interested in understanding the role of Morisco heritage in its historical and social contexts, if not also its meaning in our complex present. Morisco manuscripts have been discovered hidden under floors and behind the adobe walls of houses that the Moriscos were forced to abandon upon being exiled. Along with these rediscoveries has come the study and editing of many more Morisco manuscripts and individual texts, as well as the creation of digital archives, such as the Consejo Superior de Investigaciones Científicas Manuscript@CSIC, that include manuscripts written in Arabic, Aljamiado, Hebrew, and other languages.[41]

Both Morisco and magic manuscripts were personalized book cultures. They were personalized for the magicians who produced them in the case of grimoires, for their makers and the communities of their makers in the case of Morisco manuscripts, and occasionally for communities that were primarily, if not entirely, at odds with the Moriscos, depending on the historical moment. An essential part of this customization and personalization was fragments. The extant copies of manuscript grimoires and the large majority of Morisco manuscripts are fragmentary or composed of fragments, appearing in many cases to have lost pieces that they once had. In the case of magic manuscripts, there is some evidence that their compilers gathered a wide variety of texts and images, including at times what was seen as prestigious learned magic, which even the magician did not understand.[42] The use of fragments, which in the case of Morisco manuscripts frequently consisted not of fragments of originally composed text but of selections of existing works adapted to varying degrees to the needs and moment of the compiler, allowed for creativity and customization even in the face of a limited and sometimes very limited availability of a corpus of texts. However, the use of the same or similar texts as source texts does not necessarily entail a clean repetition. Both manuscripts featuring magic and Morisco manuscripts pose clear challenges for identification and interpretation, since even in the best cases represented by manuscripts like De Vera's, in which we can fairly clearly identify all the elements, customization reigns not just in the selection of texts but in the way in which they enter into dialogue with their referents.

Afterword

Material and Digital Tangibility

UNESCO aims to protect two types of cultural heritage: tangible and intangible. The former category, in addition to World Heritage Sites, includes Movable Heritage, which consists of all objects that are the "expression and testimony of human creation or of the evolution of nature," such as paintings, drawings, statues, sound and video recordings, engravings, manuscripts, and incunabula. A text on the UNESCO Cairo office's webpage on Tangible Cultural Heritage indicates that these objects are expected to perform a wide variety of cultural and even spiritual work that extends well beyond academic study. While this effort is both ambitious and nebulous, it is dependent on a perceived concreteness and even dependability of the objects, and on their "actuality":

> Objects are important to the study of human history because they provide a concrete basis for ideas, and can validate them. Their preservation demonstrates recognition of the necessity of the past and of the things that tell its story. Preserved objects also validate memories, and the actuality of the object, as opposed to a reproduction or surrogate, draws people in and gives them a literal way of touching the past. This unfortunately poses a danger as places and things are damaged by the hands of tourists, the light required to display them, and other risks of making an object known and available.[1]

The description of intangible heritage in the archives section of the main UNESCO website logically suggests that it requires a different sort of preservation, one that depends explicitly on a group of people who are familiar enough with its traditions, skills, and customs to pass it on to a larger community:

> ... the practices, representations, and expressions, as well as the knowledge and skills (including instruments, objects, artifacts, and cultural spaces) that communities, groups, and in some cases, individuals, recognise as part of their cultural heritage. It is sometimes called "living cultural heritage," and is manifested inter alia in the following domains: oral traditions and expressions, including language as a vehicle of the intangible cultural heritage; performing arts; social practices, rituals and festive events; knowledge and practices concerning nature and the universe; and traditional craftsmanship.[2]

Intangible heritage is thus also known as "living," in that it ceases to exist without individuals with the knowledge and skills to make it visible and externally real to contemporary audiences. Intangible heritage requires a vehicle for its expression, as opposed to the way in which tangible heritage is described as being able to manifest itself as a vehicle that requires no production or assistance in order to be present. Defined in this way, intangible heritage bears some resemblance to the digital scholarly edition, a phenomenon with many possibilities for expressing variation and for which it is difficult to determine a finishing point.

However, from a study of fragments and modern uses of manuscripts, including philological study and museum exhibits, it is clear that any absolute divide between tangible and intangible heritage is a false one. While in a practical sense these two categories function quite well, when analysed critically and in the context of a specific form of heritage, they fall apart and prompt a query of other terms used in the realm of cultural heritage. Specifically, these categories can be used to interrogate uncritical uses of the term "materiality" and to explore the meaning and limitations of something that could be called "digital tangibility." In most contexts of use, tangible fragments and even complete manuscripts require intervention and even production prior to productive use, whether in the form of physical conservation, transcription, interpretation, or the creation of paratexts that create an understanding of the main texts. At times this production does not require direct study of the manuscript or fragment's text or the creation of more texts. To cite an early modern example, as we saw with the Aljafería and shingle fragments, in some cases even invisible and inaccessible tangible objects can have presence, provided that someone knows where they are. Intangibility and tangibility exist on a continuum and are also a process, two characteristics of manuscripts and printed books. Print was dependent on manuscripts, and, as David McKitterick and others have noted, manuscripts were reliant on the press.[3]

Manuscript culture is also a process, as social bibliography has made clear in acknowledging the impact of the many actors involved in the creation, diffusion, and reception of physical forms of the text. To identify fragments as a key part of this process and to apply the notion of use to these fragments is to recognize a previously understudied and, in some contexts, wholly unrecognized part of the *variance* that Bernard Cerquiglini presented in his 1989 *Éloge de la variante* (*In Praise of the Variant*), which highlighted the rewriting and, at times, exuberant appropriation that characterizes much medieval writing.[4] This rewriting is not only textual but also material, involving both a manipulation of lines, paragraphs, and chapters, and a modification and movement of paper or parchment, a compilation and reformulation of text, and support that oftentimes yielded messy fragmentary manuscripts or, rather, those composed of fragments.

This messiness of *variance* is widely known, even if not typically framed as the result of the movement of fragments. In the context of the malleability of printed books in the years before the commercialization of binding, Jeffrey Knight has observed that the phrase "collated and perfect," used in the nineteenth and twentieth centuries to designate rare and old books that had been duly inspected and deemed orderly and clean, would not have meant much to many Renaissance readers and owners who were contingent, nonperscriptive collectors.[5] Renaissance England fostered a practice of eclectic, personalized, and even eccentric compilation. The preceding chapters have shown that eccentric compilation can at times yield eccentric texts or at least texts that can seem so to modern tastes. Long before the English Renaissance, a variety of this unusual textuality existed on the Iberian Peninsula, with one famous example being the writing of Isidore of Seville. In writing of the prose of Saint Isidore, Martin Irvine highlights the difference between early medieval and modern perceptions of originality. Irvine's postscript to a lengthy chapter on the formation of medieval textual communities recalls the discussion in the previous chapter of Mohanmad de Vera's management of his sources and, more generally, the derivative nature of Morisco literature discussed in the last chapter:

> The reason that Isidore's work has often been written off or denigrated by modern scholars – that it is a derivative, unoriginal compilation – was the very reason for its popularity throughout the Middle Ages and early Renaissance. ... The form of textuality at work can be understood through the notion of the writer as *compilator* [compiler], one who selects material from a larger cultural library and whose resulting compilation is an interpretive arrangement of the discursive traditions in which the writer intervenes. The *compilator* makes explicit the writer's function at the level of textuality: the compiler sets up a dialogue between prior texts and the interpretive discourse of his own community, isolating or bringing into focus a pattern in the larger network of texts that forms the library.[6]

Like Isidore of Seville's textuality, fragment textuality is typically unattractive and rarely seamless, or at least perceived as such, even in cases of purposeful selection, relative abundance, and readability. At times this perception of unattractiveness is primarily or even uniquely a modern one, as in the case of Saint Isidore's work, but in other instances there is evidence of an early modern distaste or a lack of appreciation for a manuscript's or folio's physical appearance, image, or textual content. Examples of fragments of this last sort are binding fragments, with the most visible being fragments of literary works that we are still interested in reading and studying; but there are many others that raise the question as to whether we should bother studying or even identifying them at all. For instance, found along with the *Tristán* fragments were some forty scraps of paper, some with text or image transfer from the *Tristán* fragments, in various formats including strips, squares, and quarter folios. These contain a wide range of partial or complete short texts, such as letters, contracts, poetry, notes, lists, pen trials, and doodles, and in some cases, two, three, or even more different partial texts that became bound together in the binding process, or a single scrap of paper with text transfer from two or more texts. These fragments have sparked little interest and likely for good reason, since, as I have shown here, we still have plenty of work to do on those fragments already known to be of interest for literary study and for which there exist intriguing if not confounding questions. Alternatively, though, these less urgent fragments may not be willfully ignored but rather have received only brief comment because we simply do not know what to do with them. Fragments of this last sort are strongly antimetonymic in the sense that while we know the pieces came from a whole, we know very little about the whole, whether for lack or information or interest, particularly in the case of letters, recipes, registers, and other personal documents. Making the fragments operable as study subjects is thus a thoroughly constructive process that may not appear to be worth the effort.

The difficulty of knowing what to do with fragments and other brief texts is often a problem with playful monkeys in the margins and other sometimes poorly understood scribal activity: adorned "scars" in parchment, marginal notes cut short by binders, and notes contained in guard folios that are of no clear hermeneutic value or not of particular hermeneutic value alone. This is evident in a Morisco composite codex found in the group discovered in Almonacid de la Sierra in 1884, which had belonged to the clandestine workshop of the aptly named Escribano family, operating in Almonacid from the mid-sixteenth century until the expulsion of the Moriscos. The codex of some 256 folios is a notebook of literary, juridical, and religious texts, some of them fragments, some copied by the Escribano family, others apparently copied and acquired elsewhere. One example of the latter is the early sixteenth-century or perhaps Mudéjar-era *Coplas del alhigante de Puey Monçón* (Songs of the pilgrim of Puey Monçon), an original Morisco or Mudejar travelogue in verse belonging to the *rihla* genre (travelogue with commentary on the people and practices of Islam), which relates the author's peregrination from Spain to Mecca.[7] Like the family's piecemeal copying and collection that produced the composite Almonacid codex, this storehouse of texts could be used to make future copies of individual texts or groups of texts of particular interest. While the texts are generally not sole extant copies, they are of interest as a collection and provide evidence of the Escribano family's compilation practices.

In addition to elucidating these practices, the codex also reveals at least one of the Escribanos' personal interests. The codex contains notes at the beginning and end written in the 1580s or 1590s pertaining to the family, specifically the life of one of its last known members, Luis Escribano. The first notes pertain to the new moon of the month of *Rajab*, the seventh month of the Islamic calendar, and the final notes list family deaths, including those of Luis's own children, the births of his children, and a notice of his marriage. Interspersed within Luis's notes on the moon and his family records are likely pen trials consisting of two cases of the word *quando* (when), in addition to one case, in Arabic, of the shortened form of the phrase recited in prayer several times a day by Muslims and usually in the reading of nearly all the suras of the Qur'an: *bismi-llahi r-rahmani r-rahim* (In the name of God, most merciful, most compassionate).[8] These notes are of interest in the sense that they can tell us of some of the personal concerns and interests of the Escribano family and their loved ones. Paired with other notes found in Morisco codices that were destined for private reading, such as birth announcements, notice of the celebration of *Eid al-Adha* (Festival of the Sacrifice), and rental agreements, the notes also tell us something about the way in which some Moriscos put their books to personal use. Montaner, Toribio Fuente Cornejo, Francisco Guillén Robles, and María José Cervera Fras are among those who have written descriptions and studies of some of the notes.[9]

While some of the Escribano notes have been studied in depth, other Iberian fragments, like the forty pieces found among the *Tristán* fragments, have not, because they have no readily apparent hermeneutic use. Perhaps some of these notes never did have a significant or even marginal hermeneutic purpose. With regard to tenuousness and purpose, the notes are thus strangely similar to fragments because they lack the one element that both defines fragments and gives them a modicum of certainty: their link to a source text. Fragments, due to their incompleteness, convey the island effect cited in previous chapters, as do the notes without referents. The point is not to compare two types of what appear to be marginal texts, since, as we have seen here, many fragments are not marginal at all, as evinced by the widespread use of intellectual fragments as portable knowledge that in some cases sought to address community needs, including the very survival of Islam. Rather, the point is to underscore that fragments are an extreme example of a characteristic of all physical manuscript texts: despite being physically tangible, they require *actualization*, to borrow from UNESCO's reference to the "actuality" of tangible heritage. What is more, like intangible heritage, these objects require a mediator, some person or group of people familiar enough with the peculiarities of manuscripts, including their hands, layout, systems of organization or apparent nonorganization, so that their traditions and customs can pass on to a "larger community."

Another point implicitly raised by the UNESCO tangible-heritage definition is that of literalness and the way in which tangible objects, unlike "surrogates," draw us in. However, the surrogate manuscript, a concept I aimed to convey in the context of glass-encased physical manuscripts, may be not only where we are or where we are headed but also in part where we have been before, even before the advent of digital manuscripts. This has come from working with poor-quality photocopied microfilms, from approaches that use physical manuscripts simply to remove the text and then place them back in the archive for long periods of time, and from certain approaches to working with fragments that see them as poor substitutes rather than study subjects in their own right. As Christoph Flüeler has recently noted, it is surprising – even astonishing – how little the relationship between physical and digital manuscripts has been examined, at least in published work.[10] It is startling in one respect due to the sense of loss that some scholars report – loss, that is, of presence, of a touchstone to the past and perhaps also of interest – when working digitally. Further, one would think that even if we had not come up with concrete solutions to the problem, we would have at least theorized about a convincing tangibility for digital manuscripts. Scholars working in the field of technology applied to artistic creation note that we are actually now in a postdigital phase, in which "we are called to reconcile this openness [of the digital] with notions such as embodiment, presence, enaction and tangibility."[11] Since 1997, Massachusetts Institute of Technology's Tangible Media Group has attempted to create user interfaces that employ physical objects, surfaces, and spaces as tangible embodiments of digital information. They write that while graphical user interfaces only allow users to interact indirectly with information, as though looking through the surface of the water to interact with the forms below, tangible user interfaces are like icebergs, in which a portion of the digital sphere emerges beyond the surface of the water into the physical realm so that users may interact directly with it.[12] Other disciplines, including art, design, and user experience for computers, tablets, and smartphones, have considered ways in which to increase the tactile feedback from electronic devices, creating a rich sense of touch for the user in a digital environment.[13]

This lack of work on material and digital manuscripts is not particularly surprising, at least in some circumstances, since some scholars have already found solutions in certain contexts. One obvious example is to use both digital and material copies of a manuscript at the same time in the archive, combining the material book with its digital counterpart, which has separate but related functions both inside and outside the library. At the same time, the material book is available to an ever-decreasing number of scholars as more and more archives, especially those that have digitized large parts of their collections, restrict access to their physical manuscripts and early printed books, and even more so to their fragmentary ones. Finally, we all must leave the archive at some point, and it is not always easy to substitute one technology for another. We can look to some of the youngest members of our society in regard to the last point. Some toddlers so accustomed to digital books and games, when given a material book, will attempt to scroll its pages.

When we do leave the archive and rely on digital reproductions of manuscripts, we could be said to benefit in several ways if the digital reproductions are of high quality or, better yet, are scholarly editions from which we can cull codicological, descriptive, structural, administrative, and digital object metadata. On a digital site, it is possible to view manuscripts and fragments distanced by time and geography concurrently. We might also reconstruct fragments to undo accidents or intentional acts that produced their current state, using the digital surrogate as a mechanical prosthesis for enhancing the physical eye. We might find information about curatorship, exhibitions in which the manuscripts are involved, and a dynamic bibliography that can be updated and revised. Ideally, we would also encounter existing printed transcriptions and editions of the text, including all necessary translations that could be called up without being obtrusive.

On a more experiential level, we might even discover a sort of presence. Drawing on Gumbrecht's notion of presence, Jan Söffner distinguishes between four types of presence: pure presence, or a "straightforward" sense of being there; fictional presence, or the experience of being there due to a presumed "as if" ontology; telepresence, or the doubling of two presences at the same place by overcoming spatial distance; and hyperpresence, or the doubling of two presences at the same time by creating a new space.[14] In the context of the philological study of manuscripts, both fragmentary and whole, there is no "pure presence" with a straightforward sense of being there, in the sense that manuscripts require actualization, a series of techniques of engagement that often involve copying the text from the manuscript and its placement in a computer file or notebook, whether to produce significant editions or a modest codicological description.

I have long thought it less than fully scholarly to sit next to a manuscript only to copy its text onto my laptop or to attempt to decipher some unclear text or strange foliation while I wait for digital reproductions that are nearly always easier to read and to transcribe than the real thing. When I am not sure what to do in this spatial and temporal gap between physical manuscript and digital reproduction, I think of something Gumbrecht said in the essay "Eat Your Fragment!" Writing of material fragments, he writes that "we can touch, caress, eat the fragment in its material presence (and we can even try to further destroy it). ... The text as a material object enhances our capacity to imagine a world of the past – although there is of course no mimetic relationship between that world of the past and the form of the text as a material object."[15] The material fragment inspires very human desires, even criminal ones, including a desire to eat, scribble on, and, most especially, to steal the fragments. These desires coexist with the academic desire to reconstitute the text with a scholarly aim. The real thing I mentioned previously has never been plainly available to me, at least the real thing that performs simultaneously all the functions I typically assign to material manuscripts: text, heritage, and object capable of evoking what Paul Zumthor, following the famed philologist Gustave Cohen, called the "medieval thing" (*la chose médiévale*), a presence of the Middle Ages. Söffner writes that there are two conditions for experiencing presence perfectly: that it is lived and also (ontologically) presumed to be nonmediated,[16] so in order to be pure a presence cannot have any element of likeness or "as if."[17] If one is to believe the notion that we have little access to the "actuality" of material manuscripts, any access to this actuality would require a suspension of disbelief regarding the pure or nearly pure presence of the manuscript. Fragments, particularly those born of practical use, force us to confront this disbelief head-on. In a fragment's defective presence, which is defective whether or not the actual fragment is present, we are always forced to make it "there" and to become aware of the constructive nature of our work.

Appendices

Correspondences between texts are noted in bold.

APPENDIX 1

Breviario Sunni, chapter 22 (Gayangos, 301 [Iça de Gebir, "Suma"]); De Vera, chapter 9 (BnF, MS 397, 25r–25v; Suárez García ed.)

Breviario Sunni:

… ase de poner el alfaquí al hombre á mitad del cuerpo y á la muger á sus ombros: para el açala echarán las manos diciendo: "'Allah ua aqbar'; las loores son ad Allah que mata y rebilca los difuntos, y á él son las graçias y las grandezas y los mayorios, y él es sobre toda cosas poderoso. ¡Señor! haz gracia y merced á Mohammad y á los de Mohammad y apiada á Mohammad y á los de Mohammad. ¡Señor! este es tu sierbo, hijo de tu sierbo, tú lo criaste y lo mantubiste y lo reblicarás; tú sabes su secreto y su paladino: benimoste á rogar por él. ¡Señor! a tí nos abedzindamos, que tú eres cumplido de omenage. ¡Señor! defiendele de la tentación de la fuessa y de las penas de Chihanama. ¡Señor! perdonale y honrrale su morada, y ensanchale su fuesa, y alimpale de sus yerros y pecados, y dale compaña mejor que la que tiene. ¡Señor! si es bueno, crecele en descanso, y si es que defaltó en tu serbiçio, da pasada de sus pecados, que tú eres sobre toda cosa poderosso. ¡Señor! afirmale su lengua al tiempo de la pregunta de la fuessa, y no le escandalizes, ni lo preubes con lo que no tiene poder para defenderse dello." Despues que a dicho **tres bezes** Allah ua aqbar, que con la primera alaquebira, serán quatro, y despues de todas dichas, diga: "¡Señor Allah! perdonea nuestros bibos y nuestro muertos, á los presentes y absenetes, grandes y pequeños, hombres y mujeres, que tu sabes nuestros fines: y pues tenemos esperança en tu piedad, da pasada de nuestros yerros y pecados. ¡Señor! defiendele de el escandalo de la fuesa y de las penas de Chihanama, y danos buen fin …

De Vera:

El açala del muerto es çuna. Obliga a todos quantos tubieren poder para ir a ella. **Y quando le izieren su açala, se á de poner el alimen, para el ombre, a la metad del cuerpo; y para la muger, en par de sus ombros; y dirán "Allau aquebar." Después dirán:**

Rogaria. **"Las lores son a Dios, que mata y rebica los difuntos; a él son las grandezas y los mayoríos; y él es sobre toda cosa poderoso. Señor, haz açala sobre Mohanmad y sobre los de Mohanmad, y apiada a Mohanmad y a los de Mohanmad."**

Y semejantes loaçiones:

"Señor, éste es tu siervo, hijo de tu siervo; tú lo criaste, y lo mantubiste, y lo rebicarás; tú sabes su secreto y su público. Venimos a te rogar por él. Señor o, a ti nos abezindamos, que tú eres cumplido de omenaje. Señor, defiéndele del tentamiento de la fuessa y de las penas del infierrno. Señor, perdónale, y ónrale su morada, y ensánçhale su sepoltura, y alímpiale de sus yerros y pecados, y dale conpañía mejor que la que tenía. Señor o, si es bueno, créçele en descanso; y si es que faltó en tu serviçio, da pasada de sus pecados; que tú eres sobre toda cosa poderosso. Señor, afírmale su lengua al tiempo de la pregunta de la sepoltura y no l'escandalizes ni le reprueves en lo que no tiene poder para defenderse. Señor, no nos desbíes de tu gualardón ni nos reprueves después d'él."

Esto á de dezir tres vezes el alimen. Y dirá el aljamaa las vezes que dixere el alimen "Alla hu aquebar," porque en el açala del muerto no ay deudo más de las ataquebiras, qu'es dezir "Allahu aquebar." Y darán açalem quando lo diere el alimen y llevarán al muerto a su sepoltura.

APPENDIX 2

Breviario Sunni, chapter 14 (Gayangos, 285–6); De Vera, chapter 9 (25v–26r)

Breviario Sunni:

No haga annefilas despues de alaçar, ni entre el pergüeno y el alicama de almagrib, y despues de almagrib puede hazer dos ó quatro arracas y despues de alatema **su alixfah, que es dos arracas con el alhamdu liehi y çabichizma, la primera, y la segunda con alhamdu lillehi y col iayuha alquefiruna**, y despues puede hazer cuantos pares pudiere y quiera, y despues haga **alguytri una arraca sola con alhamdu lillehi y coluhua y los dos culaudus.** No hagan annefilas quando el alfaqui hace annefilas, ni quando haga con alchama, ni haga alhotba, ni otro açala de deudo ó de çunna ó boto ó deboçion.

Las annefilas que se hazen de dia haganse callando, como el açala de deudo; **y quien quisiere hazer annefilas de noche, debe dexar de hazer alguetri para despues de todas las annefilas, por que alguetri es el sello de la obra del açala.** Las annefilas que se hacen entre los açalaes, basta que se hagan con solo alhamdu; y quien mas querrá hágalo con las coluhuas que quiera para yr camino, para entrar en la mar, para demandar perdon de sus pecados; para cada cosas destas y sus semejantes es muy bueno hazer dos ó quatro arracas de açala.

De Vera:

Las aracas que se azen después del açala de alatema, llamadas xafri y el güitri, dixeron los sabios de los muçlimes lo qu'es; el güitri es çuna azella cada noçhe. Qualquiere persona que lo yziere aprueva la çuna del bienaventurado. Y la izo él y su onrada çihaba, y encomendaron a su aluma la agan conforme ellos la izieron, porqu'es el gualardón en tanto colmo, que d'ella se gana, que no ay número para él.

Las dos aracas antes del güitri se azen con alhandu y açora. El güitri es una araca sola con alhando y col huga; y los dos culaudos cada una açora d'éstas una bez; y araquear; y açajedar; i dezir atahiatu; y dar açalem. **El güitri es el sello del açala; se aze entre día y noçhe.**

Adbiértese que después de aver eçho el xafri, antes de azer el güitri, pueden azer qualquiere açala de graçia que quisieren; pero después de aver eçho el güitri, no se puede azer ningún açala si no fuere después de medianoçhe, porque comiença el día venidero.

Tanbién dixeron que quien tubiere eçho el güitri y quisiere azer algunos otros açalaes de graçia los podrá azer aziendo primero una araca sola de açala con alhandu y açora, tomando en su boluntad la aze para azella par con el güitri. Y eçho, araquee, y açajede, i diga atahiatu, i dé açalem. Después podrá azer el açala que quisiere y, acabado, bolverá a hazer el güitri como antes tenía.

APPENDIX 3

Breviario Sunni, chapter 12 (Gayangos 277–81); De Vera, chapter 10 (30v–31r)

Breviario Sunni:

Los trascuerdos de l'açala son de quarto maneras: el primero es **menguamiento y se a de ymendar antes del açalem**; el segundo es creçimiento y se a de imendar despues del açalem, y el tercero es **menguamiento y creçimiento** y se a de ymendar antes del açalem, y el quatro es tal que no es menester ymienda. Las condiçiones de los trascuerdos que se an de **ymendar antes del açalem con dos açaxdas por menguamiento**, son los siguientes.

Quando se trascordare de leer en las dos arracas primeras …
Por catorçe cosas se hace la ymienda despues de açalem …
Si el leer publico no es mas de una ó dos aléas …
Los trascuerdos que no ai para que haçer ymienda en ellos, son nuebe:
Las cosas que ataxan el açala son treinta y dos, y son las siguientes: el hablar, el comer, el beber …
Las cosas que no tachan el açala son nuebe: …

De Vera:

Los trascuerdos en los açalaes son en quatro maneras. La primera es aziendo açala, suele benir a la persona ymaginaçiones de mil maneras, las quales son causa de trascordarse y unas vezes azen más de lo que deven azer y otras, menos. Y porque cosas semejantes avían de suçeder a los siervos del aluma de Mohanmad, çalei, permitió el señor poderoso se errase el annabi, çalei, en un açala, por azelle a saber las inmiendas cómo se avían de azer para que las enseñase a su aluma. Y al punto que erró y estubo en duda en lo que tenía eçho o no, deçendió Gibril, alei, por mandamiento del rey alto y dixo:

—Ya Mohanmad, tu señor te inbía el açalem. Dixo Mohanmad, çalei: —Él es el açalem, y d'él es el açalem, y a él buelve el açalem. Dixo Gibril:

—Ya Mohanmad, tu señor manda ynmiendes tu açala d'esta manera: siempre que yziendo açala eçhares de ver as eçho araca menos de lo que azer devías, **antes de dar açalem del tal açala, inmiéndalo con dos çajedas, porqu'es menguamiento i se deve inmendar antes del açalem.** La sigunda: si te suçederá aver echo o azer alguna araca de más de las que se deven azer en qualquiere açala y, antes de acabada o después de eçha, te afirmares tienes eçho más de lo que deves azer, después de aver dado açalem del tal açala, ynmiéndalo con dos çajedas, y buelve a dezir atahiatu, y buelve a dar açalem. La terçera: si te suçediere en qualquiere açala creçer en unas aracas y menguar en otras, en el propio açala, de lo que devieres azer, llámase **creçimiento y menguamiento, y dévese inmendar con dos çajedas antes del açalem.** La quarta: si te suçediere, en los açalaes que se deven azer con alhandu y açora, olvidar, en qualquiera araca, de leer açora y, asimesmo en las aracas que se deven azer con alhandu sólo, leer açora, esto es assí propio creçimiento y menguamiento donde no ay para qué; y dévese **inmendar con dos çajedas antes del açalem.** Estos quatro errores suçeden en los açalaes; inmiéndalos, ya Mohanmad, como avemos diçho y enséñalo a tu aluma como tu señor manda para que, siempre que suçediere a qualquiera d'ella cosas semejantes, lo inmienden como dicho es y cumplirán el deudo y mandamiento de Dios.

APPENDIX 4

Breviario Sunni, chapter 11 (Gayangos, 275); De Vera, chapter 10 (31r–31v)

Breviario Sunni:

… y quando la persona hiçiere açala, mire bien lo que hace y delante de quien lo hace, y aparte su persona de todos los pensamientos del mundo, tanto quanto pueda, por que quien haçe açala, es que habla con Allah el alto; y aquella es deuda que le paga; y no enbaraçe su juiçio en otra cosa, y mire que habla con Allah, y piense que tiene la muerte detrás de sí, y el peso de las animas ençima, y el puente de l'açirata baxo de sus pies y el alchanna á su mano la drecha y chihanama á su mano la izquierda: teniendo grandes deseos de alinpiar su anima con grandes xemidos y con arrepentimiento y con rretrayda boluntad, hiçiendo él mismo de sí juiçio, y pidiendo perdon ad Allah el alto, que quien perfectamente haçe açala linpiase de sus peccados; y mientras haçe açala, tenga los miembros de su persona yguales en todas las partes del açala, mirando con sus ojos al lugar de su açaxdamiento, que es donde pone la frente.

De Vera:

Por lo qual deven los muçlimes, siempre que yzieren açala, estar sobre sí i pensar en lo que yzieren, i no trascordarse. Y en caso se trascordaren, afirmen sobre lo çierto, porque no pasa en nuestro adin nada dudoso, y inmiéndese como diçho es. Por evitar semejantes dudas y errores, qualquiere persona que se **pusiere a azer açala mire bien lo que aze; i desbíe su persona de todos los pensamentos del mundo todo quanto pueda, porque quien aze açala abla con Dios verdaderamente y el açala es deuda que le paga; y no ocupe su juiçio en otra cosa; mire que abla con su señor; y piense que tiene la muerte después de sí, y el peso de las ánimas sobre ssí, y el puente del açirat baxo sus pies, y la gloria a su mano dreçha, y el infierno a su mano izquierda; tubiendo grandes deseos de alinpiar su ánima con grandes gemidos y arrepentimiento, y con retraída boluntad; haziendo él mismo de sí justiçia i pidiendo perdón a Dios, que quien perfetamente aze açala alínpiase de sus pecados. Y todo el tiempo qu'estubiere en el açala, tenga los miembros de su cuerpo yguales en todos los cabos del açala mirando con sus ojos al lugar de su açajedamento, qu'es adonde pone la frente.**

APPENDIX 5

BNM 4871 (291r–291v); De Vera, chapter 44 (232v–233r)

BNM 4871:

Diso Abdu el Malik: Reconto Ibnu Wahb, por Abdu e'r Rahman **ibnu Zayd ibnu Açlam,** que un **ermitaño de los ermitaños** se sobresubio sobre los de su tienpo, y el penso un dia **en el fuerte** de su serviçio i **su entremetimiento en la obidençia de Allah,** i diso: ¡Ya señor!, ¿ay el dia de oy **en tu servicio quien sea de mayor serviçio a tu que yo ni de más entremetimiento**? Diso: Sí. Diso: ¿I quien es? Diso: Fulano el carniçero. Diso: I devallo de su asum'a i fuese a demandar por aquel carniçero fasta que lo halló. Pues cuando lo vio el caniçero, devantóse a el, tuviéndolo en cuenta de mayor i mas onrado, i diso, ¡Ya cabdillo!, **¿qué te á fecho devallar de tu asumu'a? Diso: Tu me as fecho devallar.** Diso: ¿I por qué aquello? Diso: E venido sa saber qué es tu obra. Diso a él el tajante: Perdonete Allah, ¿es que eres tu quien me a de gualardonar por ello para que te haga a saber por mi obra, pero devallan esas palabras de ti por aflacondar a mi, Allah es mayor para que te aya de fazer a saber por mi obra. Diso a el el ermitaño: Pora Allah, no me á fecho devallar de mi asum'a otri ninguno sino tu. Diso: I fízole a saber sus nuevas. Diso: A cuanto mi obra, pues yo soy tajante todo el dia, i lo que gano en ello i queda en mi poder en la çagueria del dia, doy la terçera parte d'ello a mi padre i mi madre, y el terçio segundo para mi mujer i mis fijos y a mí, y el terçio teréro fago asadaqa con el en servicio de Allah. I volviose el ermitaño, y el diciendo: ¡ **¡Ya señor!, no cuydo que ay siervo que tome del mundo i lo dese que sea en la grada del siervo que lo desa todo i no toma del mundo cosa ninguna. Y encontrolo un almalake i disole:** Vuelve al tajante i dile que es lo que le a fecho premutar su color i tenblar su cuerpo. Pues cuando vino a el devantose el tajante i diso: ¿qué te faze tornar a mí? Diso: Que me hagas a saber que es aqeullo que te a fecho demudar tu color i tenblar tu cuerpo. Diso: La despartençia de Allah i la temor al **el'adab** de Allah, el dia que será mi aturada delate d'el el dia del juicio, el dia de su encontrada. I fuese el ermitaño **denostando** su persona i conoçio la avantalla del tajante.

De Vera:

Dixo Abdulmelique, por Abdu Rahman, que un siervo de Dios se ensoberveçó sobre los de su tiempo **y tubo por çierto era él el que más sirvía a Dios y el que mejores obras azía.** Y pensó un día en su

grande serviçio y fuerte entremetençia en serviçio de Dios, y dixo: "Ya mi señor, ¿ay el día de oy en tu serviçio siervo que mejor te sirva que yo?" **Y deçendió del çielo la palabra de Dios diziendo:** "Sí; fulano, carrniçero." Y deçendió de su açumua y fuele a buscar, y allolo. I como lo vio el carrniçero, se puso en pie, tubiéndolo por mejor siervo y más santo, y díxole: "Ya caudillo, ¿qué se te ofreçe de mí? ¿I por qué as deçendido de tu açumua?" Dixo: "Por respeto tuyo." "¿Y por qué?" Dixo: "Vengo a saber de ti **cómo sirves a Dios**." Dixo el tajante: "Perdónete Dios, ¿eres tú quien me á de gualardonar por ello para azerte a saber mi obra? ¿Quieres burlarte de mí? Sólo a Dios devo azerlo a saber y no a ti." Dixo el siervo: "Por Alla, no é deçendido de mi açumua sino **por respeto tuyo por esta y esta razón."** Y hízole a saber el caso. Entonçes dixo el tajante: "**Ya siervo de Dios,** as de saber que yo soy tajante todo el día y doy [...] dereçho como Dios bien sabe y lo que gano [...] poder doy la terçera parte d'ello a mi padre [...] **que son viejos y pobres.** El otro terçio despiénd[...] muger y hijos, y con el otro terçio ago **limosna a pobres fi cabirila**." Y fuese el ermitaño y dixo: "Ya mi señor, de sólo azérmelo a saber á perdido el color y á temblado su cuerpo." **Y bolvió al carrniçero y dixo: "Azme a saber qu'es lo que te á eçho perder tu color y temblar tu cuerpo."** Dixo: "El apartamiento de la **servitud** de mi señor y temer **el tormento** de mi señor el día será puesta mi persona en su presençia, el día del juiçio, el día de la encontrada." Y fuesse el siervo culpando su persona y conoçiendo ventaja en el tajante.

APPENDIX 6
De Vera, chapter 18 (69r–77v); BNM 4871 (6r, 7r, 12r)

Passages from the beginning, middle, and end of De Vera, chapter 38; any significant differences in proper names and content are highlighted.

I

De Vera:

Hízonos a ssaber Mohanmad hijo de Çhafar Elcuyasio, díxonos Ybrahim hijo de Yuçuf, díxonos Yzmael hijo de Abfar, **por Omar hijo de** Abdulmeli*que* Elmuzniyu, por Abulcacim, por Mohanmad hijo de Alabid, qu'el mensajero de Alla, çalei, dixo:

—Lo más temido que temo sobre vosotros es la descreençia çhica. Dixeron: —¿Qu'es la descreençia chica, ya mensajero de Dios? Dixo:

—Es la grandía ... (69r)

BNM 4871:

Fízonos a saber Muhammad fijo de Ja'far el Kurasiyyu disonos Ibrahim fijo de Yuçuf disonos Içma'il fijo de Ja'far **por Umar I Mawla al-Mutlabi el Muzniyyu**, por 'Asim por Muhmud fijo de Labid, que el mensajero de Allah, sala Allahu 'alayhi wa çallam, diso: Lo más temido **de lo que** temo sobre vosotros es la descreyençia chica. Diseron: ¿I qué es la descreyençia chica?, ¡ya mensajero de Allah! Diso: **la ufana.**[1] (6r)

II

De Vera:

Dixo **un sabio** que oyó dezir al mensajero de Dios: "Saldrán en la çaguería del tiempo unas gentes que adquirirán el mundo con el adin," quiere dezir, tomarán el mundo, y bestirán bestidos de obejas por la blandura de sus personas, tendrán las lenguas más dulçes que la miel y el açúcar, y sus coraçones serán de lobos. (70v–71r)

BNM 4871:

Fue recontado por **Abi Hurayra** que el mensajero de Allah, **sala Allahu alayhi wa çalam** [diso]: "Saldrán en la çagueria del tienpo una gentes que adquerirán mundo con el addin," queiere dezir que toman el mundo, "i visten vistiduras de ovejas," **quiere decir sus cueros d'ellas,** "por la blandura de su vestimenta, i sus lenguas más dulçes que la miel i el açúcar, i sus coraçones son coraçones de lobos." (7r)

III

De Vera:

Dixo Çilmen **Alfaraçiyu**:

Favoreçe Dios a los creyentes con la fuerça de los munefiques y **grandiosos,** i Dios da vitoria a los grandiosos por la rogaria de los creientes.

Dixo el sabio:

Yá aclararon los pasados las obras de los deudos i dixeron: "No entrará en ellas la ufana y **grandía,** porque permitió Dios adorasen con ella a sus halecados." Dixeron otros: "**Entrará en ellos** la grandí por lo qu'es las obras fuera de los deudos." Y yo digo es aquesto de una de dos maneras: si es que paga los deudos por grandeza, por *engrandeçerse* con las gentes, y, si no fuera por ellas, no aría açala, es de aquellos por quien dixo Dios en su santo Alcorán en el alea que dize: "Serán en las gradas más baxas del fuego de Alhegüiyat con Firaon y sus conpañas." Porque, aunque sea su unidad piadoso, proíbeselo los manda mientos; i por fuerça deve pagar lo que le adebdeçió. (77r–v)

BNM 4871:

I fue recontado por Çilman al-Fariçi que el diso que Allah ta'ala favoreçe a los creyentes con la fuerça de los munafiqes i que Allah ta'ala da vençita a los munafiqes por las rogaryas de los creyentes.

I diso el recontador apiadelo Allah: Ya hablaron las **jentes** en las obras de los debdos i diseron partida d'ellos: "No dentra en ellos la ufana porque Allah ta'ala fizo adurar con ella a sus halaqados." I diseron otros que dentra en'ellos la ufana i fueras d'ella de lo que dentra en las otras obidençias fuera de los debdos. I yo digo que aquesto es de dos maneras: que si es que paga los debdos por ufana a las gentes, i si no por ellos el no faria asala. **Pues este es munafiqe claramente i es de la suma de los que diso.** Allah t'ala que ellos serán en las gradas mas basa del fuego, quiere dezir en el fuego de alhawiya con Fira'un i sus compañas; porque el, aunque sea un unidad sana deviérdaselo i pastófialo lo que es sobre el fasta que pague lo que adebdeçió. (12r)

APPENDIX 7
End of De Vera's Treatise (243v–244r)

Dixo Abu Laizi, [e]stubo con el mensajero de Dios en un año muy apre[t]ado i de muçha neçesidad y estriçia, y sufrieron todos [l]a hambre, y lo tomaron con paçençia. Y les dio Dios, des[p]ués, a todos en general provisión y los remedió. Y re[m]ediará Dios a todos los que tubieren paçençia en [ro…] [...]es cosa [...] por las [...] hijos [...] por la mar y[...] y dixo: "¿Qué tienes azme [...] vas de tu biaje." "Te lo dir[...]" [...]o que no bolvió y a la buelta fue a la casa y no vio en ella riqueza ninguna, ni hijos, ni cautivos. Y alló a la muger alegre riyendo y díxole: "Sierva de Dios, siendo rica te vi triste y aora pobre te veo alegre. ¿Cómo es esto?" Dixo: "Ahogáronse mis hijos, fuéronse mis cautivos, hundiose mi azienda en el mar." Dixo: "Perdónete Dios. ¿Y por eso estás alegre?" Dixo: "Sí; porque entonçes estava rica, y temí, y tube por çierto me gualardonava Dios mis buenas obras en augmentaçión de mis bienes en el mundo; y aora que é perdido mis hijos y mi hazienda, tengo esperança en mi señor me dará el premio d'ello en la otra vida, porque lo é tomado con paçençia."

Notes

Introduction

1 Martínez de Castilla Muñoz, *Una biblioteca morisca*, 382.
2 For a codicological description of the *Roncesvalles* and its use as a carrying device, see Menéndez Pidal, "*Roncesvalles*," 106–8; reprinted in Menéndez Pidal, *Textos medievales españoles*, 7–99.
3 Thomas McFarland's translation of Schlegel in his *Romanticism and the Forms of Ruin*, 45. Peter Firchow, on the other hand, translates *hérisson* as porcupine instead of hedgehog in Schlegel, *Friedrich Schlegel's "Lucinde,"* 189. Lacoue-Labarthe and Nancy render Schlegel's simile as "the logic of the hedgehog"; Lacoue-Labarthe and Nancy, *Literary Absolute*, 44.
4 Janowitz, "The Romantic Fragment," 442.
5 Lacoue-Labarthe and Nancy, *Literary Absolute*, 43.
6 Blanchot, "Athenaeum," in *Infinite Conversation*, 359.
7 Ibid.
8 Martínez de Castilla Muñoz, *Una biblioteca morisca*, 35.
9 Gumbrecht, *Powers of Philology*, 13. For an earlier rendition of Gumbrecht's conception of fragment, see Gumbrecht, "Eat Your Fragment!"
10 Dionisotti, "On Fragments in Classical Scholarship," 1.
11 Boffey, "From Manuscript to Modern Text," 107; Dagenais, *Ethics of Reading*, 17. For a late 1990s view of manuscript culture in an Iberian setting, see the two *La corónica* forums inspired by Dagenais's book. As de Looze notes in his own Zumthorian- and Cerquiglinian-influenced work on the manuscripts of the *Conde Lucanor*, Dagenais has made the greatest use among Hispanists of Zumthor's and Cerquiglini's ideas; see the introduction to de Looze, *Manuscript Diversity*.
12 Howsam, "Practice of Book and Print Culture," 18–19.

13 Chartier, *Order of Books*, ix.

14 Nichols, "Introduction," 4. This introduction to the 1990 special issue of *Speculum* on the New Philology is a clear statement about the primary components of materialist philology. For a commentary and critique on the "newness" of New Philology, see Howard Bloch's contribution, "New Philology and Old French." For a response to the *Speculum* issue, see Busby, *Towards a Synthesis?*. Michelle Warren argues for putting philology behind us; see Warren, "Post-Philology."

15 Modern Language Association of America, "Considering the Scholarly Edition in the Digital Age." The White Paper also provides a useful list of conditions that an edition must meet to qualify as a scholarly or digital scholarly edition.

16 Chartier, *Order of Books*, x.

17 McKenzie, *Bibliography and Sociology*, 13, 29.

18 Taylor, *Three Medieval Manuscripts*, ch. 1; McGann, *Textual Condition*, 4; McGann, "The Text, the Poem, and the Problem," 285. For a clear, seminal statement on materialist philology, see Nichols and Wenzel, "Introduction," in *The Whole Book*, 1–6. On manuscript polyphony, see Sturges, "Medieval Authorship."

19 Jardine and Grafton, "'Studied for Action'"; Sherman, *Used Books*, xiii; Cormack and Mazzio, *Book Use*.

20 Twomey, "Towards a Reception History," 329.

21 Love, *Scribal Publication*; Bouza, *Corre manuscrito*.

22 While there are many studies on commonplace books, the following were particularly useful for this study: Blair, "Humanist Methods in Natural Philosophy"; Moss, *Printed Commonplace-Books*; Havens, *Commonplace Books*; Sharpe, "Uncommonplaces?"; Jardine and Grafton, "'Studied for Action'"; and Boffey and Thompson, "Anthologies and Miscellanies."

23 Bouza, *Communication*, 42–3.

24 Dagenais, *Ethics of Reading*, 171–212; Bouza, *Communication*, 42–3.

25 Gómez Bravo, "Papers Unite," ch. 5 in *Textual Agency*.

26 Ibid.; for *envoltorios*, see 94–100.

27 Martínez de Castilla Muñoz, *Una biblioteca morisca*, 29–30.

28 One notable exception in terms of the author is Chartier, "Figures of the Author," ch. 2 in *Order of Books*. For Chartier on the author, see also Chartier, "Esbozo de una genealogía."

29 As Michael F. Suarez observes, the "sociology of texts" is just one area of bibliography in which McKenzie spurred innovation. Suarez notes that while McGann's 1983 *Critique of Modern Textual Criticism* and McKenzie's 1986 *Bibliography and Sociology of Texts* are often cited as first steps towards

a "sociology of the text," McKenzie actually used the phrase in a lecture back in 1976. For a chronology of McKenzie's contributions, see Suarez, "Extended Evidence," 38–9.

30 McKenzie, *Bibliography and Sociology*, 4.

31 Isidore of Seville, *Etymologiae* 10.44, quoted and translated in Irvine, *Making*, 242.

32 Armando Petrucci reminds us that medieval miscellanies, while having in common with the scholastic model the collection of diverse texts for pedagogical purposes and their arrangement in continuous series, differ in that they use whole texts rather than fragments: see Petrucci, "Dal libro unitario al libro miscellaneo."

33 Boffey and Thompson, "Anthologies and Miscellanies," 292.

34 Gillespie, *Print Culture*, 12.

35 Lerer, "Medieval English Literature," 1254.

36 Oliver, *Poems without Names*, quoted in Lerer, "Medieval English Literature," 1254.

37 See Divizia, "Texts and Transmission"; Divizia, "Appunti di stemmatica comparata"; and Divizia, "Volgarizzamenti due–trecenteschi."

38 Glickman, *Sacred Treasure*, xv.

39 Labarta, "Supersticiones," 164.

40 Bouza, *Corre manuscrito*, 101–2.

41 The bibliography on the final scene of *Cárcel de amor* is vast. A few studies that represent the above points of view include Gerli, "Leriano's Libation" and Whinnom, "Cardona." On Leriano's consumption of the letters as a cannibalistic act involving the consumption of Laureola's body, see Chorpenning "Loss of Innocence." See also Goldberg, "Cannibalism in Iberian Narrative."

42 Mora, *Dicho de Francisco de Mora*, 374–7, quoted in Pedrosa, "Del brazo escribidor," 606.

43 Demelas, "Keep the Fragments Alive," 1.

44 For a general bibliography on the reuse of manuscripts and the fragments thus produced, Ker's classic study of Oxford bindings remains a very useful resource: Ker, *Fragments of Medieval Manuscripts*. See also the supplement to Ker's study in Pearson and Ker, *Oxford Bindings 1500–1640*. Nicholas Pickwoad is an expert on European bindings from the late-medieval period to 1900; Pickwoad, "Onward and Downward." For a concise summary of manuscript reuse for enjoyment and for economic gain with examples from both the early modern period and the late twentieth century, see Christopher de Hamel's lecture *Cutting Up*, 5–25. José Manuel Lucía Megías discusses the use of Spanish and Catalan

chivalric material in bindings in "Literatura caballeresca catalana"; and in "El *Tristán de Leonís* castellano."

45 De Hamel, *Cutting Up*, 5.

46 For a comprehensive list of the extant chivalric fragments, see Lucía Megías, "Literatura caballeresca catalana"; Lucía Megías, "Los fragmentos," 47.

47 For a collection of essays by researchers working within the BwB network (http://www.hebrewmanuscript.com/), see Lehnardt and Olszowy, *Books within Books*.

48 Erwin, "Archivist Seeks Help."

49 See Escobar's contributions and the other essays in Escobar, *El palimpsesto*. Escobar was also involved in *Rinascimento virtuale–Digitale Palimpsestforschung*, a project centred on the digitization of Greek palimpsests and the creation of electronic archiving of selected palimpsests. The project also published a bulletin, with studies pertaining to the preservation, edition and study of palimpsests; http://www.rinascimentovirtuale.eu/node/1.

50 Burón Castro, *Manual para la recuperación*.

51 In 2010, Kathryn Rudy published a piece in which she employs "use" to refer to the marks left by readers, which were discovered by using a densitometer, a machine that measures the darkness of a reflecting surface to reveal which texts a reader favoured. See Rudy, "Dirty Books."

52 Cormack and Mazzio, *Book Use*, 41; they make this observation in the context of two printed manuals, Albrecht Dürer's *Vnderweysung der Messung* (*The Art of Measurement*; 1525) and Hieronymus Hornschuch's *Orthotypographia* (1608), the first technical manual for printers.

53 Chartier, *Order of Books*, x.

54 For instance, in the first decade of the twenty-first century, two of the Hispanic Society's Qur'ans sold for around USD$2 million each at Christie's. Archer Huntington, founder of the Hispanic Society of America, studied Arabic as part of his goal to know Spain deeply. See Christie's, "Almost Complete Kufic Qur'an," price realized: £916,500 (USD$1.87 million); and Christie's, "Qur'an," price realized: £1,140,500 (USD$2,320,918).

55 Otto Ege is one of the most famous book dealers and scholars to dismantle manuscripts and to sell their individual leaves. See Cummings, "Beinecke Library"; Mauk, "Scattered Leaves."

56 On the relationship between manuscripts and museums, see the essays by Pickwoad "Museums of the Book" and "Library or Museum?"

57 UNESCO ascribes the following importance and functions to tangible heritage: "Objects are important to the study of human history because they provide a concrete basis for ideas, and can validate them. Their preservation demonstrates recognition of the necessity of the past and

of the things that tell its story. Preserved objects also validate memories; and the actuality of the object, as opposed to a reproduction or surrogate, draws people in and gives them a literal way of touching the past." UNESCO Office in Cairo, "Tangible Cultural Heritage."

58 On presence in relation to the theory of history, see the forum *On Presence*: Eelco Runia and Elizabeth J. Brouwer, ed., *History and Theory* 45 (October 2006), most particularly the articles by Runia, Ankersmit, Domanska, and Gumbrecht ("Fragment"); and Gumbrecht, *Production* and *Powers of Philology*, ch. 1. On presence in relation to conceptualizations of time and being, see Gumbrecht, *1945*. For presence applied to architecture, see Domanska, "Let the Dead Bury the Living"; and Young, "Daniel Libeskind's Jewish Museum in Berlin," in *At Memory's Edge*, 152–83. On presence as it relates to being and time, see the introduction to Nancy, *The Birth to Presence* and "Technique of the Present."

1. Fragment and Fragmentary in the Iberian Epic

1 For an analysis of Menéndez Pidal's approach to the epic, see Brown, "Relics of Menéndez Pidal"; also Menéndez Pidal, *La epopeya castellana*; the introduction to Menéndez Pidal, *Reliquias*; and Menéndez Pidal, *La leyenda de los Infantes de Lara*, 26.

2 On uses of *Roncesvalles*, see Menéndez Pidal, "*Roncesvalles*." Regarding the classification of *Roncesvalles* as a fragment, Francis Carmody proposed that it was a short and complete heroic poem, while Jane Whetnall and Roger Wright have suggested that it is a ballad. See Carmody, *Franco-Italian Sources*; Wright, *Spanish Ballads*; and Whetnall, "Question of Genre," esp. 179–80.

3 Maya Sánchez, "Chronica Adefonsi Imperatoris"; Gil, "Prefatio de Almeria." Spanish translation in Pérez González, *Crónica*; English translation in Barton and Fletcher, *World of El Cid*, 148–263. For an edition of the *Carmen Campidoctoris*, see Montaner and Escobar, "*Carmen Campidoctoris*."

4 For the dating of the Carmen, see Montaner and Escobar, "*Carmen Campidoctoris*," 130–5.

5 Deyermond, *La literatura perdida*, 37–9.

6 Ibid., 37; see also Deyermond, "Problem of Lost Epics," 30–1.

7 Deyermond, "Problem of Lost Epics," 28.

8 Brown, "Relics of Menéndez Pidal," 26; Deyermond, "Lost Genre," 231.

9 Wright, "Hispanic Epic," 416–17.

10 The *Cantar*'s two significant lacunae are both in the third *cantar*, one at verses 2337–48 and the other after verse 3507. Despite being as many as

fifty verses long each, their content has been fairly confidently deduced as the Infantes de Carrión's entry into battle, Pedro Bermúdez's attempts to disguise Fernando's cowardice, and the Cid's horse Babieca's display of speed and greatness for King Alfonso.

11 Gumbrecht, *Powers of Philology*, 18.

12 Chartier sees as a characteristic common to New Historicism and sociological approaches to manuscripts and printed books the insistence on reconnecting the text to its author, "the work with the intention and positions of its producer." This does not entail, however, "a restoration of the superb and solitary romantic figure of the sovereign author whose primary or final intention contains the meaning of the work ... as he returns in literary sociology the author is both dependent and constrained." *Order of Books*, 28.

13 McGann, *Critique*, 43–4.

14 Chartier, *Order of Books*, 25. For a history of philology with consideration of currents both in Spain and the United States, see Montaner, "La filología." A mid-twentieth-century conceptualization can be found in Carreter, *Diccionario*. Peter Richardson provides a good overview of the state of philology in the mid-1990s in "Consolation of Philology." See Gumbrecht's *Powers of Philology* for a clear conceptualization of philology in the twenty-first century.

15 McKenzie, *Bibliography and Sociology*, 3–4.

16 Menéndez Pidal, "*Roncesvalles*," 106.

17 Ibid.

18 For Horrent's thoughts on the *Carmen*, see Horrent, *Historia y poesía*, 100–3.

19 Horrent, *Roncesvalles*, 102–3.

20 Menéndez Pidal, "*Roncesvalles*," 194.

21 Ibid., 169.

22 Montaner and Escobar, "*Carmen Campidoctoris*," 69.

23 On the timing of the overwriting, see Escobar, *El palimpsesto*, 153n36.

24 Ibid., 150n11.

25 Montaner and Escobar, "*Carmen Campidoctoris*," 68–9.

26 See for instance Carmody, *Franco-Italian Sources*; Monteverdi, "Il cantare"; Riquer, "El Roncesvalles y el planto."

27 The exceptions are González Delgado, "Motivos clásicos"; Franchini, "El fragmento épico"; Rossi-Ross, "Style and Pathos."

28 Franchini, "El fragmento épico," 107.

29 Rossi-Ross, "Style and Pathos," 429.

30 Menéndez Pidal, "*Roncesvalles*," 160–89.

31 On the diversity of legends involving Charlemagne and Spain, see the recent volume edited by Matthew Bailey and Ryan Giles, *Charlemagne and His Legend*, particularly the editors' introduction, 1–12; and Bailey's study, "Charlemagne as a Creative Force in the Spanish Epic," 13–43.

32 Greetham, "Who's In," 16. Greetham notes that in the field of historical linguistics, the asterisk embodies the combination of "documentary defeat" and desire for full resolution so characteristic of fragments: "Yes, the asterisked form is unattested, but damn it, this is what should have been if the documentary caretakers had done their work properly" (17).

33 Riquer, "Roncesvalles," 623–8; Whetnall, "Question of Genre," 171–87.

34 Whetnall, "Question of Genre." See Wright, "How Old"; Carmody, *Franco-Italian Sources*, 20; and Horrent, *Roncesvalles*, 87–9; see also Wright, "Hispanic Epic," 417.

35 Whetnall, "Question of Genre," 177.

36 Whetnall, "Question of Genre," 177.

37 This two-column format is nevertheless not wide enough to allow for the correct division of verses.

38 Rodríguez-Velasco, review of the *Mocedades de Rodrigo*.

39 Funes and Tenenbaum, *Mocedades de Rodrigo*, xxi–xxii.

40 Menéndez Pelayo, *Tratado de los romances viejos*, 6:293.

41 On the oral composition of Spanish epics, see Bailey, *Poetics of Speech*.

42 On 137r, for example, the fourth and fifth stanzas are each lacking two lines. Stanza 4 is clearly incomplete, something that can be noticed in appearance, though there is no explicit indication that any text is missing. Only the first and last verses of stanza 5 are extant, but no gap appears in the text. Since the page is missing four verses, a full stanzas's worth, the page looks complete.

43 On the manuscripts, see Maya Sánchez, "Chronica Adefonsi Imperatoris," 120–32; Pérez González, *Crónica*, 27–9; Sánchez Belda, *Chronica Adefonsi Imperatoris*, lxxii–lxxviii; Rodríguez Ancieto, "Contribución al estudio."

44 These *calderóns* and the periods that mark the end of the first hemistich eventually disappear.

45 Salvador Martínez, *El "Poema de Almería,"* 127; Pérez González, *Crónica*, 143n230.

46 Gil, "Prefatio de Almería," 267. See also Wright, "First Poem," 217–19. Spanish translation in Pérez González, *Crónica*, 131–43.

47 Antonio, *Bibliotheca Hispana Vetus*, 2:22, 28, 36; Pellicer y Tovar, *Bibliotheca*, fol. 147v.

48 Pellicer y Tovar, *Bibliotheca*, fol. 147v.

49 Lowe, *Palaeographical Papers*, 2:481, paraphrased in Escobar, *El palimpsesto*, 21.
50 Escobar, *El palimpsesto*, 22.
51 Bertoni, *Il Cantare del Cid*, 197–204; Wright, "First Poem," 239–41; Higashi, "La *enmendatio*," 28; Escobar, *El palimpsesto*, 153n36.
52 Montaner and Escobar, "*Carmen Campidoctoris*," 210.
53 Ibid., 158.
54 Smith, "Dating and Relationship," 104.
55 Wright, "First Poem," 218.
56 Harney, *Epic of the Cid*, 123.
57 Bonilla y San Martín, "Reproducción de un fragmento," 318n. For Bonilla's initial presentation of the fragment, see Bonilla y San Martín, "Fragmento de un *Tristán*."
58 See, for instance, Deyermond, *Epic Poetry*; Deyermond, "La autoría"; Armistead, "*La gesta*."
59 Bailey, "*Las mocedades de Rodrigo*" (2007), 19.
60 Funes and Tenenbaum, *Mocedades de Rodrigo*, xxvi–xxvii.
61 The four sections of Palencian material consist of text on the discovery of the tomb of San Antolín and on King Sancho Abarca's acquisition of the shrine from Count Pedro of Palencia in exchange for Campó, naming Bernardo as guardian of the shrine (Bailey, "*Las mocedades de Rodrigo*" [2007], 95–135); the transfer of the bishophric from Toledo to Palencia, represented by Bishop Miro, Bernardo's uncle, and the foundation of the diocese of Palencia (143–201); the death of Bishop Miro and the naming of the second bishop of Palencia (Bernardo), and a reconfirmation of the charter by the pope and by the son of the deceased King Sancho, King Fernando I (270–9); and an incomplete passage on the expulsion of the bishop (Bernardo) by the sons of Count Pedro of Palencia and on Bernardo's plea for help to King Fernando, who laments Rodrigo's absence, which renders him unable to remedy the dispute (718–31). See "*Las mocedades de Rodrigo*," 13; and Funes and Tenenbaum, *Mocedades de Rodrigo*, xxxv. Another case in which there is a "supplementary supposition of other texts, whether or not they materially survive," noted by Brown, is Juan Victorio's 1984 edition of the *Poema de Fernán González*, in which he uses circular reasoning to substantiate the existence of an earlier *Cantar*: "Que existió tal cantar, y además con una audiencia amplia, lo prueba va el hecho de que el Arlantino se decidiera a volver a tratarlo" (quoted in Brown, "Relics of Menéndez Pidal," 20; That that poem existed, and with a large audience, proof of which is that the Arlantine poet decided to compose about it again).
62 Hook and Long, "Reflexiones," 66–7.

63 See Bailey, "*Las mocedades de Rodrigo*" (2007), particularly the "Composition of the *Mocedades*" section of the introduction, 11–14.

64 For an excellent summary of neotraditionalist and individualist scholarship, see Faulhaber, "Neo-Traditionalism"; and Armistead, "Epic and Ballad."

65 Brown, "Relics of Menéndez Pidal," 23.

2. From Bound to Metonym: Early Modern and Modern Disuse of Chivalric Fragments

1 Portions of this chapter were published in Bamford, "Fragment as Phenomenon."

2 Anthony Wood, quoted in Philip, *Bodleian Library*, 6. Wood uses "servile uses" in the context of sixteenth-century treatment of antiquities at the University of Oxford: "The ancient libraries, a glory to the University, as containing among them many rarities, the works of our own country men, besides many matters obtained from remote places, were by them or their appointment rifled. Many MSS, guilty of no other superstition than red letters in their fonts or titles, were either condemned to the fire or jakes. Others also that treated of controversial or scholastical Divinity were let loose from their chains, and given away or sold to Mechanicks for servile uses." See Wood, *History and Antiquities*, 106. For information on the motivations for the fragmentation and reuse of manuscripts, see the bibliography cited in introduction, n44 of this volume.

3 De Hamel, *Cutting Up*, 8.

4 Hulvey, "Not So Marginal," 161.

5 De Hamel (*Cutting Up*, 20) mentions a particularly provocative case in which an illuminated psalter sold at Christie's was subsequently separated, with each of its leaves selling for a 500% profit.

6 De Hamel, *Cutting Up*, 5.

7 As proposed in Cuesta Torre, "Adaptación, refundición e imitación"; and in Lucía Megías, "El *Tristán de Leonís* castellano," although Cuesta Torre makes a point of calling BNM, MSS 20262.19 and 22644/1–51 the "source" of the sixteenth-century printed editions. She also notes that some chapters in the manuscript are titled exactly as they appear in the printed edition, but that the manuscript likely has almost double the number of chapters as the printed books. In summary, Cuesta Torre, *Tristán de Leonís*, xix. For the transmission of the *Tristán de Leonís*, see also Cuesta Torre, "La transmisión textual."

8 All of the text of the *Amadís* manuscript is available in Rodríguez Moñino, Millares Carlo, and Lapesa, *El primer manuscrito*; Lucía Megías,

Antología; and the two larger fragments in Menéndez Pidal, *Crestomatía*, 2:457–9. A digital facsimile of the *Amadís* manuscript is available at the Digital Scriptorium by searching for the shelfmark UCB 115; accessed 11 December 2017, http://www.scriptorium.columbia.edu/. For the *Tristán de Leonís*, see Bonilla's transcriptions and studies on the first fragment found (BNM, MS 20262, no. 19, according to the numeration used by Carlos Alvar Ezquerra and José Manuel Lucía Megías), Bonilla y San Martín, "Reproducción de un fragmento." For Bonilla's initial presentation of the fragment, see Bonilla y San Martín, "Fragmento de un *Tristán*." See also Menéndez Pidal, *Crestomatía*, 1:352 and Alvar Ezquerra and Lucía Megías, "Hacía el códice." See Lucía Megías, *Antología* for a complete transcription and a "critical" presentation of most of the text, save two very brief fragments, as well as descriptions of the miniatures. See Lucía Megías, "El *Tristán de Leonís* castellano" for a more developed description of the miniatures. A study of the narrative units of the *Tristán* and analysis of the unique qualities of the manuscripts can be found in Gómez Redondo, *Historia*, v.II.1527–40.

9 Rodríguez Moñino, Millares Carlo, and Lapesa, *El primer manuscrito*, 25n15.
10 Lucía Megías, "El *Tristán de Leonís* castellano," 2.
11 Lucía Megías, "Los fragmentos," 47.
12 Pickwoad, "Use of Fragments," 1–2.
13 Ibid., 2.
14 See Clark, "Print." For a summary of the demise and later temporary resurgence of Spanish chivalric manuscripts in the sixteenth century, see Hook, "Arthur Goes Global."
15 For a copy of the complete letter, see Andrés de Uztarroz and Dormer, *Progresos de la historia*, 488–9.
16 Flórez, *Viage de Ambrosio de Morales*, 170.
17 Ibid., 40, 38.
18 Ibid., 173.
19 McMunn, "Illustrated Fragments," 112.
20 Ibid., 98.
21 Ibid., 100–2.
22 Pickwoad, "Use of Fragments," 4–5.
23 *Reused, Rebound, Recovered*.
24 Lowe, *Paleographical Papers*, 481.
25 Declercq, "Introduction."
26 I refer to the *Tristán* fragments according to the numeration used by the BNM and in work by Manuel Alvar and Lucía Megías.
27 Lucía Megías, "El *Tristán de Leonís* castellano," 8–9.

28 Additional examples include King Arturo and Lanzarote coming to Tristán's tent and walking around it, listening (fol. 14); King Arturo, Tristán, King Mares, and Queen Iseo going to the city of Camelot (fol. 18); King Mares going to the court of King Arturo with twenty knights (20abc); and King Arturo and his knights journeying to a monastery where Tristán and his friend Lanzarote were staying (fol. 25).

29 Lucía Megías, "El *Tristán de Leonís* castellano," 10.

30 Ibid., 8.

31 On the highly patterned system of illumination in the *Cifar* and symbolic elements of the miniatures, see Planas Badenas, "El manuscrito de Paris" and Bernías, "El manuscrito de Paris," in the same volume; and Ayerbe-Chaux, "Las *Islas Dotadas*."

32 Donahue, "Notes on the Illumination," 6.

33 This point of view contrasts with that of Lucía Megías, "El *Tristán de Leonís* castellano," 10–11.

34 This is a method that Garnier develops, beginning in the mid-1970s, with *La guerre au Moyen Âge* up through his two-volume study on the meaning and grammar of gestures in the medieval image. See Garnier, *La guerre au Moyen Âge* and *La langage de l'image*.

35 Donahue, "Notes on the Illumination," 2.

36 Camille, *Mirror in Parchment*.

37 Lucía Megías, "El *Tristán de Leonís* castellano," 11.

38 Ibid.

39 The episodes are discussed in the introduction to Cuesta Torre's edition, *Tristán de Leonís*, xix–xxiii.

40 For a thorough summary of these debates and discussion of work by Sharrer, Bonilla, Lida, Waley, Seidenspinner-Nuñez, Gwara, and others, see Cuesta Torre, *Tristán de Leonís*, xxiii–xxvii.

41 Apart from Rodríguez Moñino's transcription and study and the accompanying works by Agustín Millares Carlo and Rafael Lapesa (Rodríguez Moñino, Millares Carlo, and Lapesa, *El primer manuscrito*), the most comprehensive examination is Alberto Montaner's work on differences in the use of emblematic elements in the manuscript and in Montalvo's edition, Montaner, "Del Amadís primitivo."

42 Rodríguez Moñino, Millares Carlo, and Lapesa, *El primer manuscrito*, 216.

43 All citations from the *Amadís* come from Juan Manuel Cacho Blecua's edition, Rodríguez de Montalvo, *Amadís de Gaula*.

44 I cite Edwin Place and Herbert Behm's translation, Rodríguez de Montalvo, *Amadis of Gaul*, 35.

45 I resolve all abbreviations and put hypothetical reconstituted text in brackets with a question mark.

46 Montaner, "Del Amadís primitivo," 2.

47 The passage in Montalvo's edition reads:

> Y Amadís vio venir descontra ellos a Ardián, el su enano; y como vio el escudo de Amadís, conosciólo luego, y dixo a grandes bozes:
>
> –¡O señor Amadís, socorred a vuestro hermano don Galaor, que lo matan, y a su amigo, el rey Cildadán!
>
> Cuando esto oyeron, moviéronse al más correr de sus cavallos, juntos uno con otro, que don Bruneo a su poder a él ni a otro en tal menester no daría la aventaja. Y yendo assí, vieron venir a Madarque, el bravo gigante que era señor de la ínsola, y venía en un gran cavallo y armado de hojas de muy fuerte azero y loriga de muy gruessa malla, y en lugar de yelmo una capellina gruessa y limpia y reluziente como espejo, y en su mano un muy fuerte venablo tan pesado, que otro cualquier cavallero o persona que sea apenas y con gran trabajo lo podría levantar, y un escudo muy grande y pesado. (3.65.976)
>
> (And Amadís saw Ardan, his dwarf, coming toward them; and when he saw the shield of Amadís, he recognized it at once, and shouted: "Oh, Sir Amadís, help your brother Don Galaor, for they are killing him, and his friend, King Cildadan!" When they heard this, they went forward at the top speed of their horses, neck and neck, for Don Bruneo with all his strength would not yield any advantage in such an emergency to him or to any other. And going thus, they saw Madarque, the fierce giant, coming, who was the lord of the island, and he came on a big horse, and armed with plates of very strong Steel and coat of mail of very thick mesh, and instead of a helmet a thick armored hood as clear and shining as a mirror; and in his hand a very strong javelin so heavy that any other knight or person who might exist could scarcely with great effort lift it, and a very large, heavy shield. [Rodríguez de Montalvo, *Amadis of Gaul*, trans. Place and Behm, 1:36])

48 Montaner, "Del Amadís primitivo," 2.

49 Rodríguez de Montalvo, *Amadis of Gaul*, 38–9. Other examples include the reporting of this chance encounter to Amadís's beloved Oriana's mother, Queen Brisena: "–Amigos, lo que a mí me plazería es que os vais a la reina Brisena y le digáis cómo os embía el su cavallero de la Ínsola Firme, y que

fallé a don Galaor mi hermano, y besadle las manos por mí" (Rodríguez de Montalvo, *Amadís de Gaula*, ed. Cacho Blecua, 980; Friends, what will please me is that you go to Queen Brisena and tell her how the knight of the Firm Island sent you, and that I have found Don Galaor my brother; and kiss her hands for me [Rodríguez de Montalvo, *Amadis of Gaul*, trans. Place and Behm, 2:39]); and later in Queen Brisena's meeting of her two sons, not seen together since their early encounter with another giant: "–¡Ay, Virgen María Señora!, ¿y qué es esto, que mis hijos veo ante mí?" (984; Oh, Lady Virgen Mary! And how does it happen that I see my sons before me! [2:42]).

50 "Los antiguos originales que estavan corruptos y mal compuestos en antiguo estilo, por falta de los diferentes y malos escriptores, quitando muchas palabras superfluas y poniendo otras de más polido y elegante estilo tocantes a la cavallería y actos della." (Rodríguez de Montalvo, *Amadís de Gaula*, ed. Cacho Blecua, book 1, prologue, 225; He corrected the ancient originals which were corrupt and poorly composed in the antique style through the fault of diverse poor scribes, taking out many superfluous words and putting in others of a more polished and elegant style pertaining to chivalry and the deeds thereof. [Rodríguez de Montalvo, *Amadis of Gaul*, trans. Place and Behm, 1:21])

51 Lucía Megías, "Literatura caballeresca catalana," 247–56.

3. Used to Pieces: The Muwashshahas and Their Romance Kharjas from Al-Andalus to Cairo

1 As Federico Corriente has recently reiterated, the number of kharjas in Romance is often overestimated. He cites inaccuracies in the three most commonly used dictionaries of the Spanish language: María Moliner's *Diccionario de uso del español*, the dictionary of the Real Academia Española, and the *Diccionario D. Manuel Seco del español actual*. Corriente and Sáez-Badillos, "Review Essay of Bossong," esp. 304–5n7.

2 Corriente, "The *Kharjas*," esp. 116–17. The debate about whether the kharjas and their muwashshahas had Romance or Eastern origins produced a significant amount of scholarship in the second half of the twentieth century. For a summary of these debates, see Armistead, "Brief History"; Corriente, "By No Means"; Hitchcock, "The Fate of the *Kharjas*."

3 García Gómez, "Métrica de la moaxaja," following his mentor Julián Ribera y Tarragó, "El cancionero"; Alonso, "Cancioncillas"; Menéndez Pidal, "Cantos"; Monroe and Swiatlo, "Ninety-Three Arabic *Ḫargas*."

4 Gorton, "The Metre of Ibn Quzmān"; Abu Haidar, "*Kharja*" and "*Muwashshaḥāt*"; Jones, "Romance Scansion"; Derek Latham, "New Light" and "Prosody"; and Hitchcock, "Some Doubts." Samuel Stern's landmark publication that brought the kharjas to light is *Les chansons mozarabes.*

5 *Tasmit* is a pattern in which there is an independent changing rhyme in all but the last segment, which has common rhyme.

6 Corriente, *Poesía dialectal*; Zwartjes, *Love Songs;* Corriente "*Kharjas*," 113.

7 Armistead, "Brief History," 11.

8 Jones, *Romance "Kharjas,"* 7. For a good introduction to the Romance kharjas in Hebrew script, see Benabu, "Orthography."

9 Espòsito, "Dismemberment," 8.

10 Ibid., 6.

11 Espòsito, "Monkey," 474.

12 Hamilton, "Hispanism," 184.

13 Mallette, *European Modernity*, 232; for Mallette's chapter on kharja studies, with a focus on García Gómez, see 162–97. See also Mallette, "Misunderstood."

14 Rosen, "Muwashshah," 169.

15 Samuel Armistead wrote in the late 1980s that this was a moot point, a "non-problem," following James Monroe's assessment of the issue as a "beached whale"; Armistead and Monroe, "Beached Whales." A clear statement of García Gómez's reasons for editing the Romance kharjas in their frame appears in a footnote in the prologue of the second edition of his *Las jarchas romances*, 17n5: "Si no fuera por la razón 'exclusivamente métrica', y no solo en tanto en cuanto se reproduce en árabe y en calco rítmico la 'estructura prosódica' de la 'composición entera' (en la que la combinación de la jarcha se repite varias veces) habría carecido de sentido traducir íntegramente todas las moaxajas, pues–salvo algún caso excepcional–habría bastado traducir nada más que la estrofa de preparación o transición (*tamhid*) a la jarcha. Sin el calco rítmico, habría yo gastado en balde cacumen, tinta y papel, puesto que no se trataba de estudiar el arte literario de la moaxaja, objetivo muy distinto del mío de entonces." (If it were not for the "exclusively metrical" reason, and not only in so far as it is reproduced in Arabic and in the metre, the "prosodic structure" of the "entire composition" [in which the combination of the *jarcha* is repeated several times] it would not have made sense to translate the *moaxajas* in their entirety, since – except for in exceptional cases – it would have been sufficient to translate only the preparation or transition [*tamhid*] stanza to the *jarcha.* Without the rhythmic pattern, I would have wasted wits, ink, and paper, since my objective was not to study the

literary art of the *moaxaja*, a very different objective than mine at that time.) See also Bamford, "Romance *Kharja*" and Bamford, "Ruins in Motion."

16 Bamford, "Romance *Kharja*."

17 Rosen, "Muwashshah," 165.

18 Glickman, *Sacred Treasure*, 4; Reif, *Jewish Archive*, 10; Cole and Hoffman, *Sacred Trash*, 16.

19 Cole and Hoffman, *Sacred Trash*, 27.

20 Ibid., 12.

21 Glickman, *Sacred Treasure*, 9.

22 The Mishnah indicates: "Any of the Holy Scriptures may be saved from burning [by bearing them from one domain to another on the Sabbath], whether they are such that are read [on the Sabbath] or not. In no matter what language they are written [if they become unfit for use], they need to be hidden away [in the Genizah]" (II Shabbath>, 16:1). For a clear explanation of the difference between Rabbinic and Karaite interpretations of Exod. 35:3, "You shall kindle no fire in all of your habitations on the Sabbath day," see Frank, "Karaite Ritual."

23 Reif, *Jewish Archive*, 12; Cole and Hoffman, *Sacred Trash*, 13.

24 Quoted in Glickman, *Sacred Treasure*, 11.

25 Quoted in Cole and Hoffman, *Sacred Trash*, 13.

26 Ibid., 15.

27 Ibid., 16–17.

28 Ibid., 15.

29 Benabu and Yahalom, "Importance of the Genizah Manuscripts," 140.

30 This manuscript is known as the "Colin manuscript," named after the French philologist Georges Colin. It was available to García Gómez via photocopy for his *Jarchas romances*. The manuscript is now only known through Alan Jones's introduction and edition, *Uddat al-jalīs*. The *Uddat al-jalīs* is the most complete and important anthology of Andalusian Arabic muwashshahas, with more than 280 muwashshahas copied by at least six different scribes. Ibn Baqi's muwashshaha occurs in a section of the manuscript containing eleven other muwashshahas with Romance kharjas.

31 Corriente, "*Kharjas*," 126.

32 Ibid., 141.

33 Jones, *Romance "Kharjas,"* 171.

34 Corriente, "*Kharjas*," 122.

35 Jones, *Romance "Kharjas,"* 171.

36 Corriente, "*Kharjas*," 125.

37 Ibid., 126.

38 Jones, *Romance "Kharjas,"* xi.

39 Benabu and Yahalom, "Importance," 154.
40 Ibid., 155.
41 Ibid. The other three Hebrew manuscripts of Halevi's kharja are fairly consistent with the Genizah fragment, with only the slight differences noted below:

MS Oxford 1971:	bnyd lpškh 'ywn šn'lw / km knd mwqdgwn pdylw
MS Schocken 37:	'g'm bnyd lpškh 'ywn šn'lw / bm knd mwqrgwn pdylw
MS Oxford 1970:	bnyd lpškh 'ywn šn' lw / bsr nd mw qrgwn pry lw

42 Solà-Solé, *Corpus*, 197.
43 Corriente, *Romania arábica*, 243.
44 Jones, *Romance "Kharjas,"* 102.
45 One explanation for this one-letter difference between Ibn Baqi's and Halevi's kharja is that the *ya* in the Arabic was an error for *ba*, due to the palaeographic similarity of medial *ba* and *ya*. The use of *ba* for *ya* could also explain the presence of *nbd* instead of *bnyd* in the Arabic manuscript: a simple instance of haplography of the first *ba* and confusion of *ya* with *ba*.
46 Jones, *Romance "Kharjas,"* 105.
47 Confusion of *bet* for *kaf* in one case (Schocken 37) and confusion for *bet* for *kaf* and *resh* for *kaf* in the other (Oxford 1970).
48 Benabu and Yahalom, "Importance," 155.
49 Jones, *Romance "Kharjas,"* 105.
50 Corriente, "*Kharjas*," 121.
51 Benabu and Yahalom, "Importance," 154.
52 Ibid., 155.
53 As Linda F. Compton has argued, muwashshahas that end with Romance or bilingual kharjas more frequently end with the voice of a woman than Arabic kharjas do: see Compton, *Andalusian Lyrical Poetry*. For women in Hebrew lyric of the Iberian Peninsula, see Rosen, *Unveiling Eve*, 30–63.
54 I base the English translation on García Gómez, *Jarchas romances*, 2nd ed., 96–9; Solà-Solé, *Corpus*, 195; Jones's facsimile of the final stanza, *Romance "Kharjas,"* 101–2; and Jones's critical edition of the Colin manuscript, *'Uddat al-jalīs*, 254. For the kharja, I cite Corriente, "*Kharjas*," 121, with the exception of the interpretation of *pashkah*.
55 See Menéndez Pidal, "Cantos," 233; García Gómez, *Jarchas romances*, 2nd ed., 96–9; and Corriente, *Romania arábica*, 243–4.
56 In 1985, Armistead and Monroe suggested that the kharja is a quotation from a previous *zajal*. See Armistead and Monroe, "Beached Whales"; and Monroe, "Which Came First."

57 Ibn Quzman, *Gramática*, 338.

58 English translation based on Corriente's Spanish version in Ibn Quzman, *El cancionero hispanoárabe*, 138.

59 Ibn al-Xabbaz, quoted in Corriente, *Poesía dialectal*, 127.

60 Ibn Nizar, quoted in ibid., 128.

61 Halkin, *Yehuda Halevi*, 76. For a translation of Halevi's poem of friendship to Moshe Ibn Ezra, see Cole, *Dream of the Poem*, 152–3.

62 See Halkin, *Yehuda Halevi*, 76–7. The other poem featuring Yosef is a short, nostalgic elegy for Yehudah Ibn Ezra. Halkin translates the poem as follows: "Because it sees man is but a vain thing, / Time turns on him. Like Abel killed by Cain, / It lays the splendidest of our sons low / And slays the darlings of our hearts. / Souring our wine until our tears taste sweet, / It has breached the Ibn Ezra's foursquare lines. / For two of them, now far away, I pine, / And for the days in which they won the palm, / While asking for Yosef, I'm told to wait, / And for Yehuda, 'He is gone.'"

63 I base the English translation primarily on Angel Sáenz-Badillos and Judit Targarona's translation in Ha-Levi, *Yehudah ha-Levi: Poemas*, 203–5, but also on Solà-Solé, *Corpus*, 194–5; and Hayyim Brody's edition of Halevi's diwan, Brody, *Dīwān*, 168–9. For the kharja, I cite Corriente's recent interpretation, "Updated Survey," 121, and Benabu and Yahalom's reading.

64 Bossong, *Poesía*, 189.

65 Ibid., 91–162; for a summary see 93–5. Another analysis of muwashshaha intertextuality can be found in Valencia and Boyarin, "*Ke adame filiolo alieno*."

66 Benabu and Yahalom, "Importance," 147.

67 Bossong, *Poesía*, 146; Benabu and Yahalom, "Importance," 147.

68 Bossong, *Poesía*, 146.

69 Ibid., 146–9.

70 Corriente, *Poesía dialectal*, 288.

71 Jones, *Romance "Kharjas,"* 131; kharja from Corriente, *Poesía dialectal*, 312.

72 On these Jewish intellectuals, see Ossorio, "Ibn Dayyān"; Saénz-Badillos "Ibn Muhājir" and "Ibn Ferruziel." See also Corriente and Sáenz-Badillos, "A vueltas," esp. 171–3. For Hebrew imitations of Arabic muwashshahas, see Almbladh, "Ma laḏḏā lī sharbu r-rāḥi"; Elinson, "Contrapuntal Composition"; as well as the bibliography cited by Bossong, *Poesía*, 92 and Corriente and Sáenz-Badillos, "Review Essay," 319n38.

73 Ibn Bassam writes: "The first to make in our country these meters of the *muwaššaḥ* and to invent their method of poetical composition was, as I learned, Muḥammad b. Maḥmūd al-Qabrī the Blind. He composed them

on the meters [hemistichs] of the classical poetry, except that he usually chose the neglected and less frequently used meters. He also used to take vernacular and ʻajamī [non-Arabic] phrases, calling them *markaz*, and built upon them the *muwashshaḥ* ..." Samuel Stern's translation in Stern, *Hispano-Arabic Strophic Poetry*, 64.

74 The section reads *km knd* in the Genizah fragment, in Oxford 1971, and with a minor emendation in Schocken 37.

75 Corriente, "*Kharjas*," 121.

76 Ibid., 125.

77 Corriente, *Romania arabica*, 243.

78 Corriente, *Poesía dialectal*, 311.

79 Benabu and Yahalom, "Importance," 144.

80 Ibid., 141.

81 Fleisher, "Additional Data," 140.

82 On the dating of R. El'azar ben Chalfon's work, see ibid., 138.

83 Ibid., 137, 144. For the poems in Hebrew, see Scheiber, "Fragment."

84 Corriente, *Poesía dialectal*, 315. For the complete muwashshaha, see Brody, *Dīwān*, 2:324–5. The kharja translation is in Corriente, "*Kharja*," 125.

85 Benabu and Yahalom, "Importance," 141–2; see also Benabu, "Poetry in Two Languages," 128.

86 The identification of the poet of this composition is up for debate; according to Brody, it is by Halevi, but according to Fleisher, Ibn Zaddiq.

87 Corriente, *Poesía dialectal*, 313; Corriente, "*Kharja*," 125. For Halevi's complete muwashshaha, see Brody, *Dīwān*, 2:321–2.

88 Fleisher, "Additional Data," 140.

89 While the examples here support what appears to have been a phasing out of the Romance kharjas in Egypt, in some cases the Romance kharjas continued to be copied with their corresponding Andalusian muwashshahas even after they were no longer understood. Benabu notes that there is a twelfth-century copy of one of Halevi's diwans, owned by a *gaon* (honourable sage) of the Palestinian Academy, Rabbi Abraham Abu Takir, which shows a concerted attempt to preserve the Romance kharjas; Benabu, "Poetry in Two Languages," 128–9. In a section of fifteen Andalusian muwashshahas by Hebrew poets, the Romance kharja was eliminated in all cases but one (in which the *gaon* himself appears to have added and also slightly misunderstood the Romance kharja "¿Qué hare, madre? Este amado mío está a la puerta" (kharja in Corriente, *Poesía dialectal*, 317; What shall I do, mother? This lover of mine is at the door).

90 Scheindlin, "Mid-Life Repentance," 41.

91 Brann, *Compunctious Poet*, 90; Brann's translation of D.H. Baneth and H. Ben Shammai's edition of the *Kuzari* (Ha-Levi, *Kuzari*); my emphasis.
92 Schönle, "Ruins and History," 649.
93 Hill, *Maurice Blanchot*, 8–9.
94 Carmi, *Penguin Book*, 347. The Hebrew is in Yefim Schirmann's anthology *Ha-Shirah*, 2:489 (#208b).

4. Faith in Fragments

1 Specifically, the workers were cleaning the ceiling. On the discovery of the Qur'an folios, see Cervera Fras, "Palabras árabes." See also Borrás Gualis, *Mudéjar*.
2 Cervera Fras, "Palabras árabes," 451.
3 Ibid., 449.
4 Also known as Saint Margaret, Marina was a popular saint in the Middle Ages known for her defeat of devils that appeared to her in the form of dragons.
5 On extending the possibility of dating the tile to the fifteenth century, see Isabel Velázquez, author of the most recent comprehensive study on the tile, which appears on the occasion of a public exhibition of the tile organized by the Instituto Castellano y Leonés de la Lengua and the Fundación Villalar; Velázquez, *La teja*, 24. Jose Hernando Pérez identified the script as a type of Gothic cursive called *letra de albalaes* that is actually associated with a specific notarial form used for economic and administrative concerns associated with Pedro I's reign (1350–9) but previously used as a script of payment in commercial settings; see Hernando Pérez, "Nuevos datos." Since *letra de albalaes* has been used to describe script from the thirteenth century, Antonio Millares Carlo prefers gothic cursive; see Millares Carlo and Ruiz Asencio, *Tratado*, 193. On *albalaes* script, see also Casado Quintanilla, "De la escritura."
6 Velázquez concurs with Hernando Pérez regarding the tile's text being that of the *PFG*, but Gwara challenges this attribution, as well as the attribution of the very first line to the *Libro de Apolonio*, citing the highly formulaic character of *mester de clerecía* verse, with reference to Dana Nelson's work: Gwara, "*Poema*."
7 For a good overview on the *Ordo commendationis animae*, as well as a detailed analysis of its use in the *Cantar de Mio Cid*, see Gerli, "*Ordo Commendationis*."
8 Hernando Pérez, "Nuevos datos," 144n; Velázquez, *La teja*, 34–6.
9 On presence, see the bibliography in introduction n58 above.

10 On the effects of climatic conditions on parchment and paper manuscripts, see Clemens and Graham, *Introduction*, particularly the section on damaged manuscripts; and De Hamel, *Scribes and Illuminators*, esp. ch. 3.
11 For instance, see Ciruelo, *Reprovación*, II, I, 17v or Pereira, *Adversus fallaces*, I, prœm., 1. On "magia benéfica," see Cardaillac-Hermosilla, *La magie en Espagne*, 48.
12 El-Bourdrari, "Magie." One of the most popular forms of sorcery in the Prophet Muhammad's lifetime was to tie knots in a rope and then to recite incantations over the knots, thus bewitching or harming another person. This sort of sorcery is mentioned in the penultimate chapter of the Qur'an, in which Muslims are instructed to seek refuge from this sort of evil: "And from the evil of those who practice witchcraft when they blow on knots" (113:4). According to lore, Muhammad once thought that he was suffering as a result of a spell that a man had cast upon him. The man's daughters tied the spell into a cord with eleven knots and hid the cord in a well. Muhammad fell ill, and God sent him two suras (containing eleven verses) about sorcery, as well as the archangel Gabriel with instructions on how to use the suras. Muhammad recited the eleven verses of the two suras over the cord, and with each verse, a knot was untied. He recovered when all eleven knots were undone and the spell broken.
13 Dols, "Theory of Magic," 216.
14 Canaan, "Decipherment," 129.
15 Ibid., 132.
16 Labarta, *Libro de los dichos maravillosos*, 0.42, cited in López Baralt, *La literatura secreta*, 242.
17 Roza, "Recetarios."
18 Viladrich, "Fablamiento del Alcorán," 189.
19 López Baralt, *La literatura secreta*, 257–8.
20 *Libro de los dichos maravillosos*, Biblioteca Tomás Navarro Tomás (CCHS-CSIC); *El fablamiento del Alcoran*, BNM, MS 5081; *El libro de las suertes*, BNM, MS 5300.
21 Labarta, "Supersticiones," 167.
22 Roza, "Recetarios," 564.
23 Asín Palacios, *La espiritualidad*, 162–3.
24 Antonio Ballesteros-Beretta cites a portion of Alfonso X's last will and testament in which he states that the *Cantigas* were to be kept in the church where his body was to be buried in Seville, or in the case of a Murcia burial, in the cathedral there; see Ballesteros-Beretta, *Alfonso X*, 1053.
25 The recipe reads: "Alherze para aborrençia a quien querrás. Escriberás estos alawatimes en-una caña i crebarás la caña en la casa que tienen amor,

pues no se ajuntarán jamás" (BNM, MS 4937, fols. 3r–v; Talisman for whomever you may abhor. You will write these magic words on a cane and break it in the house in which he and his woman make love, then they will never get together again), quoted in Roza, "Recetarios," 564.

26 Jones, "Ten Dedications."

27 See studies by Vakaloudi, "Kinds and the Special Function," cited in Skemer, *Binding Words*, 165.

28 On the Astorga inscription, see Paz de Hoz, "Henoteísmo." On Christian inscriptions on Syrian lintels, see Prentice, "Magical Formulae."

29 On the presence of Iao in amulets, see Bonner, *Studies in Magical Amulets*; and Delatte and Derchain, *Les intailles magiques*, catalogue numbers 208, 254, and 381.

30 "It is a universal custom to write the word *Shad-dai* (Almighty) on the other side of the mezuzah, opposite the blank space between the two sections. As this word is written on the outside, the practice is unobjectionable. They, however, who write names of angels, holy names, a Biblical text, or inscriptions usual on seals within the mezuzah, are among those who have no portion in the world to come. For these fools not only fail to fulfill the commandment, but treat an important precept that expresses the Unity of God, the love of Him, and His worship, as if it were an amulet to promote their own personal interests; for, according to their foolish minds, the mezuzah is something that will secure for them advantage in the vanities of the world" (Maimonides, *Mishneh Torah* 5.4 94–5; translation from Twerskey, *Maimonides Reader*, 94–5.

31 Trachtenberg, *Jewish Magic*, 147.

32 Isaac ben Moses of Vienna, *Sefer Or Zarua*.

33 Frazer and Fraser, *Golden Bough*, 3.1.

34 Skemer, *Binding Words*, 144, citing Ciruelo, *Reprovación*, 75.

35 Gumbrecht, *Production*, esp. xv, 2, 18–19, 49, 107–11, 116.

36 The most recent study appears in ch. 3 of Ryan Giles's *Inscribed Power: Amulets and Magic in Early Spain*, in which he examines the tile in the context of other works composed in cuaderna vía, most particularly the *Libro de Apolonio* and the *Libro de buen amor*. See Giles, *Inscribed Power*, 87–108.

37 I cite the inscription in the *Hispania Epigraphica* database, record 2436, which cites the *Corpus Inscriptionum Latinarum* (CIL) 112/5= HEp, Armin U. Stylow et al., *Corpus Inscriptionum Latinarum*, vol. 2.

38 Velázquez, *La teja*, 54–5 n34.

39 Skemer, *Binding Words*, 305–7.

40 Velázquez, *La teja*, 26–7; Hernando Pérez, *Hispano Diego García*, 108.

41 Gwara, "*Poema*," 116–17, 127, 131.

42 Gómez Moreno, "La poesía épica," 2:88; Hernando Pérez, *Hispano Diego García*, 108.
43 Gwara, "*Poema,*" 127.
44 Weiss, "*Mester de Clerecía,*" 144–5.
45 I quote Menéndez Pidal's transcription in *Reliquias*, 47–8, 58.
46 I quote the English translation in Such and Rabone, *Poem of Fernán González*.
47 Skemer, "Amulet Rolls," 197–8.
48 While Maimonides cautions about the use of the mezuzah as an amulet and the addition of other text and seals, Fray Martín de Castañega wrote that it was acceptable to use quotations of scripture and other texts if they were used to fight the Devil in a spirit of pure Catholic faith and devotion; Castañega, *Tratado*.
49 Gwara, "*Poema,*" 122.
50 Ibid., 130, 132.
51 Ibid., 132.
52 All quotations from the *Libro de Apolonio* come from Manuel Alvar's edition, *Libro de Apolonio*; references refer to stanza numbers. This riddle also appears in Latin in the *Historia Apolonii Regis Tyrii*: "Item ait ad eum puella: / Non sum compta comis et non sum compta capillis / Intus enim mihi crines sunt, quos nos uidet ullus. / Me manibus mittunt, manibusque remittor in auras," cited in Alvar, *Libro de Apolonio*, 2:259.
53 Tarsiana's ability to save herself from sex slavery by telling her traumatic story and playing her viola evinces this motif, as well as the scene in which she, still a virgin and a relatively well-treated slave, is identified to her father.
54 The word *raída* is used in legal documents contemporary with the shingle, including the *Siete Partidas* (Seven-Part Code), to refer to dilapidated documents whose appearance renders them no longer valid. For instance, in Title XIX, Law VIII of the third *Partida*, as part of the law declaring the necessity of registers and of making and maintaining perfect records, *raída* means incomplete and unlawful, in contrast with the whole of the register, by which the unusable and incomplete can be renewed: "E dezimos que registro tanto quiere dezir como libro que es fecho para remembrança de las cartas e de los preuilejos que son fechos. E tiene pro porque si el preuilejo, o la carta se pierde o se rompe, o se deffaze la letra, por vejez o por otra cosa: o si viniere alguna dubda sobre ella por ser rayda, o de otra manera qualquier: por el registro se puedan cobrar las perdidas e renouarse las viejas" (Alfonso X, *Las siete partidas*, XIX.viii, 2:124; We declare that a register means a book made to preserve the remembrance of ordinances and privileges which are granted. It is the advantage for the

reason that if the privilege or ordinance is lost, or defaced, or the writing becomes illegible through age or where any doubt arises concerning it on account of its being erased, or for any other reason whatsoever; what is lost can be ascertained, and what is illegible through age can be renewed by means of the register [translation from "Notaries" in *Las Siete Partidas*, trans. Scott, 762]).

55 Skemer, "Amulet Rolls," 197–8.
56 Skemer, *Binding Words*, 182.
57 Bühler, "Prayers," 271.
58 Darío Álvarez quoted in Mateos Paramio, "Palabras," 9.
59 Lord, "From the Document," 365.
60 Hernando Pérez, "Nuevos datos," 137.
61 Luck, *Arcana mundi*, 33.
62 Malinowski, "Magic," 67–9.

5. The Fragment among the Moriscos: Mohanmad de Vera's Culture of Compilation

1 For a critical edition of De Vera's text, as well as detailed studies of his use of sources, linguistic aspects of his treatise, and a glossary, see Suárez García, "El tratado." De Vera's treatise is held at the BnF, MS 397. Suárez García has recently published this edition, study, and glossary as *El compendio islámico de Mohanmad de Vera*, which I have not yet been able to consult. All page numbers referenced in this chapter and in the rest of the book thus refer to the dissertation.
2 As López Baralt reminds us by noting the presence of Arabic grammars translated into Aljamiado, such as Ibn al-Yurrum's *Yarrumiyya*, the Moriscos did not lose their Arabic without a fight. López Baralt, *La literatura secreta*, 44.
3 Mancebo de Arévalo, *Tratado*, 104.
4 On the category of Aljamiado literature, see Montaner, "La literatura aljamiada."
5 Martínez de Castilla Muñoz, "Manuscritos," 146. Martínez de Castillo Muñoz's definition is consistent with Francisco Rico's in his "Entre el códice," 152: "Manuscritos que agavillan obras distintas y en general de dispar autoría, pero copiados por un mismo amanuense, en una misma oficina, por comisión de un mismo patrono ... Para ahorrarnos distingos, pueden quedar aparte ahora los facticios y los formados por aluvión, a través de aportaciones independientes y separadas en el tiempo." (Manuscripts that bind different works, and in general, works of disparate

authorship, but copied by the same scribe, in the same workshop, by commission of the same patron ... To save us distinctions, the factitious manuscripts and those formed by alluvium can be set apart, through independent and separate contributions over time.)

6 Wiegers, *Islamic Literature*, 164.

7 See Fonseca, *Sumario*, 34; on the Mancebo's reading of the *Celestina*, see Narváez, "El mancebo."

8 For a catalogue of Mudejar and Morisco manuscripts in Latin characters, see Casassas Canals, "La literatura islámica."

9 For information on the manuscripts of the *Breviario*, see Wiegers, *Islamic Literature*, ch. 4.

10 On the influence of the *Breviario* on the *Breve compendio*, see ibid., 161–73.

11 As Suárez García notes, "purified" and, I would say, "cortada" as well refer to Castilian as opposed to Aragonese or the linguistic variants in his source texts, and more generally to the modernization of the text. See Suárez García, "El tratado," 47.

12 Wiegers, *Islamic Literature*, ch. 5.

13 Gayangos's edition, Iça de Gebir, "Suma"; Wiegers, *Islamic Literature*, 122. On Aljamiado manuscripts in the library of the Real Academia de la Historia, see Gálmes de Fuentes, *Los manuscritos*.

14 Iça de Gebir, "Suma," 272–5.

15 Bernabé Pons, "Taqiyya,"

16 When quoting the *Breviario*, I cite Gayangos's edition, Iça de Gebir, "Suma," 272.

17 There is also a version at the Bibliothèque Nationale in Algeria that Karima Bouras, who studied the manuscript in depth for her thesis, says is quite similar to the text in T-13: see Bouras, "La *Wasiyya*." On the 1969 Ocaña discovery, see Martínez Ruiz and Albarracín Navarro, "Libros árabes"; Albarracín Navarro, "Los manuscritos"; and Hofman Vannus, "Los manuscritos." Both Ocaña manuscripts are held in the private library of Rafael del Águila Goicoechea and Luisa Tejerina.

18 For a comprehensive glossary of terms used in De Vera's treatise, including *aparçero*, see Suárez García, "El tratado," 335–634; English translation from Abdel Haleem, *Qur'an*, 190.

19 Harvey, "Literary Culture," 166.

20 Fragmentary Junta 6, which modernizes the language of the text in BNM, MS 4781, reduces the *isnad* (list of authorities) and eliminates certain phrases, is De Vera's closest referent.

21 See Suárez García, "El tratado," 32–44.

22 In BNM 4871, regarding the butcher, the *siervo* relates to an angel the following: "¡Ya señor!, no cuydo que ay siervo que tome del mundo i lo dese que sea en la grada del siervo que lo desa todo i no toma del mundo cosa ninguna. Y encontrolo un almalake i disole." (290r; Oh, Lord! I can't believe there is a servant who has lived in the world and then abandons everything in the same manner as the one who abandons everything and doesn't take anything from the world. And then he was found by an angel who said to him.)

23 Suárez García's definition of *munefiqe*, "El tratado," 520.

24 Parkes, "Influence," 128.

25 Passage from *Commentarius in primum librum sententiarum Petrii Lombardi, Opera Omnia* (Quaracchi: Ex Typographia Collegi S. Bonaventurae, 1882), 1:14–15, quoted and translated in Hult, *Self-Fulfilling Prophecies*, 61n99.

26 For an English edition of Mancebo's explanation, see Harvey, "Mancebo de Arévalo," 263–4.

27 Bernabé Pons, "Interferencias."

28 Jesús Rodríguez Velasco's work on the dialectic between main text and glosses is an interesting analogy to the referent-intellectual fragment relationship; see, for instance, "La Bibliotheca."

29 Suárez García, "El tratado," 25, following Wiegers, *Islamic Literature*, 120.

30 Busto Cortina, "El Alkitab de Çamarqandí," 192.

31 See the first chapter of López Baralt's *Literatura secreta* entitled "Al revés de los cristianos: La España invertida de la literatura aljamiado-morisca," 37–68.

32 Barletta writes that these structures and practices are "symbolic tools employed by Castilian and Aragonese alfakíes to regiment the cultural practice of their neighbors and legitimate their position as purveyors of Islamic knowledge within these communities." Barletta, *Covert Gestures*, 154.

33 For Christian attitudes towards the Qur'an, see Burman, *Reading the Qur'an*.

34 For a summary of the editions and some scholarship on these works, see López Baralt, *La literatura secreta*, 239–40.

35 Ibid., 265, 24.

36 Morales Estévez, "Los grimorios," 548–9.

37 Ibid., 538–9.

38 Ibid.

39 Pedraza García, "De libros clandestinos," 80.

40 One relatively well-known notebook containing magic material that has survived is Jaime Manobel's *Dietario mágico* (Archivo Histórico Nacional Inquisición MPD.442), which served as both leger and magic compilation. Manobel was a necromancing cleric and also a swindler, born in 1572 in

Huesca and detained and imprisoned by the Inquisition in 1590. His magic book is some forty pages; its cover bears no title, but its interior covers contain images of Saint John and Mary Magdalene. Manobel's *Dietario* is centred on two main areas in which he hoped magic would have an effect: to cure the sick and to mediate relationships between men and women.

41 The Manuscript@CSIC portal (http://manuscripta.bibliotecas.csic.es/) contains digital copies of manuscripts in the CSIC libraries, as well as codicological descriptions and METS-PREMIS metadata for the manuscripts, with the aim of making the holdings more accessible. The initial stage of the digitization process has been restricted to the CSIC's own collections of Arabic, Hebrew, Persian, and Turkish manuscripts.

42 The meaning of reading was variable in Morisco magic manuscripts. In addition to the use of pseudo-Kufic letters and the combination of *nomina* (magic names) with magic symbols in illicit magic spells, the Moriscos employed cryptic words without semantic content in licit ones as well. In the case of the latter, as López Baralt notes, in the *Libro de dichos maravillosos*, there is a spell to control a storm, in which the user must pronounce a series of magic words of uncertain or no meaning while performing a series of actions. The words are vocalized in both extant manuscripts, such that the *tempestarius* (conjurer of storms) can read, even if not totally understand them. In regard to illicit spells, Joaquina Albarracín Navarro and Juan Martínez Ruiz have noted that in cases in the *Misceláneo de Salomón*, unintelligible words or those whose form may not simply be abbreviations or mnemonic devices, as in other traditions of magic, served to awaken intuition and dull analytic thought. See Martínez Ruiz, *Medicina*, 142–3, cited in López Baralt, *La literature secreta*, 250.

Afterword

1 UNESCO Office in Cairo, "Tangible Cultural Heritage."

2 See also the document related to the Convention for the Safeguarding of the Intangible Cultural Heritage (29 September–17 October 2003), the convention that established UNESCO's interest in intangible heritage: UNESCO, "Text."

3 McKitterick, Print, 47. By the mid 1990s, early modern manuscript studies was an established field. McGann's well-known *A Critique of Modern Textual Criticism* (1983) and McKenzie's often-cited *Bibliography and Sociology of Texts* (1986) both proposed theoretical frameworks that

emphasized social and historical contexts of production and reception instead of a manuscript/print divide, and many other studies followed.

4 English translation: Cerquiglini, *In Praise of the Variant.*

5 Knight, "Epilogue: Collated and Perfect," in *Bound to Read*, 180–1.

6 Irvine, *Making*, 243.

7 For a study on the tradition of the *rihla* in the Spanish context, see Paradela, *El otro laberinto*, esp. 1–15.

8 Montaner, "Anotaciones familiares," 177.

9 In addition to Montaner (cited above), see also Fuente Cornejo, "Las anotaciones"; Guillén Robles, *Catálogo*, nos. XC, LI and LXXVII; and Cervera Fras, "Descripción." On Morisco scribes and copyists, see López Morillas, "Copistas"; and, by the same author, "Más sobre los escribanos."

10 Flüeler, "Digital Manuscripts."

11 Cadoz et al., "Tangibility," 754.

12 Ishii et al., "Radical Atoms," 38.

13 For MIT, see for instance, ibid., 38–51.

14 Söffner, "What Production."

15 Gumbrecht, "Eat Your Fragment!," 320, 321.

16 As reported in an interview with Helen Solterer, "Performer le passé," 138.

17 Söffner, "What Production," 11.

Appendices

1 Transcription from Busto Cortina, "El Alkitāb de Çamarqandī: Edición."

Bibliography

MANUSCRIPT SOURCES

Bancroft Library, University of California, Berkeley (UCB)

115, *Amadís de Gaula*

Biblioteca del Monasterio de El Escorial, Madrid

b-IV-21, *Poema de Fernán González*

Biblioteca Nacional de España, Madrid (BNM)

590, *Chronica Adefonsi Imperatoris*
1279, *Chronica Adefonsi Imperatoris*
1505, *Chronica Adefonsi Imperatoris*
4871, *Libro de Samarqandi*
4937, Medical instructions and prescriptions
5223, "Rrogarya sacada del libro segovyano"
12915, Works of canon law; binding from which *Tristán de Leonís* fragments were extracted
20262/19, First folio found of the *Tristán de Leonís* manuscript
22644/1–51, Folios of the *Tristán de Leonís* manuscript extracted from 12915

Bibliothèque nationale de France, Paris (BnF)

Fonds espagnol, 12, *Mocedades de Rodrigo*
Fonds espagnol, 397, Mohamnad de Vera's treatise
Fonds latin, 5132, *Carmen Campidoctoris*

Cambridge University Library, Taylor-Schechter Genizah Collection

T-S H15.46, Halevi's poem containing the kharja containing *Pascua*

Bodleian Library, University of Oxford

Neubauer, Cat. Bodl. Hebr. 1970.1, copy of Halevi's *Diwan*
Neubauer, Cat. Bodl. Hebr. 1971, copy of Halevi's *Diwan*

Real Academia de la Historia, Madrid

11/9410 (olim T-13), *Ecomiendas de Alí*, Arabic-character version
11/9393 (olim S-1), *Ecomiendas de Alí*, Latin character version

Schocken Library, Jerusalem

37, Halevi's *Diwan*, derived from Oxford 1971

Private Collections

Rafael del Águila Goicoechea and Luisa Tejerina

Ocaña (1969), vol. 1, *Encomiendas de Alí*

The Library of the Late Georges Colin

"Colin" manuscript, unique copy of the *Uddat al-jalis* of Ali Ibn Bishri

PRINTED SOURCES

Abdel Haleem, M.A.S., ed. and trans. *The Qur'an*. Oxford: Oxford University Press, 2010.

Abu Haidar, Jarfer. "The *Kharja* of the *Muwaššaḥ* in a New Light." *Journal of Arabic Literature* 9 (1978): 1–13.

– . "The *Muwashshaḥāt* and the *Kharjas* Tell Their Own Story." *Al-Qanṭara* 26, no. 1 (2005): 43–98.

Albarracín Navarro, Joaquina. "Los manuscritos en árabe de Ocaña (Toledo)." In Viguera and Castillo Castillo, *Los manuscritos árabes*, 55–9.

Alfonso X. *Las siete partidas*. Edited by Gregorio López. Salamanca: Andrea de Portonariis, 1555.

Almbladh, Karin. "Ma laḏḏā lī sharbu r-rāḥi: An Arabic muwashshaḥa and its Hebrew muʿāraḍāt." *Orientalia Suecana* 41–2 (1992–3): 5–16.

Alonso, Dámaso. "Cancioncillas 'de amigo' mozárbes: Primavera temprana de la lírica europea." *Revista de Filología Española* 33 (1949): 297–349.

Alvar, Manuel, ed. *Libro de Apolonio*. 3 vols. Madrid: Fundación Juan March, 1976.

Alvar Ezqerra, Carlos, and José Manuel Lucía Megías. "Hacia el códice del *Tristán de Leonís*, cincuenta y nueve nuevos fragmentos manuscritos en la Biblioteca Nacional de Madrid." *Revista de Literatura Medieval* 11 (1999): 9–135.

Andrés de Uztarroz, Juan Francisco, and Diego J. Dormer. *Progresos de la historia en Aragon y vidas de sus cronistas: Desde que se instituyó este cargo hasta su extinción. Primera parte que comprende la biografía este de Gerónimo Zurita*. Saragossa: Impr. del Hospicio, 1878.

Ankersmit, Frank. R. "Presence and Myth." *History and Theory* 45, no. 3 (2006): 328–36.

Antonio, Nicolás. *Bibliotheca Hispana Vetus: Sive Hispani scriptores qui ab Octaviani Augusti aevo ad annum Christi 1500 flornerunt*. 2 vols. Madrid: Joachimuum de Ibarra, 1788.

Aquinas, Thomas. *Summa theologiae*. Vol. 40, *Superstition and Irreverence, 2a2ae. 92–100*. Edited by Thomas Franklin O'Meara and Michael John Duffy. Cambridge: Cambridge University Press, 2006.

Armistead, Samuel. "A Brief History of *Kharja* Studies." *Hispania* 70, no. 1 (1987): 8–15.

–. "Epic and Ballad: A Traditionalist Perspective." *Olifant* 8 (1981): 376–88.

–. "*La gesta de las Mocedades de Rodrigo*: Reflections of a Lost Epic Poem in the *Crónica de los reyes de Castilla* and the *Crónica general de 1344*." PhD diss., Princeton University, 1955. (*Dissertation Abstracts International* 15, 2198–9).

–, and James T. Monroe. "Beached Whales and Roaring Mice: Additional Remarks on the Hispano-Arabic Strophic Poetry." *La corónica* 13, no. 2 (1985): 206–42.

Asín Palacios, Miguel. *La espiritualidad de Algazel y su sentido cristiano*. Vol. 1. Madrid: Maestre, 1934.

Ayerbe-Chaux, Reinaldo. "Las *Islas Dotadas*: Texto y miniaturas del manuscrito de París, clave para su interpretación." In *Hispanic Studies in Honor of Alan D. Deyermond: A North American Tribute*, edited by John S. Miletich, 31–50. Madison: HSMS, 1996.

Bailey, Matthew, ed. *"Las mocedades de Rodrigo": Estudios críticos, manuscritos y edición*. London: King's College London, Centre for Late Antique & Medieval Studies, 1999.

–, ed. *"Las mocedades de Rodrigo": The Youthful Deeds of Rodrigo, the Cid*. Toronto: University of Toronto Press and Medieval Academy of America, 2007.

–. *The Poetics of Speech in the Medieval Spanish Epic*. Toronto: University of Toronto Press, 2010.

–, and Ryan Giles, eds. *Charlemagne and His Legend in Early Spanish Literature and Historiography*. Cambridge: D.S. Brewer, 2016.

Ballesteros-Beretta, Antonio. *Alfonso X el Sabio*. Barcelona: Salvat Editores, 1963.

Bamford, Heather. "A Romance *Kharja* in Context." *Journal of Medieval Iberian Studies* 5, no. 2 (2013): 169–83.

–. "Fragment as Phenomenon and Philological Subject: Two Cases of Chivalric Binding Fragments." *La corónica* 39, no. 2 (2011): 29–60.

–. "Ruins in Motion." *Postmedieval: A Journal of Medieval Cultural Studies* 4, no. 2 (2013): 192–204.

Barletta, Vincent. *Covert Gestures: Crypto-Islamic Literature as Cultural Practice in Early Modern Spain*. Minneapolis: University of Minnesota Press, 2005.

Barton, Simon, and Richard Fletcher, eds., *The World of El Cid: Chronicles of the Spanish Reconquest*. Manchester: Manchester University Press, 2000.

Benabu, Isaac. "Orthography in the Hispano-Romance Kharjas in Hebrew Characters." In Corriente and Sáenz-Badillos, *Poesía estrófica*, 31–42.

–. "Poetry in Two Languages: The *Kharja* and Its *Muwaššaḥ*." In *Iberia and Beyond: Hispanic Jews between Cultures: Proceedings of a Symposium to Mark the 500th Anniversary of the Expulsion of Spanish Jewry*, edited by Bernard D. Cooperman, 123–42. Newark: University of Delaware Press, 1998.

–, and Joseph Yahalom. "The Importance of the Genizah Manuscripts for the Establishment of the Text of the Hispano-Romance Kharjas in Hebrew Characters." *Romance Philology* 40, no. 2 (1986): 139–58.

Bernabé Pons, Luís F. "Interferencias entre el árabe y el romance en los textos coránicos aljamiados." In *Lenguas en contacto: El testimonio escrito*, edited by Pedro Bádenas de la Peña, Sofía Torallas Tovar, Eugenio R. Luján, and María Ángeles Gallego, 119–22. Madrid: CSIC, 2004.

–. "Taqiyya, niyya y el islam de los moriscos." *Al-Qantara* 34, no. 2 (2013): 491–527.

Bernías, Carmen. "El manuscrito de Paris: Las miniaturas." In *Libro del caballero Zifar: Codice de París*, edited by Francisco Rico, 193–244. Barcelona: Moleiro Editor, 1996.

Bertoni, Giulio. *Il "Cantare del Cid": Introduzione, versione, note, con due appendici*. Bari: Laterza & Figli, 1912.

Blair, Ann. "Humanist Methods in Natural Philosophy: The Commonplace Book." *Journal of the History of Ideas* 53, no. 4 (1992): 541–51.

Blanchot, Maurice. *The Infinite Conversation*. Translated by Susan Hanson. Minneapolis: University of Minnesota Press, 1993.

Bloch, Howard R. "New Philology and Old French." *Speculum* 65, no. 1 (1990): 38–58.

Boffey, Julia. "From Manuscript to Modern Text." In *A Companion to Medieval English Literature and Culture, c.1350–c.1500*, edited by Peter Brown, 107–22. Malden, MA: Blackwell, 2007.

–, and John Thompson. "Anthologies and Miscellanies: Production and Choice of Texts." In *Book Production and Publishing in Britain 1375–1475*, edited by Jeremy Griffiths and Derek Pearsall, 279–315. Cambridge: Cambridge University Press, 1989.

Bonaventure, Saint. *Commentarius in primum librum Sententiarum magistri Petri Lombardi, Opera omnia*. Quaracchi: Ex Typographia Collegi S. Bonaventurae, 1882.

Bonilla y San Martín, Adolfo. "Fragmento de un *Tristán* castellano del siglo XIV." In *Anales de la literatura española (años 1900–1904)*, edited by Adolfo Bonilla y San Martín, 25–9. Madrid: Tello, 1904.

–, ed. "Reproducción de un fragmento de un *Tristán* castellano del siglo XIV." *Libro del esforçado cauallero don Tristan de Leonis y de sus grandes fechos en armas, Valladolid, 1501*, edited by Adolfo Bonilla y San Martín, 318–20. Madrid: Sociedad de Bibliófilos Madrileños, 1912.

Bonner, Campbell. *Studies in Magical Amulets: Chiefly Graeco-Egyptian*. Ann Arbor: University of Michigan Press, 1950.

Borrás Gualis, Gonzalo M., ed. *Mudéjar: El legado andalusí en la cultura española*. Saragossa: Universidad de Zaragoza, 2010. Catalogue of exhibition shown at the Paraninfo, Universidad de Zaragoza, 6 October 2010 to 9 January 2011.

Bossong, Georg. *Poesía en convivencia: Estudios sobre la lírica árabe, hebrea, y romance en la España de las tres religiones*. 4th ed. Bibliotheca Arabo-Romanica et Islamica. Girón: Ediciones TREA, 2010.

Bouras, Karima. "La *Wasiyya* de Ali del manuscrito aljamiado 614 de la Bibliothèque nationale d'Algérie (estudio, edición y materiales)." PhD diss., Universidad Complutese de Madrid, 2007.

Bouza, Fernando. *Communication, Knowledge, and Memory in Early Modern Spain*. Philadelphia: University of Pennsylvania Press, 2004.

–. *Corre manuscrito: Una historia cultural del Siglo de Oro*. Madrid: Marcial Pons, Historia, 2001.

Brann, Ross. *The Compunctious Poet: Cultural Ambiguity and Hebrew Poetry in Muslim Spain*. Baltimore: Johns Hopkins University Press, 1991.

Brody, Heinrich, ed. *Dīwān des Abū-l-Ḥasan Jehuda ha-Levi* [Yehūdā halevī: The diwan]. 4 vols. Schriften des Vereins Mekize Nirdamim, 1894–1930. Reprinted with introduction, bibliography, additions, and indices by A.M. Habermann. Fransborough: Gregg International, 1971.

Brown, Catherine. "The Relics of Menéndez Pidal: Mourning and Melancholia in Hispanomedieval Studies." *La corónica* 24, no. 1 (1995): 15–41.

Brownrigg, Linda L., and Margaret M. Smith, *Interpreting and Collecting Fragments of Medieval Books*. Los Altos Hills, CA: Anderson-Lovelace, 1998.

Bühler, Curt F. "Prayers and Charms in Certain Medieval English Scrolls." *Speculum* 39, no. 2 (1964): 270–8.

[Burgos, Juan de, ed.] *El libro del esforcado cauallero don* Tristán de Leonis *y de sus grandes fechos en armas*. Valladolid: Juan de Burgos, 1501.

Burman, Thomas E. *Reading the Qur'an in Latin Christendom, 1140–1560*. Philadelphia: University of Pennsylvania Press, 2007.

Burón Castro, Taurino. *Manual para la recuperación de fragmentos de manuscritos, impresos y otros documentos especiales*. León: T. Burón, 2002.

Busby, Keith, ed. *Towards a Synthesis? Essays on the New Philology*. Amsterdam: Rodopi, 1993.

Busto Cortina, Juan Carlos. "El Alkitab de Çamarqandí." In Mateos Paramio and Villaverde Amieva, *Memoria de los Moriscos*, 190–3.

——. "El Alkitāb de Çamarqandī: Edición del ms. aljamiado 4871 de la BNM, con un vocabulario completo y un estudio de algunos cuentos que en él aparecen." PhD diss., Universidad de Oviedo, 1992. 3 microfilms. http://coteam.herokuapp.com/corpus.html.

Cadoz, Claude, Annie Luciani, Jérôme Villeneuve, Alexandros Kontogeorgakopoulos, and Iannis Zannos. "Tangibility, Presence, Materiality, Reality in Artistic Creation with Digital Technology." Paper presented at the 40th International Computer Music Conference/11th Sound and Music Computing Conference, Athens, Greece, 14–20 September 2014. Accessed 9 December 2017. https://hal.archives-ouvertes.fr/hal-01085958.

Camille, Michael. *Mirror in Parchment: The Luttrell Psalter and the Making of Medieval England*. Chicago: University of Chicago Press, 1998.

Canaan, Tewfik. "The Decipherment of Arabic Talismans." In *Magic and Divination in Early Islam*, edited by Emilie Savage-Smith, 125–78. Aldershot: Ashgate/Variorum, 2004.

Cardaillac-Hermosilla, Yvette. *La magie en Espagne: Morisques et vieux chrétiens aux XVIe et XVIIe siècles*. Zaghouan: Fondation Temini pour la Recherche Scientifique et l'Information (FTERSI), 1996.

Carmi, T., ed. and trans. *The Penguin Book of Hebrew Verse*. New York: Viking Press, 1981.

Carmody, Francis. *Franco-Italian Sources of the "Roncesvalles."* Publications of the Institute of French Studies 50. New York: Columbia University, 1934.

Carreter, Fernando Lázaro. *Diccionario de términos filológicos*. Madrid: Gredos, 1953.

Casado Quintanilla, Blas. "De la escritura de Albalaes a la Humanística, un paréntesis en la historia de la escritura." In *II Jornadas científicas sobre documentación de la Corona de Castilla (siglos XIII–XV)*, edited by Juan Carlos Galende Díaz, 11–40. Madrid: Universidad Complutense de Madrid, 2003.

Casassas Canals, Xavier. "La literatura islámica castellana: Siglos XIII–XVII (Catálogo de textos de mudéjares y moriscos escritos en caracteres latinos)." *Al-Andalus Magreb* 16 (2009): 89–113.

Castañega, Fray Martín de. *Tratado de las supersticiones y hechizerias y de la posibilidad y remedio dellas*. Edited by Juan Robert Muro Abad. Logroño: Instituto de Estudios Riojanos, 1994.

Cerquiglini, Bernard. *Éloge de la variante: Histoire critique de la philologie*. Paris: Seuil, 1989.

–. *In Praise of the Variant: A Critical History of Philology*. Translated by Betsy Wing. Baltimore: Johns Hopkins University Press, 1999.

Cervera Fras, María José. "Descripción de los manuscritos mudéjares de Calanda (Teruel)." In *Homenaje a la profesora emérita María Luisa Ledesma Rubio*, edited by Maria Luisa Ledesma Rubio, 165–87. Saragossa: Universidad de Zaragoza, 1993.

–. "Palabras árabes en el artesonado del Salón del Trono de los Reyes Católicos." In *La Aljafería*, edited by Antonio Beltrán Martínez, 2:447–51. Saragossa: Cortes de Aragón, 1998.

Chartier, Roger. "Esbozo de una genealogía de la 'función-autor.'" *Artefilosofia Ouro Preto* 1 (2006): 187–98.

–. *Order of Books: Readers, Authors, and Libraries in Europe between the Fourteenth and Eighteenth Centuries*. Stanford: Stanford University Press, 1994.

Chorpenning, Joseph F. "Loss of Innocence, Descent into Hell, and Cannibalism: Romance Archetypes and Narrative Unity in 'Carcel de Amor.'" *Modern Language Review* 87, no. 2 (1992): 343–51.

Christie's. "An Almost Complete Kufic Qur'an: North Africa or Near East, Early 10th Century." Lot 10/Sale 7428. 23 October 2007, London, King Street. Accessed 27 January 2017. http://www.christies.com/LotFinder/lot_details.aspx?intObjectID=4979407.

–. "Qur'an: Signed Yahya bin Muhammad ibn 'Umar, Probably Mesopotamia, Dated 17 Ramadan AH 599/6 June 1203 AD." Lot 20/Sale 7428. 23 October 2007. Accessed 27 January 2017. http://www.christies.com/LotFinder/lot_details.aspx?intObjectID=4979417.

Ciruelo, Pedro. *Reprovación de las supersticiones y hechicerías: Libro muy necesario [a todos los buenos cristianos, [1538]. Agora de nuevo hechos ciertos apuntamientos que van con una X señalados*. Salamanca: Pedro de Castro, 1541.

Clark, James. "Print and Pre-Reformation Religion: The Benedictines and the Press, c. 1470–c. 1550." In *The Uses of Script and Print, 1300–1700*, edited by Julia Crick and Alexandra Walsham, 71–92. Cambridge: Cambridge University Press, 2004.Clemens, Raymond and Timothy Graham, eds. *Introduction to Manuscript Studies*. Ithaca: Cornell University Press, 2007.

Cole, Peter. *The Dream of the Poem: Hebrew Poetry from Muslim and Christian Spain, 950–1492*. Princeton: Princeton University Press, 2007.

–, and Adina Hoffman. *Sacred Trash: The Lost and Found World of the Cairo Geniza*. New York: Nextbook, 2011.

Compton, Linda Fish. *Andalusian Lyrical Poetry and Old Spanish Love Songs: The Muwashshaḥ and Its Kharja*. New York: New York University Press, 1976.

Cormack, Bradin, and Carla Mazzio. *Book Use, Book Theory, 1500–1700*. Chicago: University of Chicago Library, 2005.

Corriente, Federico. "By No Means '*jarchas mozárabes*.'" *Romance Philology* 1, no. 1 (1996): 46–61.

–. *Poesía dialectal árabe y romance en Alandalús: Cejeles y xarajāt de muwaššaḥāt*. Biblioteca románica hispánica 407. Madrid: Gredos, 1997.

–. *Romania arábica: Tres cuestiones básicas. Arabismos, "mozárabe" y "jarchas."* Madrid: Editorial Trotta, 2008.

–. "The *Kharjas*: An Updated Survey of Theories, Texts, and Their Interpretation." *Romance Philology* 63, no. 1 (2009): 109–29.

Corriente, Federico, and Angel Saénz-Badillos. "A vueltas con las xarajāt con texto romance de la serie hebrea." *Vox Romanica* 67 (2008): 169–82.

–. "Review Essay of Bossong, *Poesía en convivencia: Estudios sobre la lírica árabe, hebrea y romance en la España de las tres religiones* [2010]." *La corónica* 40, no. 1 (2011): 301–24.

Cuesta Torre, María Luzdivina. "Adaptación, refundición e imitación: De la materia artúrica a los libros de caballerías." *Revista de poética medieval* 1 (1997): 35–70.

–. "La transmisión textual de don Tristán de Leonís." *Revista de literatura medieval* 5 (1993): 63–94.

–, ed. *Tristán de Leonís*: *Valladolid, Juan de Burgos 1501*. Alcalá de Henares: Centro de Estudios Cervantinos, 1999.

Cummings, Mike. "Beinecke Library acquires 'treasure trove' of medieval manuscripts from a famed 'book breaker.'" *Yale News*, 15 November 2015. https://news.yale.edu/2015/11/15/beinecke-library-acquires-treasure-trove-medieval-manuscripts-famed-book-breaker.

Dagenais, John. *The Ethics of Reading in Manuscript Culture: Glossing the "Libro de buen amor."* Princeton: Princeton University Press, 1994.

Declercq, Georges. "Introduction: *Codices rescripti* in the Early Medieval West." In *Early Medieval Palimpsests*, Bibliologia: Elementa ad librorum studia pertinentia 26, edited by Georges Declercq, 7–22. Turnhout: Brepols, 2007.

De Hamel, Christopher. *Cutting Up Manuscripts for Pleasure and Profit*. The 1995 Sol M. Malkin Lecture in Bibliography. Charlottesville: Book Arts Press, 1996.

–. *Scribes and Illuminators*. Toronto: University of Toronto Press, 1992.

Delatte, Armand, and Philippe Derchain. *Les intailles magiques gréco-égyptiennes*. Paris: Bibliothèque nationale de France, 1964.

De Looze, Lawrence. *Manuscript Diversity, Meaning, and Variance in Juan Manuel's "El Conde Lucanor."* Toronto: University of Toronto Press, 2006.

Demelas, Delphine. "Keep the Fragments Alive: Manuscript Rescue Practices. An Example of the 18th Century." Paper presented at the International Congress on Medieval Studies, Kalamazoo, Michigan, 12–15 May 2016. Accessed 27 January 2017. https://www.academia.edu/16984731/Keep_the_fragments_alive._Manuscript_rescue_practices_an_example_of_the_18th_century.

Deyermond, Alan. *Epic Poetry and the Clergy: Studies on the "Mocedades de Rodrigo."* London: Tamesis, 1969.

–. "La autoría de las Mocedades de Rodrigo: Un replanteamiento." In Bailey, *"Las mocedades de Rodrigo"* (1999), 1–15.

–. *La literatura perdida de la Edad Media castellana: Catálogo y estudio*. Vol. 1, *Épica y romances*. Salamanca: Ediciones Universidad de Salamanca, 1995.

–. "The Lost Genre of Medieval Spanish Literature." *Hispanic Review* 43 (1975): 231–59.

–. "The Problem of Lost Epics: Evidence and Criteria." In *"Al que en buen hora naçio": Essays on the Spanish Epic and Ballad in Honour of Colin Smith*, edited by Brian Powell, Geoffrey West, and Dorothy Severin, 27–43. Modern Humanities Research Association, Hispanic Studies TRAC 12. Liverpool: Liverpool University Press, 1996.

Digital Scriptorium. Entry for UCB, MS 115. Accessed 27 January 2017. http://vm136.lib.berkeley.edu/BANC/digitalscriptorium/.

Dionisotti, A.C., "On Fragments in Classical Scholarship." In Most, *Collecting Fragments*, 1–33.

Divizia, Paolo. "Appunti di stemmatica comparata." *Studi e Problemi di Critica Testuale* 78 (2009): 29–48.

–. "Texts and Transmission in Late Medieval and Early Renaissance Italian Multi-text Codices." In *The Dynamics of the Medieval Manuscript: Text Collections from a European Perspective (Utrecht, 25–28 April 2013)*, edited by Bart Besamusca, Matthias Meyer, Karen Pratt, and Ad Putter, 101–10. Göttingen: Vandenhoeck & Ruprecht, 2015. https://www.academia.edu/3210930/Texts_and_Transmission_in_Late_Medieval_and_Early_Renaissance_Italian_Multi-text_Codices

–. "Volgarizzamenti due-trecenteschi da Cicerone e Aristotele in un codice poco noto (Kórnik, Polska Akademia Nauk, Biblioteka Kórnicka, 633)." *Italia Medioevale e Umanistica* 55 (2014): 1–31.

Dols, Michael. "The Theory of Magic in Healing." In *Magic and Divination in Early Islam*, edited by Emilie Savage-Smith, 87–101. Aldershot: Ashgate/ Variorum, 2004.

Domanska, Ewa. "Let the Dead Bury the Living: Daniel Libeskind's Monumental Counterhistory." In *History of Historiography Reconsidered: Essays in Honor of Georg G. Iggers*, edited by Edward Wang, Franz L. Fillafer, and Georg G. Iggers, 437–54. New York: Berghahn Books, 2007.

–. "The Material Presence of the Past." *History and Theory* 45, no. 3 (2006): 337–48.

Donahue, Christopher. "Notes on the Illumination of Espagnol 36, BnF (*Libro del cauallero Çifar*)." *Hispanofilia* 150 (2007): 1–14.

El-Bourdrari, Hassan. "Magie: Islam. Positions de la magie dans la pensée musulmane." In *Dictionnaire critique de l'ésotérisme*, edited by Jean Servier, 772a–775b. Paris: Presses Universitaires de France, 1998.

Elinson, Alexander. "Contrapuntal Composition in a Muwashshaḥ Family, or Variations on a Panegyric Theme." *Medieval Encounters* 7 (2001): 174–96.

Erwin, Micah. "Archivist Seeks Help in Identifying Website Material." *Ransom Center Magazine*, 26 July 2012. Accessed 27 January 2017. http://blog.hrc.utexas.edu/2012/07/26/manuscript-waste/.

Escobar, Ángel, ed. *El palimpsesto grecolatino como fenómeno librario y textual*. Saragossa: Institución Fernando el Católico, 2006.

Espòsito, Antonio. "Dismemberment of Things Past: Fixing the *jarchas*." *La corónica* 24, no. 1 (1995): 4–14.

–. "The Monkey in the *jarcha*: Tradition and Canonicity in the Early Iberian Lyric." *Journal of Medieval and Early Modern Studies* 30, no. 3 (2000): 463–77.

Faulhaber, Charles. "Neo-Traditionalism, Formulism, Individualism, and Recent Studies on the Spanish Epic." *Romance Philology* 30 (1976–7): 83–101.

Fleisher, Ezra. "Additional Data Concerning the Poetry of R. El'azar Chalfon." In *Occident and Orient: A Tribute to the Memory of Alexander Scheiber*, edited by Robert Dan, 137–53. Leiden: Brill, 1988.

Flórez, Henrique, ed. *Viage de Ambrosio de Morales por orden del Rey d. Phelipe II a los Reynos de Leon y Galicia y principado de Asturias*. Madrid: Antonio Marin, (1572) 1765.

Flüeler, Christoph. "Digital Manuscripts as Critical Edition." *Schoenberg Institute for Manuscript Studies* (blog), University of Pennsylvania. 30 June 2015. https://schoenberginstitute.org/2015/06/30/digital-manuscripts-as-critical-edition/.

Fonseca, Gregorio. *Sumario de la relación y ejercicio espiritual sacado y declarado por el Mancebo de Arévalo en nuestra lengua castellana*. Madrid: Fundación Ramón Menéndez Pidal, 2002.

Franchini, Enzo. "El fragmento épico de *Roncesvalles*: Estado de la cuestión y nuevas observaciones." *La corónica* 24, no. 1 (1995): 90–110.

Frank, Daniel. "Karaite Ritual." In *Judaism in Practice: From the Middle Ages through the Early Modern Period*, edited by Lawrence Fine, 248–64. Princeton: Princeton University Press, 2001).

Frazer, James G., and Robert Fraser. *The Golden Bough: A Study in Magic and Religion*. Oxford: Oxford University Press, 1998.

Fuente Cornejo, Toribio. "Las anotaciones en caracteres latinos de las guardas del ms. Aljamiado-morisco J. XIII." *Sharq Al-Andalus* 8 (1991): 135–52.

Funes, Leonardo, and Felipe Tenenbaum, eds. *Mocedades de Rodrigo: Estudio y edición de los tres estados del texto*. Colección Tamesis, Serie B: Textos 45. Woodbridge: Tamesis, 2004.

Galmés de Fuentes, Álvaro. *Los manuscritos aljamiado-moriscos de la Biblioteca de la Real Academia de la Historia (legado Pascual de Gayangos)*. Madrid: Real Academia de la Historia, 1998.

García Gómez, Emilio. *Las jarchas romances de la serie árabe en su marco*. Madrid: Sociedad de estudios y publicaciones, 1965.

–. "Métrica de la moaxaja y métrica española: Aplicación de un nuevo método de medición completa al 'Gaiš' de Ben al-Jaṭīb.'" *Al-Andalus* 39, no. 1 (1974): 1–256.

Garnier, François. *La guerre au Moyen Âge: XIe–XVe siècle: L'histoire par les documents iconographiques*. Poitiers: INRDP, CRDP-poitiers, 1976.

–. *La langage de l'image au Moyen Âge*. Vol. 1, *Signification et symbolique*; Vol. 2, *Grammaire des gestes*. Paris: Léopard d'Or, 1982–9.

Gerli, E. Michael. "Leriano's Libation: Notes on the *Cancionero* Lyric, *Ars moriendi*, and the Probable Debt to Boccaccio." *MLN* 96, no. 2 (1981): 414–20.

–. "The *Ordo commendationis animae* and the Cid Poet." *MLN* 95, no. 2 (1980): 436–41.

Gil, Juan, ed. "Prefatio de Almeria." In *Chronica Hispana saeculi XII*, 1:251–67. Corpus Christianorum, Continuatio Mediaevalis 71. Turnholt: Brepols, 1990.

Giles, Ryan. *Inscribed Power: Amulets and Magic and Early Spain*. Toronto: University of Toronto Press, 2017.

Gillespie, Alexandra. *Print Culture and the Medieval Author: Chaucer, Lydgate, and Their Books, 1473–1557*. Oxford English Monographs. Oxford: Oxford University Press, 2009.

Glickman, Mark. *Sacred Treasure – The Cairo Genizah: The Amazing Discoveries of Forgotten Jewish History in an Egyptian Synagogue Attic*. Woodstock, VT: Jewish Lights, 2011.

Goldberg, Harriet. "Cannibalism in Iberian Narrative: The Dark Side of Gastronomy." *Bulletin of Hispanic Studies* 1 (1997): 107–22.

Gómez Bravo, Ana M. *Textual Agency: Writing Culture and Social Networks in Fifteenth-Century Spain*. Toronto: University of Toronto Press, 2013.

Gómez Moreno, Ángel. "La poesía épica y de clerecía medievales." In *Historia crítica de la literatura hispánica*, edited by Juan Ignacio Ferreras, Carlos Alvar, and Ángel Gómez Moreno, 2:71–98. Madrid: Taurus, 1988.

Gómez Redondo, Fernando. *Historia de la prosa medieval castellana: El desarrollo de los géneros. La ficción caballeresca y el orden religioso*. Crítica y Estudios Literarios 2. Madrid: Cátedra, 1999.

González Delgado, R. "Motivos clásicos en el *Cantar de Roncesvalles* y en la gesta del abad don Juan de Montemayor." *Revista Portuguesa de Humanidades* 15, no. 2 (2011): 47–58.

Gorton, Theodor. "The Metre of Ibn Quzmān: A 'Classical' Approach." *Journal of Arabic Literature* 6 (1975): 1–29.

Greenia, George, ed. "Forum: Letters on 'Manuscript Culture in Medieval Spain.'" *La corónica* 27, no. 1 (1998): 123–247.

–, ed. "Forum: Letters and Responses on 'Manuscript Culture in Medieval Spain.'" *La corónica* 27, no. 2 (1998): 171–232.

Greetham, David. "Who's In, Who's Out: The Cultural Politics of Archival Exclusion." *Studies in the Literary Imagination* 32, no. 1 (1999): 1–28.

Guillén Robles, Francisco. *Catálogo de los manuscritos árabes existentes en la Biblioteca Nacional de Madrid*. Madrid: Imprenta y Fundación de M. Tello, 1889.

Gumbrecht, Hans Ulrich. "Eat Your Fragment! About Imagination and the Restitution of Texts." In Most, *Collecting fragments*, 315–27.

–. *The Powers of Philology: Dynamics of Textual Scholarship*. Urbana: University of Illinois Press, 2003.

–. "Presence Achieved in Language." *History and Theory* 45, no. 3 (2006): 317–27.

–. *Production of Presence: What Meaning Cannot Convey*. Stanford: Stanford University Press, 2004.

–. *1945: Latency as Origin of the Present*. Stanford: Stanford University Press, 2012.

Gwara, Joseph. "The *Poema de Fernán González*, the Villamartín Tile and the Diffusion of *cuaderna vía* Verse." In *Historicist Essays on Hispano-Medieval Narrative: In Memory of Roger M. Walker*, edited by Barry Taylor and Geoffrey West, 115–34. London: Modern Humanities Research Association, 2004.

Ha-Levi, Yehuda. *The Kuzari*. Edited by D.H. Baneth and H. Ben Shammai. Jerusalem: Magnes Press, 1977.

–. *Yehudah ha-Levi: Poemas*. Edited by Angel Sáenz-Badillos and Judit Targarona Borrás. Madrid: Clásicos Alfaguara, 1994.

Halkin, Hillel. *Yehuda Halevi*. New York: Nextbook/Schocken, 2010.

Hamilton, Michelle. "Hispanism and Sephardic Studies." *Journal of Medieval Iberian Studies* 1, no. 2 (2009): 179–94.

Harney, Michael, ed. *The Epic of the Cid, with Related Texts*. Indianapolis: Hackett, 2011.

Harvey, Leonard Patrick. "The Literary Culture of the Moriscos (1492–1609): A Study Based on the Extant Manuscripts in Arabic and Aljamía." PhD diss., Magdalen College, Oxford, 1958.

–. "The Mancebo de Arévalo and his Treatises on Islamic Faith and Practice." *Journal of Islamic Studies* 10, no. 3 (1999): 249–76.

Havens, Earle. *Commonplace Books: A History of Manuscripts and Printed Books from Antiquity to the Twentieth Century*. New Haven: Beinecke Rare Book and Manuscript Library, 2001.

Hernando Pérez, J. *Hispano Diego García en la interpretacion del ostrakon de Villamartin sobre el "Poema de Fernán González."* Burgos: Facultad de Teología del Norte de España, 1995.

–. "Nuevos datos para el estudio del *Poema de Fernán González*." *Boletín de la Real Academia Española* 66, no. 237 (1986): 135–52.

Higashi, Alejandro. "La *emendatio ope ingenii* y un poema latino sobre el Cid." *Incipit* 15 (1995): 23–44.

Hill, Leslie. *Maurice Blanchot and Fragmentary Writing: A Change of Epoch*. New York: Continuum, 2012.

Hispania Epigraphica Online Database. "Roman Inscriptions from the Iberian Peninsula." http://eda-bea.es/.

Hitchcock, Richard. "The Fate of the *Kharjas*: A Survey of Recent Publications." *Bulletin for the British Society for Middle Eastern Studies* 12 (1985): 172–90.

–. "Some Doubts about the Reconstruction of the *Kharjas*." *Bulletin of Hispanic Studies* 50 (1973): 109–19.

Hofman Vannus, Iris. "Los manuscritos de Ocaña: Paradigma de peripecias y peculiaridades de la memoria escrita." In *Colecciones madrileñas: Transmisiones moriscas. Actas: Jornadas sobre manuscritos árabes*, edited by Nuria Martínez de Castilla, José Luis Garrot, Ana Isabel Beneyto, and María Jesús Viguera, 63–76. Anaquel de Estudios Árabes Anejos 1. Madrid: Universidad Complutense, 2008.

Hook, David. "Arthur Goes Global: Arthurian Material in Hispanic and Portuguese America and Asia." In *The Arthur of the Iberians: The Arthurian Legends in the Spanish and Portuguese Worlds*, edited by David Hook, 382–407. Cardiff: University of Wales Press, 2015.

–, and Antonia Long. "Reflexiones sobre la estructura de las *Mocedades de Rodrigo*." In Bailey, "*Las mocedades de Rodrigo*" (1999), 53–67.

Horrent, Jules. *Historia y poesía en torno al "Cantar del Cid."* Barcelona: Ariel, 1973.

–. *Roncesvalles: Étude sur le fragment de cantar de gesta conservé à l'Archivo de Navarra (Pampelune)*. Paris: Les Belles Lettres, 1951.

Howsam, Leslie. "The Practice of Book and Print Culture: Sources, Methods, Readings." In *The Perils of Print Culture: Book, Print, and Publishing History in Theory and Practice*, edited by Eve Patten and Jason McElligott, 17–34. New York: Palgrave, 2014.

Hult, David F. *Self-Fulfilling Prophecies: Readership and Authority in the First "Roman de la Rose."* Cambridge: Cambridge University Press, 1986.

Hulvey, Monique. "Not So Marginal: Manuscript Annotations in the Folger Incunabula." *Papers of the Bibliographical Society of America* 92 (1998): 159–76.

Ibn Quzman. *El cancionero hispanoarabe*. Edited by Federico Corriente. Madrid: Editora Nacional, 1984.

–. *Gramática, métrica y texto del cancionero hispanoárabe de Aban Quzman*. Edited by Federico Corriente. Madrid: Instituto Hispano-Árabe de Cultura, 1980.

Iça de Gebir. "Suma de los principales mandamientos y devedamientos de la ley y çunna." In *Memorial histórico español: Colección de documentos, opúsculos y antigüedades*, edited by Pascual de Gayangos, 5:247–417. Madrid: Real Academia de la Historia, 1853.

Irvine, Martin. *The Making of Textual Culture: "Grammatica" and Literary Theory, 350–1100*. Cambridge: Cambridge University Press, 1994.

Isaac ben Moses of Vienna. *Sefer Or Zarua*. Vol. 2. Zhitomir: Shapiro, 1862.

Ishii, Hiroshi, Dávid Lakatos, Leonardo Bonanni, and Jean-Baptiste Labrune. "Radical Atoms: Beyond Tangible Bits, toward Transformable Materials." *Interactions* 19, no. 1 (January 2012): 38–51.

Isidore of Seville. *Etymologiae*. Edited by W.M. Lindsay. Oxford: Clarendon, 1911.

Janowitz, Anne. "The Romantic Fragment." In *A Companion to Romanticism*, edited by Duncan Wu, 442–51. Oxford, Blackwell, 1998.

Jardine, Lisa, and Anthony Grafton. "'Studied for Action': How Gabriel Harvey Read His Livy." *Past and Present* 129 (1990): 30–78.

Jones, Alan. *Romance "Kharjas" in Andalusian Arabic* Muwaššaḥ *Poetry: A Paleographic Analysis*. Oxford Oriental Institute Monographs 9. London: Ithaca Press, 1988.

–. "Romance Scansion and the *Muwashshaḥāt*: An Emperor's New Clothes?" *Journal of Arabic Literature* 11 (1980): 36–55.

–. *Uddat al-jalīs of Alī ibn Bishrī: An Anthology of Andalusian Arabic Muwaššaḥāt*. Cambridge: Trustees of the E.J.W. Gibb Memorial, 1992.

Jones, Christopher. "Ten Dedications 'To the gods and goddesses' and the Antonine Plague." *Journal of Roman Archaeology* 18 (2005): 293–301.

Ker, Neil Ripley. *Fragments of Medieval Manuscripts Used as Pastedowns in Oxford Bindings: With a Survey of Oxford Binding c. 1515–1620*. Oxford: Printed for the Oxford Bibliographical Society by A.T. Broome, 1954.

Knight, Jeffrey T. *Bound to Read: Compilations, Collections, and the Making of Renaissance Literature*. Philadelphia: University of Pennsylvania Press, 2013.

Labarta, Ana, ed. *Libro de los dichos maravillosos: Misceláneo morisco de magia y adivinación*. Madrid: Consejo Superior de Investigaciones Científicas, 1993.

–. "Supersticiones moriscas." *Awraq* 5–6 (1982–3): 161–90.

Lacoue-Labarthe, Philippe, and Jean-Luc Nancy. *The Literary Absolute: The Theory of Literature in German Romanticism*. Albany: State University of New York Press, 1988.

Lara, Eva, and Alberto Montaner, eds. *Señales, portentos y demonios: La magia en la literatura española del renacimiento*. Salamanca: SEMYR, 2014.

Latham, Derek. "New Light on the Scansion of an Old Andalusian *Muwaššaḥ*." *Journal of Semitic Studies* 27 (1982): 61–75.

–. "The Prosody of an Andalusian *Muwaššaḥ* Re-examined." In *Arabian and Islamic Studies: Articles Presented to R.B. Serjeant*, edited by R.I. Bidwell and G.R. Smith, 86–99. London: Longmans, 1983.

Lehnardt, Andreas, and Judith Olszowy, eds., *Books within Books: New Discoveries in Old Book Bindings*. Leiden: Brill, 2014.

Lerer, Seth. "Medieval English Literature and the Idea of the Anthology." *PMLA* 118, no. 5 (2003): 1251–67.López Baralt, Luce. *La literatura secreta de los últimos musulmanes de España*. Madrid: Editorial Trotta, 2009.

López Morillas, Consuelo. "Copistas y escribanos moriscos." In *Actes du II Symposium International du CIEM: Religion, identité et sources documentaires sur les morisques andalous*, edited by Abdeljelil Temimi, 71–8. Tunis: Institut Supérieur de Documentation, 1984.

–. "Más sobre los escribanos moriscos." In *La littérature aljamiado-morisque: Hybridisme linguistique et univers discursif*, edited by Abdeljelil Temimi, 105–7. Tunis: Centre de recherches en bibliothéconomie et sciences de l'information, 1986.

Lord, Beth. "From the Document to the Monument: Museums and the Philosophy of History." In *Museum Revolutions: How Museums Change and*

Are Changed, edited by Simon J. Knell, Suzanne Macleod, and Sheila E.R. Watson, 355–66. London: Routledge, 2007.

Love, Harold. *Scribal Publication in Seventeenth-Century England*. Oxford: Clarendon Press, 1993.

Lowe, Elias A. *Palaeographical Papers, 1907–1965*. Edited by Ludwig Bieler. 2 vols. Oxford: Clarendon Press, 1972.

Lucía Megías, José Manuel, ed. *Antología de libros de caballerías castellanos*. Alcalá de Henares: Centro de Estudios Cervantinos, 2001.

–. "Los fragmentos del *Tristán* de la Biblioteca Nacional: Los tesoros de las encuadernaciones." In *Amadís de Gaula, 1508: Quinientos años de libros de caballerías*, 47–9. Madrid: Biblioteca Nacional de España, Sociedad Estatal de Conmemoraciones Culturales, 2008.

–. "El *Tristán de Leonís* castellano: Análisis de las miniaturas del códice BNM ms. 22.644." *eHumanista: Journal of Iberian Studies* 5 (2005): 1–47.

–. "Literatura caballeresca catalana: De los testimonios a la interpretación (un ensayo de crítica ecdótica)." *Caplletra: Revista Internacional de Filología* 39 (2005): 231–56.

–, Emma Cadalhia, and José María Moreno, eds. *Amadís de Gaula, 1508: Quinientos años de libros de caballerías*. Madrid: Biblioteca Nacional de España, 2008.

Luck, Georg. *Arcana mundi: Magic and the Occult in the Greek and Roman Worlds. A Collection of Ancient Texts*. Baltimore: Johns Hopkins University Press, 1985.

Malinowski, Bronislaw. "Magic, Science and Religion." In *Magic, Science and Religion: And Other Essays*, 1–71. Glencoe, IL: The Free Press, 1948.

Mallette, Karla. *European Modernity and the Arab Mediterranean: Toward a New Philology and a Counter-Orientalism*. Philadelphia: University of Pennsylvania Press, 2010.

–. "Misunderstood." *New Literary History* 34, no. 4 (2003): 677–97.

Mancebo de Arévalo. *Tratado (Tafsira) del Mancebo de Arévalo*. Edited by María Teresa Narváez. Madrid: Trotta, 2003.

Martínez de Castilla Muñoz, Nuria. *Una biblioteca morisca entre dos tapas*. Saragossa: Instituto de Estudios Islámicos y del Oriente Próximo, 2010.

–. "Manuscritos musulmanes misceláneos y facticios del Aragón del siglo XVI." In *Manuscritos para comunicar culturas*, edited by Mostafa Ammadi, Francisco Vidal-Castro, and María Jesús Viguera Molins, 141–50. Bouregreg: Casablanca, Universidad Hassan II-Aïn Chock, Faculté des Lettres et des Sciences Humaines, 2013.

Martínez Ruiz, Juan. *Medicina, farmacopea y magia en el "Misceláneo de Salomón": Texto árabe, glosas aljamiadas y glosario*. Granada: Universidad de Granada, 1987.

–, and Joaquina Albarracín Navarro, "Libros árabes, aljamiado mudéjares y bilingües descubiertos en Ocaña (Toledo)." *Revista de Filología Española* 55, no. 1 (1972): 63–6.

Mateos Paramio, Alfredo. "Palabras más perdurables que las casas." In Mateos Paramio and Villaverde Amieva, *Memoria de los Moriscos*, 17–24.

–, and Juan Carlos Villaverde Amieva, eds. *Memoria de los Moriscos: Escritos y relatos de una diáspora cultural*. Madrid: Biblioteca Nacional and Sociedad Estatal de Conmemoraciones Culturales, 2010.

Mauk, Ben. "Scattered Leaves." *New Yorker*, 7 January 2014. Accessed 27 January 2017. https://www.newyorker.com/business/currency/scattered-leaves.

Maya Sánchez, Antonio, ed. "Chronica Adefonsi Imperatoris." In *Chronica Hispana saeculi XII*, Corpus Christianorum, Continuatio Mediaevalis 71, 1:109–248. Turnholt: Brepols, 1990.

McFarland, Thomas. *Romanticism and the Forms of Ruin: Wordsworth, Coleridge, and Modalities of Fragmentation*. Princeton: Princeton University Press, 1981.

McGann, Jerome J. *A Critique of Modern Textual Criticism*. Chicago: University of Chicago Press, 1991.

–. *The Textual Condition*. Princeton: Princeton University Press, 1991.

–."The Text, the Poem, and the Problem of Historical Method." *New Literary History* 12, no. 2 (1981): 269–88.

McKenzie, Donald F. *Bibliography and Sociology of Texts*. Cambridge: Cambridge University Press, 1999.

McKitterick, David. *Print, Manuscript and the Search for Order, 1450–1830*. Cambridge: Cambridge University Press, 2003.

McMunn, Meradith T. "The Illustrated Fragments of the *Roman de la Rose*." In Brownrigg and Smith, *Interpreting*, 97–113.

Menéndez Pelayo, Marcelino. *Tratado de los romances viejos*. In *Antología de poetas líricos castellanos*, edited by Enrique Sánchez Reyes, Edición Nacional 6, 22–4. Santander: Consejos de Investigaciones Científicas, 1944.

Menéndez Pidal, Ramón. "Cantos románicos andalusíes, continuadores de una lírica latina vulgar." *Boletín de la Real Academia Española* 31 (1951): 187–270.

–. *Crestomatía del español medieval*. 2nd ed. Vols. 1–2. Madrid: Editorial Gredos, 1971–6.

–. *La epopeya castellana a través de la literatura española*. Buenos Aires: Espasa-Calpe Argentina, 1945.

–. *La leyenda de los Infantes de Lara*. Vol. 1. Madrid: Espasa-Calpe, 1971.

–, ed. *Reliquias de la poesía épica española*. Madrid: CSIC, Instituto de la Cultura Hispánica, 1951.

–. "*Roncesvalles*: Un nuevo cantar de gesta español del siglo XIII." *Revista de Filología Española* 4 (1917): 105–204.

–. *Textos medievales españoles: Ediciones críticas y estudios*. Madrid: Espasa-Calpe, 1976.

Millares Carlo, Antonio, and José Manuel Ruiz Asencio. *Tratado de paleografía española*. Vol. 1. Madrid: Espasa-Calpe, 1983.

Modern Language Association. "Considering the Scholarly Edition in the Digital Age: A White Paper of the Modern Language Association's Committee on Scholarly Editions." June 2015, revised September 2015. Accessed 27 January 2017. https://scholarlyeditions.mla.hcommons.org/2015/09/02/cse-white-paper/v.

Monroe, James T. "Which Came First, the *Zajal* or the *Muwaššḥa*? Some Evidence for the Oral Origins of Hispano-Arabic Strophic Poetry." *Oral Tradition* 4, nos. 1–2 (1989): 38–64.

–, and David Swiatlo. "Ninety-Three Arabic *Ḫarjas* in Hebrew *Muwaššaḥs*: Their Hispano-Romance Prosody and Thematic Features." *Journal of the American Oriental Society* 97, no. 2 (1977): 141–63.

Montaner, Alberto. "Anotaciones familiares." Entry for M-CCHS RES RESC/13. In Mateos Paramio and Villaverde Amieva, *Memoria de los Moriscos*, 176–7.

–. "Del *Amadís* primitivo al de Montalvo: Cuestiones de emblemática." *Amadís de Gaula: Quinientos años de libros de caballería. Estudios en homenaje a Juan Manuel Cacho Blecua*, edited by José Manuel Lucía Megías and Ma. Carmen Marín Pina, 541–64. Alcalá de Henares: Centro de Estudios Cervantinos, 2008.

–. "La filología." In *La España del siglo XXI, literatura y bellas artes*, directed by Salustino del Campo and José Félix Tezanos, edited by Francisco Rico, Jordi García, and Antonio Bonet Correa, 5:287–311. Madrid: Fundación Sistema, 2009.

–. "La literatura aljamiada." In Mateos Paramio and Villaverde Amieva, *Memoria de los Moriscos*, 45–55.

–, and Ángel Escobar, eds. *"Carmen Campidoctoris" o poema latino del Campeador*. Madrid: España Nuevo Milenio, 2001.

Monteverdi, Angelo. "Il cantare degli Infanti di Salas." *Studi Medievali* 13 (1934): 113–50.

Mora, Francisco de. *Dicho de Francisco de Mora para el proceso remisorial de la canonización de santa Teresa*. In *Obras de santa Teresa de Jesús*, edited by Silverio de Santa Teresa, 1:370–94. Burgos: El Monte Carmelo, 1915.

Morales Estévez, Roberto. "Los grimorios y recetarios mágicos: Del mítico Salomón al clérigo nigromante." In Lara and Montaner, *Señales*, 537–78.

Moss, Ann. *Printed Commonplace Books and the Structuring of Renaissance Thought*. Oxford: Clarendon Press, 1996.

Most, Glenn, ed. *Collecting Fragments/Fragmente sammeln*. Aporemata: Kritische Studien zur Philologiegeschichte 1. Gottingen: Vandenhoeck & Rupprecht, 1997.

Nancy, Jean-Luc. *The Birth to Presence*. Stanford: Stanford University Press, 1993.

–. "The Technique of the Present: On Kawara." In *Multiple Arts: The Muses II*, 191–206. Stanford: Stanford University Press, 2006.

Narváez, María Teresa. "El mancebo de Arévalo, lector morisco de *La Celestina*." *Bulletin of Hispanic Studies* 72 (1995): 255–72.

Nelson, Charles L., ed. and trans. *The Book of the Knight Zifar: A Translation of "El Libro del Cavallero Zifar."* Lexington: University Press of Kentucky, 2014.

Nichols, Stephen G. "Introduction: Philology in a Manuscript Culture." *Speculum* 65, no. 1 (1990): 1–10.

–, and Siegfried Wenzel, eds. *The Whole Book: Cultural Perspectives on the Medieval Miscellany*. Ann Arbor: University of Michigan Press, 1996.

O'Callaghan, Joseph F., ed. and trans. *The Latin Chronicle of the Kings of Castile*. Medieval and Renaissance Texts and Studies 236. Tempe: Arizona State University, 2002.

Oliver, Raymond. *Poems without Names: The English Lyric, 1200–1500*. Berkeley: University of California Press, 1970.

Ossorio, Salvatierra. "Ibn Dayyān." In *Encyclopedia of Jews in the Islamic World*, edited by Norman A. Stillman. Brill Online, 2013. Accessed 27 January 2017. http://referenceworks.brillonline.com/entries/encyclopedia-of-jews-in-the-islamic-world/ibn-al-dayyan-abu-amr-SIM_0010260.

Paradela, Nieves. *El otro laberinto español: Viajeros árabes a España entre el siglo XVII y 1936*. Madrid: Siglo XXI de España Editores, 2005.

Parkes, Malcolm B. "The Influence of the Concepts of *Ordinatio* and *Compilatio* on the Development of the Book." In *Medieval Learning and Literature: Essays Presented to Richard William Hunt*, edited by J.J.G. Alexander and M.T. Gibson, 115–141. Oxford: Clarendon Press, 1976.

Paz de Hoz, María. "Henoteísmo y magia en una inscripción de Hispania." *Zeitschrift für Papyrologie und Epigraphik* 118 (1997): 227–30.

Pearson, David, and N.R. Ker. *Oxford Bookbinding 1500–1640: Including a Supplement to Neil Ker's Fragments of Medieval Manuscripts Used as Pastedowns in Oxford Bindings*. Oxford Bibliographical Society Publications 3, 3rd series 3. Oxford: Oxford Bibliographical Society, 2000.

Pedrosa, José Manuel. "Del brazo escribidor al libro escrito por santa Teresa." In Lara and Montaner, *Señales*, 599–625.

–. "De libros clandestinos y nigromantes: En torno a la posesión y transmisión de grimorios en dos procesos inquisitoriales entre 1509 y 1511." *Revista General de Información y Documentación* 17, no. 1 (2007): 63–80.

Pellicer y Tovar, José de. *Bibliotheca formada de los libros i obras publicas de Don Ioseph Pellicer de Ossau y Tovar*. Valencia: Geronimo Vilagrasa, 1671.

Pereira, Benito. *Adversus fallaces et superstitiosas artes, id est, de magia, de observatione somniorum, et de divinatione astrologica libri tres*. Ingolstadt: Sartori, 1591.

Pérez González, Maurilio, ed. *Crónica del emperador Alfonso VII*. León: Universidad de León, 1997.

Petrucci, Armando. "Dal libro unitario al libro miscellaneo." In *Società romana e impero tardoantico: Tradizione dei classici, trasformazione della cultura*, edited by Andrea Giardina, 4:271–4. Rome: Editori Laterza, 1986.

Philip, Ian Gilbert. *The Bodleian Library in the Seventeenth and Eighteenth Centuries*. Oxford: Clarendon Press, 1983.

PhiloBiblon database. Dir. Charles Faulhaber. Berkeley: University Library, 1997–. Accessed 27 December 2017. http://vm136.lib.berkeley.edu/BANC/philobiblon/index.html. The following manuscripts were accessed 26–7 December 2017: Berkeley, Bancroft Library, University of California, Berkeley, MS 115 (BETA manid 1182); Madrid, Biblioteca del Monasterio de El Escorial, MS B-iv-21 (BETA manid 1307); Madrid, Biblioteca Nacional de España, MS 2244/1–51 (BETA manid 4507) and MS 20262/19 (BETA manid 1462); Paris, Bibliothèque nationale de France, Espagnol 12 (BETA: manid 1232).

Pickwoad, Nicholas. "Library or Museum? The Future of Rare Book Collections and its Consequences for Conservation and Access." In *New Approaches to Book and Paper Conservation and Access*, edited by Patricia Engel, 113–30. Vienna: Berger, 2011.

–. "Museums of the Book." *Advances in Librarianship* 24 (2000): 81–101.

–. "Onward and Downward: How Binders Coped with the Printing Press Before 1800." In *A Millennium of the Book*, edited by Robin Myers and Michael Harris, 61–106. New Castle, DE: Oak Knoll, 1994.

–. "The Use of Fragments of Medieval Manuscripts in the Construction and Covering of Bindings of Printed Books." In Brownrigg and Smith, *Interpreting*, 1–20.

Planas Badenas, Josefina. "El manuscrito de Paris: Estudio arqueológico." In *Libro del caballero Zifar: Códice de París*, edited by Francisco Rico, 137–92. Barcelona: Moleiro Editor, 1996.

El poema de Fernán González. Edited by Juan Victorio. Madrid: Cátedra, 1948.

Prentice, William. "Magical Formulae on Lintels of the Christian Period in Syria." *American Journal of Archaeology* 10, no. 2 (1906): 137–50.

Reif, Stefan. *A Jewish Archive from Old Cairo: The History of Cambridge University's Genizah Collection*. Richmond, UK: Curzon, 2000.

Reused, Rebound, Recovered: Medieval Manuscript Fragments in Law Book Bindings. Exhibit curated by Benjamin Yousey-Hindes and Mike Widener. Rare Book Exhibition Gallery, Level L2, Lillian Goldman Law Library, Yale Law School. February–May 2010.

Ribera y Tarragó, Julián. "El cancionero de Abencuzmán." In *Discursos leídos ante la Real Academia Española*, 3–92. Madrid: Imprenta Ibérica, 1912.

Richardson, Peter. "The Consolation of Philology." *Modern Philology* 92, no. 1 (1994): 1–13.

Rico, Francisco. "Entre el códice y el libro (notas sobre los paradigmas misceláneos y la literatura del siglo XIV)." *Romance Philology* 51 (1997–8): 151–69.

Riquer, Martín de. "El *Roncesvalles* y el planto de Gonzalo Gústioz." In *Studi in onore di Angelo Monteverdi*, edited by Giuseppina Gerardi Maruzzo, 2:623–28. Modena: Società tipografica editrice modenese, 1959.

Rodríguez Ancieto, Cipriano. "Contribución al estudio de los textos latinos de la Edad Media española: El poema latino *Prefacio de Almería*." *Boletín de la Biblioteca Menéndez Pelayo* 13 (1931): 40–175.

Rodríguez de Montalvo, Garci. *Amadís de Gaula*, 2 vols. Edited by Juan Manuel Cacho Blecua. Letras hispánicas. Madrid: Cátedra, 1987.

–. *Amadis of Gaul, Books III and IV*. Translated by Edwin Place and Herbert Behm. Lexington: University of Kentucky Press, 2000.

Rodríguez Moñino, Antonio R., Agustín Millares Carlo, and Rafael Lapesa. *El primer manuscrito del Amadís de Gaula, noticia bibliográfica*. Madrid: Impr. de S. Aguirre Torre, 1957.

Rodríguez Velasco, Jesús D. "La Bibliotheca y los márgenes: Ensayo teórico sobre la glosa en el ámbito cortesano del siglo XV en Castilla. I: Códice, dialéctica y autoridad." *eHumanista* 1 (2001): 119–34.

–. Review of *Mocedades de Rodrigo: Estudio y edicion de los tres estados del texto*, edited by Leonardo Funes and Felipe Tenenbaum. *The Medieval Review*, 8 March 2006. https://scholarworks.iu.edu/journals/index.php/tmr/article/view/16122/22240.

Rosen, Tova. "The Muwashshah." In *The Literature of Al-Andalus*, edited by Maria Rosa Menocal, Raymond P. Scheindlin, and Michael Anthony Sells, 165–89. Cambridge: Cambridge University Press, 2000.

–. *Unveiling Eve: Reading Gender in Medieval Hebrew Literature*. Philadelphia: University of Pennsylvania Press, 2003.

Rossi-Ross, Elena. "Style and Pathos in the Spanish Epic Planctus: An Aesthetic Critique of the Roncesvalles." *Revista Canadiense de Estudios Hispánicos* 12, no. 3 (1988): 429–45.

Roza, Pablo. "Recetarios mágicos moriscos: Brebajes, talismanes y conjuros aljamiados." In Lara and Montaner, *Señales*, 555–78.

Rudy, Kathryn M. "Dirty Books: Quantifying Patterns of Use in Medieval Manuscripts Using a Densitometer." *JHNA* 2 (2010): 1–2. https://www.jhna.org/index.php/past-issues/volume-2-issue-1-2/129-dirty-books.

Runia, Eelco. "Spots of Time." *History and Theory* 45, no. 3 (2006): 305–16.

Saénz-Badillos, Angel. "Ibn Ferruziel, Joseph ha-Nasi (Cidellus, Cidiello)." In *Encyclopedia of Jews in the Islamic World*, edited by Norman A. Stillman. Brill Online, 2013. Accessed 27 January 2017. http://referenceworks.brillonline.com/entries/encyclopedia-of-jews-in-the-islamic-world/ibn-ferruziel-joseph-ha-nasi-cidellus-cidiello-SIM_0010560.

–. "Ibn Muhājir, Abraham (Abū Iṣḥāq) Ben Me'ir." In *Encyclopedia of Jews in the Islamic World*, edited by Norman A. Stillman. Brill Online, 2013. Accessed 27 January 2017. http://referenceworks.brillonline.com/entries/encyclopedia-of-jews-in-the-islamic-world/ibn-muhajir-abraham-abu-ishaq-ben-meir-SIM_0010920.

Salvador Martínez, Heraclio. *El "Poema de Almería" y la épica románica*. Madrid: Gredos, 1975.

Sánchez Belda, Luís, ed. *Chronica Adefonsi Imperatoris*. Madrid: CSIC, 1950.

Scheiber, Alexander. "A Fragment of the Diwan of El'azar Kohen." *Sinai* 55 (1954): 184–6.

Scheindlin, Raymond P. "Mid-Life Repentance in a Poem by Judah Halevi." *The Maghreb Review* 29 (2004): 40–52.

Schirmann, Yefim. *Ha-Shirah ha-Ivrit bi-Sefarad Uvi-Provence*. 2 vols. Jerusalem: Dvir, 1955.

Schlegel, Friedrich. *Friedrich Schlegel's "Lucinde" and the Fragments*. Translated by Peter Firchow. Minneapolis: University of Minnesota Press, 1971.

Schönle, Andreas. "Ruins and History: Observations on Russian Approaches to Destruction and Decay." *Slavic Review* 65, no. 4 (2006): 649–69.

Sharpe, Kevin. "Uncommonplaces? Sir William Drake's Reading Notes." In *The Reader Revealed*, edited by Sabrina Alcorn Baron, 59–65. Seattle: University of Washington Press, 2001.

Sherman, William H. *Used Books: Marking Readers in Renaissance England*. Philadelphia: University of Pennsylvania Press, 2008.

Las Siete Partidas. Vol. 3: *The Medieval World of Law, Lawyers and Their Work (Partida III)*. Translated by Samuel Parsons Scott. Edited by Robert I. Burns, S.J. Philadelphia: University of Pennsylvania Press, 2001.

Skemer, Don C. "Amulet Rolls and Female Devotion in the Late Middle Ages." *Scriptorium* 55, no. 2 (2001): 197–227.

–. *Binding Words: Textual Amulets in the Middle Ages*. University Park: Pennsylvania State University Press, 2006.

Smith, Colin. "The Dating and Relationship of the *Historia Roderici* and the *Carmen Campi Doctoris*." *Olifant* 9 (1986): 99–112.

Söffner, Jan. "What Production of Presence and Mimesis Have in Common." In *Proceedings of the 9th International Workshop on Presence, Cleveland State University, Cleveland, OH, August 24–26*, edited by Cheryl Campanella Bracken and Matthew Lombard, 6–17. Cleveland: Cleveland State University, 2006.

Solà-Solé, José María. *Corpus de poesía mozárabe*. Barcelona: Ediciones Hispam., 1973.

Solterer, Helen. "Performer le passé: Rencontre avec Paul Zumthor (entretien)." In *Paul Zumthor, ou l'invention permanente: Critique, histoire, poésie*, edited by Jacqueline Cerquiglini-Toulet and Christopher Lucken, 117–59. Geneva: Droz, 1998.

Stern, Samuel M. *Les chansons mozarabes: Les vers finaux-kharjas-en espagnol dans les muwashshahs arabes et hébreux. Édités avec introduction, annotation, sommaires et glossaire*. Palermo: Manfredi, 1953. Reprint, Oxford, 1964.

–. *Hispano-Arabic Strophic Poetry: Studies*. Edited by L.P. Harvey. Oxford: Clarendon Press, 1974.

Sturges, Robert S. "Medieval Authorship and the Polyphonic Text." In *Bakhtin and Medieval Voices*, edited by Thomas J. Farrell, 122–37. Gainesville: University Press of Florida, 1995.

Suarez, Michael F. "Extended Evidence, D.F. McKenzie and the Forms of Bibliographical Knowledge." In *Books and Bibliography: Essays in Commemoration of Don McKenzie*, edited by John Thompson, 36–56. Wellington: Victoria University Press, 2002.

Suárez García, Raquel. *El compendio islámico de Mohanmad de Vera*. Oviedo: Ediuno, 2016.

–. "El tratado de materia religiosa de Mohanmad de Vera (Ms. 397 de la Bibliothèque nationale de France)." PhD diss., Universidad de Oviedo, 2004.

Such, Peter, and Richard Rabone, trans. *The Poem of Fernán González*. Oxford: Oxbow Books, 2015.

Taylor, Andrew. *Three Medieval Manuscripts and Their Readers*. Philadelphia: University of Pennsylvania Press, 2002.

Trachtenberg, Joshua. *Jewish Magic and Superstition: A Study in Folk Religion*. Philadelphia: University of Pennsylvania Press, 2004.

Twerskey, Isadore. *Maimonides Reader*. Springfield, NJ: Behrman House, 1972.

Twomey, Michael. "Towards a Reception History of Western Mediaeval Encyclopedias in England Before 1500." In *Pre-Modern Encyclopaedic Texts:*

Proceedings of the Second COMERS Congress, Groningen, 1–4 July, 1996, edited by Peter Binkley, 329–62. Brill: Leiden, 1997.

UNESCO. "Text of the Convention for the Safeguarding of the Intangible Cultural Heritage." Accessed 27 January 2017. https://ich.unesco.org/en/convention.

UNESCO Office in Cairo. "Tangible Cultural Heritage." Accessed 27 January 2017. http://www.unesco.org/new/en/cairo/culture/tangible-cultural-heritage/.

Vakaloudi, Anastasia. "The Kinds and the Special Function of the ἐπωδαί (epodes) in Apotropaic Amulets of the First Byzantine Period." *BYZANTINOSLAVICA: International Journal of Byzantine Studies* 59, no. 2 (1998): 222–38.v

Valencia, Adriana, and Shamma Boyarin. "*Ke adame filiolo alieno*: Three Muwaššaḥāt that Share the same Kharja." In *Wine, Women and Song: Hebrew and Arabic Literature of Medieval Iberia*, edited by Michelle Hamilton, S.J. Portnoy, and David Wacks, 75–86. Newark, DE: Juan de la Cuesta, 2004.

Velázquez, Isabel. *La teja de Villamartín de Sotoscueva (Burgos): Los versos más antiguos del "Poema de Fernán González."* Burgos: Instituto Castellano y Leonés de la Lengua, 2006.

Viguera, María Jesús, and Concepción Castillo Castillo, eds. *Los manuscritos árabes en España y Marruecos: Homenaje de Granada y Fez a Ibn Jaldún. Actas del congreso internacional, Granada, 2005*. Granada: Fundación El Legado Andalusí, 2006.

Viladrich, Merce. "Fablamiento del Alcorán." In Mateos Paramio and Villaverde Amieva, *Memoria de los Moriscos*, 189–90.

Warren, Michelle. "Post-Philology." In *Postcolonial Moves: Medieval through Modern Times*, edited by Patricia Clare Ingham and Michelle R. Warren, 19–46. New York: Palgrave, 2003.

Weiss, Julian. *The "Mester de Clerecía": Intellectuals and Ideologies in Thirteenth-Century Castile*. Woodbridge, UK: Tamesis, 2006.

Whetnall, Jane. "A Question of Genre: *Roncesvalles* and the *Siete Infantes* Connection." In *The Age of the Catholic Monarchs, 1474–1516: Literary Studies in Memory of Keith Whinnom*, edited by Alan Deyermond and Ian Macpherson, 171–87. Liverpool: Liverpool University Press, 1989.

Whinnom, Keith. "Cardona, the Crucifixion and Leriano's Last Drink." In *Studies on the Spanish Sentimental Romance (1450–1550): Redefining a Genre*, edited by Joseph J. Gwara and E. Michael Gerli, 207–15. Rochester, NY: Tamesis, 1997.

Wiegers, Gerard. *Islamic Literature in Spanish and Aljamiado: Yça of Segovia (fl. 1450), His Antecedents and Successors*. Brill: Leiden, 1994.

Wood, Anthony. *The History and Antiquities of the University of Oxford in Two Books*. Edited by John Gutch. Oxford: University of Oxford, 1792.

Wright, Roger. "Hispanic Epic and Ballad." In *Medieval Oral Literature*, edited by Karl Reichl, 411–28. Berlin: De Gruyter, 2012.

–. "The First Poem of the Cid – The *Carmen Campi Doctoris*." In *Papers of the Liverpool Latin Seminar*, edited by Francis Cairns, 2:213–48. Liverpool: University of Liverpool, 1979.

–. "How Old Is the Ballad Genre?" *La corónica* 14, no. 2 (1986): 251–7.

–, ed. and trans. *Spanish Ballads with English Verse Translations*. Warminster, UK: Aris and Phillips, 1995.

Young, James E. *At Memory's Edge: After-Images of the Holocaust in Contemporary Art and Architecture*. New Haven: Yale University Press, 2000.

Zwartjes, Otto. *Love Songs from al-Andalus: History, Structure, and Meaning of the Kharja*. Leiden: Brill, 1997.

Index

Page numbers in italics refer to figures.

TORONTO IBERIC

1 Anthony J. Cascardi, *Cervantes, Literature, and the Discourse of Politics*
2 Jessica A. Boon, *The Mystical Science of the Soul: Medieval Cognition in Bernardino de Laredo's Recollection Method*
3 Susan Byrne, *Law and History in Cervantes'* Don Quixote
4 Mary E. Barnard and Frederick A. de Armas (eds), *Objects of Culture in the Literature of Imperial Spain*
5 Nil Santiáñez, *Topographies of Fascism: Habitus, Space, and Writing in Twentieth-Century Spain*
6 Nelson R. Orringer, *Lorca in Tune with Falla: Literary and Musical Interludes*
7 Ana M. Gómez-Bravo, *Textual Agency: Writing Culture and Social Networks in Fifteenth-Century Spain*
8 Javier Irigoyen-García, *The Spanish Arcadia: Sheep Herding, Pastoral Discourse, and Ethnicity in Early Modern Spain*
9 Stephanie Sieburth, *Survival Songs: Conchita Piquer's* Coplas *and Franco's Regime of Terror*
10 Christine Arkinstall, *Spanish Female Writers and the Freethinking Press, 1879–1926*
11 Margaret E. Boyle, *Unruly Women: Performance, Penitence, and Punishment in Early Modern Spain*
12 Evelina Gužauskytė, *Christopher Columbus's Naming in the* diarios *of the Four Voyages (1492–1504): A Discourse of Negotiation*
13 Mary E. Barnard, *Garcilaso de la Vega and the Material Culture of Renaissance Europe*
14 William Viestenz, *By the Grace of God: Francoist Spain and the Sacred Roots of Political Imagination*
15 Michael Scham, Lector Ludens*: The Representation of Games and Play in Cervantes*
16 Stephen Rupp, *Heroic Forms: Cervantes and the Literature of War*

17 Enrique Fernandez, *Anxieties of Interiority and Dissection in Early Modern Spain*
18 Susan Byrne, *Ficino in Spain*
19 Patricia M. Keller, *Ghostly Landscapes: Film, Photography, and the Aesthetics of Haunting in Contemporary Spanish Culture*
20 Carolyn A. Nadeau, *Food Matters: Alonso Quijano's Diet and the Discourse of Food in Early Modern Spain*
21 Cristian Berco, *From Body to Community: Venereal Disease and Society in Baroque Spain*
22 Elizabeth R. Wright, *The Epic of Juan Latino: Dilemmas of Race and Religion in Renaissance Spain*
23 Ryan D. Giles, *Inscribed Power: Amulets and Magic in Early Spanish Literature*
24 Jorge Pérez, *Confessional Cinema: Religion, Film, and Modernity in Spain's Development Years, 1960–1975*
25 Joan Ramon Resina, *Josep Pla: Seeing the World in the Form of Articles*
26 Javier Irigoyen-García, *"Moors Dressed as Moors": Clothing, Social Distinction, and Ethnicity in Early Modern Iberia*
27 Jean Dangler, *Edging Towards Iberia*
28 Ryan D. Giles and Steven Wagschal (eds), *Beyond Sight: Engaging the Senses in Iberian Literatures and Cultures, 1200–1750*
29 Silvia Bermúdez, *Rocking the Boat: Migration and Race in Contemporary Spanish Music*
30 Hilaire Kallendorf, *Ambiguous Antidotes: Virtue as Vaccine for Vice in Early Modern Spain*
31 Leslie J. Harkema, *Spanish Modernism and the Poetics of Youth: From Miguel de Unamuno to* La Joven Literatura
32 Benjamin Fraser, *Cognitive Disability Aesthetics: Visual Culture, Disability Representations, and the (In)Visibility of Cognitive Difference*
33 Robert Patrick Newcomb, *Iberianism and Crisis: Spain and Portugal at the Turn of the Twentieth Century*
34 Sara J. Brenneis, *Spaniards in Mauthausen: Representations of a Nazi Concentration Camp, 1940–2015*
35 Silvia Bermúdez and Roberta Johnson (eds), *A New History of Iberian Feminisms*
36 Steven Wagschal, *Minding Animals in the Old and New Worlds: A Cognitive Historical Analysis*
37 Heather Bamford, *Cultures of the Fragment: Uses of the Iberian Manuscript, 1100–1600*

www.ingramcontent.com/pod-product-compliance
Lightning Source LLC
LaVergne TN
LVHW041112090826
844660LV00061B/814/J